A CITY DIVIDED

A City Divided

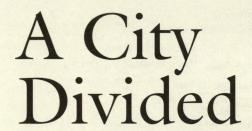

The Racial Landscape of Kansas City, 1900–1960

SHERRY LAMB SCHIRMER

University of Missouri Press
Columbia and London

Cataloging-in-Publication data available from the Library of Congress.
ISBN 0-8262-1391-X

∞™ This paper meets the requirements of the
American National Standard for Permanence of Paper
for Printed Library Materials, Z39.48, 1984.

Designer: Stephanie Foley
Typesetter: BOOKCOMP, Inc.
Printer and binder: Thomson-Shore, Inc.
Typefaces: ITC Galliard and Myriad MM

Title-page image courtesy Special Collections, Kansas City Public Library,
Kansas City, Missouri.

To my husband, Steve Schirmer,
for his editing and his endurance

CONTENTS

A CITY DIVIDED

INTRODUCTION

With Race in Mind

■ ■ ■

THIS STUDY BEGAN in a boundless accumulation of documents that I felt sure would yield a dissertation topic—probably about school segregation. After all, *Jenkins v. State of Missouri*, the suit that generated those many boxes of paper, was all about the segregation of Kansas City, Missouri, schools, and I had focused much of my graduate study on the social history of childhood and family. It seemed a good fit. Many file boxes into my search, however, I was finding little to add to the story of school segregation. That topic already had been examined thoroughly. Instead, my attention was drawn over and over again to the white mentality revealed in the depositions and documents the case generated. There, whites talked about and thought about race in peculiar yet consistent patterns. I decided that this was the story I wanted to explore—to find the historical origins of those patterns, to identify the historical experiences in a local context that gave rise to whites' perceptions and behavior regarding race, and to discover how those perceptions shaped the spatial and social structure of the city. That is the purpose of this book.[1]

1. The *Jenkins v. State of Missouri* suit originated in 1977 when the Kansas City, Missouri, School District [KCMSD] sued the State of Missouri and eighteen suburban school districts seeking a metropolitan-wide desegregation plan. U.S. District Judge Russell G. Clark revised the suit, designating KCMSD a defendant in a class action on behalf of KCMSD students. In 1984, Judge Clark eliminated the suburban districts as defendants. Later that year, he found KCMSD and the State of Missouri guilty of failing to desegregate the district, and he subsequently ordered a magnet school plan to overcome racial imbalance in KCMSD's enrollments. Plaintiffs' attorney in the suit, Arthur Benson, later deposited his voluminous case files with the Western Historical Manuscripts Collection. The collection is designated "Arthur Benson Papers," KC 250, Western Historical Manuscripts Collection, hereafter cited as "Benson Papers."

Specifically, four themes that seemed to be important recurred throughout the volumes of evidence and testimony in the *Jenkins* case. First, concerns about the use, occupancy, and control of urban space shaped race relations to a significant degree. Second, key decision makers and ordinary white citizens were inclined to use the magician's tactic of misdirection, either by denying that race was a factor in their behavior or by claiming that their actions were necessary to forestall racial unrest among whites. Third, many whites encoded African Americans in a set of collective images so negative and so widely held that they provided an effective and politically acceptable rationale for racial exclusion and racial isolation. Finally, a minority of whites sought interracial contacts in the belief that integration would uplift individual and community values.

Issues of urban land use and attitudes about city space were clearly central to creating and preserving school segregation. The familiar pattern of white flight produced a sprawling Kansas City metropolitan area that, by 1977, encompassed nineteen separate school districts and twenty-five municipalities in two states. Other public agencies, including housing authorities and urban renewal and highway construction agencies, assisted in the spatial sorting of the population with policies that targeted integrated neighborhoods for disruption while subsidizing white flight. Most remarkable about these policy decisions was that they were founded on the assumption that whites would always behave like bigots—abandoning integrated neighborhoods, resisting public housing in their locale, or defecting from integrated schools.[2] In 1977, for example, the city of Independence, Missouri, protested the busing of pupils in and out of the KCMSD schools that lay within Independence city limits because it could incite whites to "destruction of property, personal injury, and general degradation of the educational process."[3] Judging by this variety of excuse-making, local whites were not just bigots but potentially violent bigots. Segregation might be regrettable, but it did at least keep the lid on rampaging bigotry.

It was also evident in these case records that decision makers and mem-

2. "Plaintiffs' Synopsis of Contentions and Supporting Facts," Desegregation Notebook, folder 8; "Statement of the Case," 14–26, Benson Papers. School district boundaries were so manipulated that they did not correspond to municipal boundaries. Thus five of these districts lay entirely or almost entirely within the city limits of Kansas City, Missouri. See also, Deposition of Jimmie Miller Haff, Box 107; Deposition of Vincent O'Flagherty, Box 113; Deposition of Louise Reeves, 40, Box 114; Deposition of Gwendolyn Marie Dunlap-Wells, 28–30, Box 119; Deposition of A. Odell Thurman, 18, Box 117, Benson Papers.

3. "Summons in *City of Independence, Missouri v. School District of Kansas City, Missouri*," 3, Box 354, Benson Papers.

bers of the public habitually engaged in denial and misdirection. Dozens of personnel from key public agencies testified that they never considered the discriminatory results of decisions they made because "civil rights" was the responsibility of some other agency or some other staff member. Others denied that race was a factor in their behavior, since to admit race as a motive would be divisive and discreditable. Whites opposed the construction of subsidized housing in their neighborhoods, for example, because the occupants would abuse neighborhood amenities, overcrowd local schools with underachieving pupils, and increase neighborhood crime. "Race is also an issue, although it's never mentioned," one housing executive noted. "You hear the same thing, group after group."[4]

A third pattern of behavior made these misdirection tactics possible: whites used a coded language to refer obliquely to African Americans, without direct reference to race. After all, who could condemn parents for wanting to shield their families from low-achieving, crime-prone despoilers of neighborhood amenities, or their schools from undisciplined, violent students with low test scores, apathetic parents, and a fondness for vandalism? The code worked because it articulated a shared set of assumptions that black people were disorderly, dishonest, and immoral. "You couldn't help but read between lines," a former school board member recalled, because everyone knew whom the labels were supposed to fit.[5]

By contrast, a fourth pattern evident in the testimony revealed a segment of the white population that not only accepted integration but saw it as a social nostrum, for they expected integration to improve individual character and to strengthen the social order. Speaking of children in racially balanced schools, school administrator Jack Casner asserted, "These kids learn how to respect each other, get along together, and work together. I think that it is vital to the country, and I think it is vital for them as human beings." Stated educator Wayne Dotts, "The future is going to depend upon people's ability to interact effectively with people of different cultures." In fact, a number of

4. Deposition of William R. Southerland, 32, Box 116; Deposition of Thomas Stephen Kilbride, 30–31, Box 110, Benson Papers. See also, U.S. Department of Housing and Urban Development Memorandum, August 5, 1974, in "Summary of Deposition of John E. Bridges, Jr.," Box 102, Benson Papers. Commenting on school desegregation in Boston in the 1970s, pundit Andrew Kopkind noted an "inane refusal to admit" what should have been apparent, namely, "that 'race' was an issue in the busing controversy." Quoted in George R. Metcalf, *From Little Rock to Boston: The History of School Desegregation,* 243.

5. "Deposition of Della M. Hadley," 38, Box 107; Deposition of Jack Casner, 27–28, Box 103, Benson Papers. This entire set of assumptions emerged most clearly in defense attorneys' line of questioning of deponents. See for example, Deposition of Wayne Dotts, Box 105, Benson Papers.

white parents went to considerable lengths to ensure that their youngsters would have multiracial contacts in the belief that children developed tolerance, trust, and humility as a result. Protesting that school desegregation was not meant solely to assist African Americans, Richard Dawson asserted, "I consider it to be just as much a matter of giving my daughter, and people like my daughter to come, equal opportunity."[6]

These perceptual and behavior patterns intrigued me and suggested that a social historian might shed light on the character of race relations in Kansas City by asking questions about the historical origins of these attitudes and actions. Specifically, what circumstances in Kansas City's past made issues of urban space salient? What historical experiences induced some whites to associate African Americans with criminality, disorganized family life, and the deterioration of property values, while other whites equated integration with community betterment? In what ways did the collective demands of African Americans shape white attitudes and responses to racial issues, and what political or social conditions gave rise to the tactics of misdirection, concealment, and subterfuge in thwarting those demands? If, in fact, historical experiences in a local context did shape whites' racial mentalities, how were those perceptions and behaviors communicated to new residents across time?

There is, of course, a single, straightforward answer to these questions, namely that each of those phenomena is the product of racism. By "racism" I mean a complex of feelings and beliefs that members of other racial groups are innately inferior. Many scholars have attributed white racism to uniquely personal factors, such as patterns of personality formation, low levels of career mobility, or the quality of individual social contacts.[7] Understanding how child-rearing patterns, education levels, or interpersonal relationships shaped individuals' feelings about race does not, however, explain why large and disparate populations of whites, whose personality formation and personal experiences may have differed widely, translated some—but not all—of those feelings into publicly expressed myths about race.

Nor does racism explain "racialism," that is, how a social structure came to be stratified by race. As John Cell notes, racism can motivate a wide range of

6. Deposition of Jack Casner, 33; Deposition of Wayne Dotts, 25, Box 105; Deposition of Richard Dawson, 32, Box 104, Benson Papers. See also, Deposition of Judith Y. Walthall, 9, Box 118; Deposition of Patricia Soden, 18–19, 54–68, Box 115, Benson Papers.

7. Proponents of psychosocial explanations of racism include Seymour Martin Lipset, *Political Man: The Social Bases of Politics;* Peter Loewenberg, "The Psychology of Racism," 186–201; Bruno Bettelheim and Morris Janowitz, *Dynamics of Prejudice: A Psychological and Sociological Study of Veterans;* Joel Kovel, *White Racism: A Psychohistory.*

discriminatory practices, from slavery or segregation to deportation or extermination. Racism, by itself, cannot explain every one of such disparate forms
of inequity. Moreover, people who possess the deepest personal antagonisms
toward another race may not have much to do with constructing a system of
discrimination, either because they have little to gain by doing so or because
they lack the political power to translate their antagonisms into public policy.[8]

Instead, models that focus on the *public* formation of racial perceptions
and their impact in the *public* arena are more helpful in interpreting the data
and suggesting answers to the questions I posed. Specifically, those models
suggest that systems of racial discrimination and the ideas that underpin them
are "functional." They exist because they get something done. Many scholars
have proposed, for example, that racism originated among Europeans in the
eighteenth century as the solution to a very practical problem: the need to
find some culturally satisfying justification for slavery. In recent times, Herbert Blumer argues, various groups have erected systems of racial inequality
because they believe that they have something to gain by the system. Their
social, cultural, or material needs will be served, or they will acquire what
Blumer calls "group social position," which entitles them to "exclusive or
prior rights in many important areas of life."[9]

Such a *system* of racial domination requires collective image making about
the subordinate racial group that legitimates its subordination. By ascribing
negative qualities to a subordinate group, other scholars argue, a dominant
group "manufactures" a reality in which social harmony and order seem to
require the subordination of one by the other. Thus it aims to "comfort those
whom the system rewards and to justify the system to those who fail." Although the image making appears calculated, dominant ideologies are powerful, in part, because "dominant groups develop such an ideology without
contrivance: it flows naturally from their side of experience as they seek to
impose a sense of order on the pattern of social relations."[10] In other words,
it is a historical product.

8. Cell, *The Highest Stage of White Supremacy: The Origins of Segregation in South
Africa and the American South*, 4.
9. Blumer, "Race Prejudice as a Sense of Group Position," 3–7. For functional explanations of the origins of racism, see for example, Thomas F. Gossett, *Race: The History of an Idea in America*, 3; George M. Fredrickson, *White Supremacy: A Comparative
Study in American and South African History*, 70–79. See also, George Fredrickson, *The
Arrogance of Race: Historical Perspectives on Slavery, Racism, and Social Inequality*, 5.
Winthrop Jordan denies that slavery caused prejudice but maintains that they "caused
each other." Jordan, *The White Man's Burden: Historical Origins of Racism in the United
States*, 45.
10. Joan Huber and William H. Form, *Income and Ideology: An Analysis of the Amer-
ican Political Formula*, 99. See also, Mary R. Jackman and Michael J. Muha, "Education

Historians disagree, however, about what privileges and entitlements whites actually won by their "racial group position." Some point to the economic benefits that employers enjoyed from a population of permanently cheap labor or cite the advantages of political domination that segregation afforded to the southern elite.[11] Others argue that working-class whites reached higher wages by standing on the backs of black labor.[12] Preferring Weber to Marx, other scholars argue that racialism helped whites establish social status or, in Craig Steven Wilder's terms, to obtain the "social power" to "hoard social benefits while people of color became the primary consumers of social ills."[13] Numerous other historians have pointed out that gender relations and sexual advantage were also central to systems of racial domination, from which white men garnered the prestige of a racially pure lineage or compensated for their failure as breadwinners by serving as "defender of the purity of white women" against the "black beast rapist."[14] Along with political cohesiveness and psychic consolation, gender-based racialism gave white men almost unlimited sexual access to black women.[15] The ideal model, of course, balances the categories of race, status, and gender in its analysis, as John Dollard did so effectively more than sixty years ago, when his examination of racial caste in a small southern city revealed that the white middle class were the principal beneficiaries of what he called "economic gain," "prestige gain," and "sexual gain."[16]

---

and Intergroup Attitudes: Moral Enlightenment, Superficial Democratic Commitment, or Ideological Refinement?" 759.

11. Harold Baron and John Cell assert, for example, that economic elites employed segregation and the racial segmentation of the labor force to secure the cooperation of white workers and to extract the maximum economic benefit from black and white labor. Baron, "Racism Transformed: The Implications of the 1960s," 10–33; Cell, *Highest Stage,* 17. Proponents of the political benefits include C. Vann Woodward, *The Strange Career of Jim Crow,* and J. Morgan Kousser, *The Shaping of Southern Politics: Suffrage Restriction and the Establishment of the One-Party South, 1880–1910.*

12. See, for example, David R. Roediger, *The Wages of Whiteness: Race and the Making of the American Working Class.*

13. Wilder, *A Covenant with Color: Race and Social Power in Brooklyn,* 216.

14. Joel Williamson, *The Crucible of Race: Black-White Relations in the American South since Emancipation,* 301. See also, Ronald Takaki, "The Black Child-Savage in Ante-bellum America," 33.

15. See for example, Angela Y. Davis, *Women, Culture, and Politics;* Ann Firor Scott, *The Southern Lady: From Pedestal to Politics, 1830–1930;* Catherine Clinton, *The Plantation Mistress: Women's World in the Old South;* and Catherine Clinton, "Caught in the Web of the Big House." Studies that show the role of gender and race in maintaining white male prestige include Bertram Wyatt-Brown, *Southern Honor: Ethics and Behavior in the Old South;* Bill Cecil-Fronsman, *Common Whites: Class and Culture in Ante-bellum North Carolina;* Charles L. Flynn, Jr., *White Land, Black Labor: Caste and Class in Late Nineteenth-Century Georgia.*

16. Dollard, *Caste and Class in a Southern Town.*

I have used the term *class* throughout this work, in part because it is a conveniently familiar one. Most readers share roughly common notions about the meaning of "working class" or "middle class." However, I use a broad definition of class that includes factors of prestige, culture, social and familial organization, and political aspiration. As Burton Bledstein has noted, class in the United States has been as much a "state of mind" as a marketplace relationship. Thus, I find Max Weber's understanding of a class as a "status" group more helpful, because it describes a collective of individuals who define themselves as a group by social as well as economic means (including education, living standard, moral values, child rearing and family patterns, and cultural norms).[17] Unfortunately, historians often lack the richness and immediacy of the sociologist's resources. We cannot interview hundreds of subjects to determine their education level, cultural values, or aspirations. Consequently, I have had to rely on the blunt instrument of occupational category to determine the status group identities of certain populations.

Surprisingly few studies of white racial mentality exist, and nearly all of those focus on the rural south.[18] Consequently, Kansas City, Missouri, provides a fitting context in which to examine white mentality, for the city partook of two cultural legacies. Situated in a slaveholding state and originally populated by first- and second-generation migrants from the upper south, Kansas City claimed a tenuous southern heritage. After the Civil War, however, the city drew most of its burgeoning population from midwestern and northeastern states. Its booming commercial and industrial sectors and its dependence on Boston and Chicago investors linked the city economically to the industrial north and helped shape its economic and social development according to the pattern of northern urban dynamism. As late as the 1950s, local residents liked to say that theirs was "a Northern town with a Southern exposure." As such, Kansas City provides an ideal laboratory in which to observe how a variety of assumptions about race interacted within a modern urban setting. It was, in many respects, a composite of urban America. Or, as other local citizens used to boast, it was an "all-American city."

Paradoxically, while this is an examination of white racial mentalities, I have relied often on blacks to tell whites' story. Because a code of civility and

17. Bledstein, *The Culture of Professionalism: The Middle Class and the Development of Higher Education in America*, 5; S. M. Miller, ed., *Max Weber*, 49–53.

18. Kenneth Kusmer notes that the class and racial attitudes of urban whites is one of the most significant and underanalyzed topics in current historiography. Kusmer, "Urban Black History at the Crossroads," 468. The notable exception is Chicago. For example, James R. Grossman's account of black Chicagoans' experience of the Great Migration devotes a chapter to understanding whites' responses to the migrants. Grossman, *Land of Hope: Chicago, Black Southerners, and the Great Migration.*

concealment governed whites' discussion and handling of contentious racial issues, they seldom articulated their racial attitudes or motives openly. Black leaders, however, had to be astute observers and judicious analysts of white mentality and behavior. Their analyses, or at least those of the black middle class, appeared in print more often, and I have relied on their discernment to help me understand whites. Thus, this study of whites is often told from the black perspective.

I have organized that story in the following way. Chapter 1 provides a prologue by identifying the factors that made the use and control of urban space salient issues in Kansas City before 1920, particularly in regard to the delineation of status. Chapter 2 describes the place blacks occupied in the city's social and physical landscape between 1900 and 1920. Chapter 3 examines more closely the dynamics by which issues of urban space and social status came to be linked to race between 1900 and 1920. Specifically, it explores the efforts of the middle class to define its group position by distancing its members from poverty and urban squalor, from shifting land uses, and from urban crime and immorality between 1900 and 1920. As middle-class whites' anxieties over these factors mounted, and as the local black population grew larger and more assertive, the white middle class increasingly associated blacks with these fearsome qualities of urbanism and sought to distance itself from its anxieties by distancing itself from and exerting control over black people.

Chapters 4 and 5 recount the critical decade of the 1920s, when whites fully elaborated the image making process that portrayed blacks as crime prone, immoral, and antithetical to secure property values. At the same time, white Kansas Citians institutionalized these myths in a racialist social structure that provided a mechanism for transmitting those images across time to new generations of white Kansas Citians. Also in the 1920s, these chapters maintain, white Kansas City fully developed protocols of concealment and misdirection to divert blacks' protests against racialism and to prevent white racial antipathies from flaring into violence or disorder. Because African Americans strove to dismantle racialism or ameliorate its effects, Chapter 6 assesses the impact of blacks' collective actions in reshaping white racial perceptions between 1920 and 1940. Chapters 7 and 8 examine civil rights activism in Kansas City between 1941 and 1958, the formative period for the civil rights movement in the city. These chapters focus on the ways in which black Kansas Citians devised direct action tactics that were peculiarly suited to confronting misdirection and trace the emergence of an "integration ethos" by which white liberals hoped to transform human personality.

1

Social Status and the Control of Urban Space

■ ■ ■

A N ORDINARY MAN in so many ways, Clarence Burton was remarkable in one respect: he wrote an autobiography recounting his ordinary life. Burton came to Kansas City in 1878. As a bachelor just out of his teens, the middle-class Burton roomed in the same neighborhood as his fellow workers, near the machine shop where they worked in the city's industrial West Bottoms. He spent his leisure time with those same blue-collar young men and enjoyed the company of their sisters and girlfriends at church socials. These working-class girls were a jolly and decent lot, he recalled, but the ambitious young machinist rejected them as potential mates. Convinced he would never find a suitable wife at such gatherings, he enrolled in one of the city's commercial dancing schools. Apparently, Burton's resort to dancing embarrassed him, for he took pains in his memoirs to explain that dance schools offered one of the few places where unmarried strangers could meet in decorous surroundings. There he hoped to come "into contact with a select crowd." In fact, he found a young woman at the school who met his expectations, unromantic though they were. "She appealed to me in the strongest way," he remembered. "She was sensible and a good housekeeper and there was nothing about her that would apparently make a young man regret that she became his partner."[1]

Even as a young family man on his way up, Burton continued to worry about associating with the right sort. That was not easy to do in a city with the inchoate social structure so typical of burgeoning western towns. Burton carefully narrowed his social contacts, joining fraternal lodges and the

1. Burton, *Autobiography of Clarence A. Burton: A Story of His Life and Experiences,* 252–53.

Rotary Club because these organizations brought him into association with men of good standing in the business community and earned his boss's approval. Finding the right home for his family proved to be more difficult. As a prospective bridegroom, Burton had thought about renting a home for his bride, but his sense of his present status and future prospects led him to buy a house and furnish it prior to his wedding in 1880. Alas, home ownership was fraught with risks. Burton quickly found that monthly mortgage payments on this first home took half his salary, and he had to go into debt just to complete his wedding arrangements. Any future decline in the value of his property would inflict a painful loss. "It showed that my judgment had pretty much lost its bearings," he confessed, "and I was so carried away with the idea of a home of my own that I did not make a good financial arrangement."[2] The house itself lacked "bathroom conveniences" and streetcar connections, but its location overlooking the future site of the city's Union Station stood at a satisfying distance from the disagreeable sights and inhabitants of the central city in 1880.

Within a few years, however, African Americans and impoverished immigrants began filling up the subdivision just north of Burton's home, and he prepared to move his family. Over the next fifty years, the vagaries of the Kansas City housing market would keep the Burtons on the move. Initially, the collapse of a real estate boom in 1888 showed how precarious his investment in a home could be. Things scarcely improved for him when housing construction revived around the turn of the century. Easily built "pattern" houses filled in areas left vacant by the boom's collapse, particularly along the city's eastern flank, where Burton settled his family in 1900. Homes in these new subdivisions were priced to sell to middle-class and prosperous blue-collar purchasers. Because these subdivisions lacked property restrictions to protect resale value, however, amenities deteriorated quickly and turnover was high.[3] By the time he wrote his memoirs in 1927, Burton would uproot his own family a half dozen more times, moving from one equally disappointing neighborhood to another in his quest for security.

The things that mattered to Burton mattered to countless other Kansas Citians: ambition for advancement; respectability and decorum; association with people like himself; and location—namely, an investment in a home

---

2. *Ibid.*, 255.
3. Fletcher Cowherd, "Experiences and Observations of a Long-Time Kansas City Realtor," Vertical File, Missouri Valley Room–Kansas City Public Library [hereafter MVR-KCPL], 6–7; Clifford Naysmith, "Population in Kansas City, Missouri," folder 4, 54, 69, A. Theodore Brown Collection, Western Historical Manscript Collection [hereafter WHMC].

and neighborhood that secured his family physically, financially, and socially. By the early decades of the twentieth century, concerns about social status and urban space had fused. They were sides of the same coin—at least in Kansas Citians' thinking. Matters of space became a preoccupation that shaped, among other things, the ways in which white, mainly middle-class Kansas Citians responded to race as an issue and to African Americans in particular.

■ ■ Space, Status, and the Upper Class

Initially, Kansas Citians had good cause to worry about the urban space they occupied. From its beginnings in 1838, theirs was an ugly town, even by western standards. Theodore Case recalled his arrival to establish a medical practice in 1857:

> The first view of Kansas City was by no means prepossessing, as it consisted principally of a line of shady looking brick and frame warehouses, dry goods stores, groceries, hotels, saloons, restaurants, etc. strung along the levee, from Wyandotte street to a little east of Walnut, the whole backed up and surrounded by a rugged and precipitous bluff, from 100 to 150 feet high covered with old dead trees, brush, dogfennel and "jimson" weeds, with an occasional frame or log house scattered between and among them, and a few women and children, principally darkies, looking down at the boat.[4]

Making way for growth meant that residents had to carve streets upward and then across the rocky promontories and brush-filled ravines that towered above the town's Missouri River levee. The result was a series of man-made canyons cutting south from the river, with buildings perched precariously as much as fifty feet above the roadway below. Jerry-built and mud-choked, the town was a risk to life and limb and an offense to the eye.[5]

The best Case could say of the town's leading citizens was that they were "civilized people who wore store clothes and claimed to possess most of the Christian virtues." The city's development as a transportation and commercial hub after the Civil War added some tone to Kansas City society. Yet Sarah Coates remembered fondly that local "high society" still lacked pretensions and rigid protocols in the 1870s, and membership was open to anyone who

4. Case, "Kansas City before and during the War," 106.
5. James J. Schlafly, "A History of the Catholic Church in the Diocese of Kansas City."

possessed "absolute respectability" and "full allegiance to the town whose welfare was the vital issue."[6] Within a decade things had changed dramatically. The wife of real estate developer Kersey Coates and thus a member of that high society, the Quaker-reared Sarah grew increasingly critical of local nabobs' snobbery and wanton expenditure on entertainment. Impromptu suppers that highlighted the city's early social calendar gave way to more select and lavish gatherings in the 1880s as the local elite began to establish social and physical distance between its members and the average run of Kansas Citians. Now the high point in the social schedule was the New Year's Day open house, when prominent hostesses put on duchesse lace and "dripping diamonds" to greet friends and usher them to refreshment tables heaped nearly to the candelabra with delicacies. Despite the title "open house," no one who lacked the proper social credentials dared to send in a card, for those who attended came from an exclusive set.[7] But the local newspapers carried column after column describing the appointments, favors, and dress at these occasions so that the common folk learned who their social betters were, and how magnificently better at that. In years to follow, the Kansas City Club, the University Club, the Kansas City Country Club, and a dozen other select organizations also served to anoint the chosen, though in less publicized ceremonies.

Presumably, the distinguished members of these clubs could proclaim their status even more tangibly in the bricks and mortar of a home. Instead, they found it difficult to establish homesites that provided both a lasting expression of their social place and a reliable barrier to the unsavory aspects of urban life. Repeatedly, the wealthy settled in distinguished residential enclaves, only to find themselves surrounded by blight within a few years and forced to move to newer, more fashionable precincts. The migratory habits of the elite were dictated in part by the transient character of Kansas City's business centers. As Figure 1.1 shows, city boundaries had to expand considerably to keep up with the migration of trade and residence. When the streets were graded in the 1850s, commerce shifted from the river levee to the adjacent heights south of the river. There the expanding business hub gradually encroached on Knob Hill, the first of the city's enclaves of wealth. Worse, the neighboring business center also sported honky-tonks, lewd theatricals, a clutch of gambling parlors, and most of the bawdy houses, where visiting cattlemen made nightly riot. Just east of Knob Hill, an impoverished

6. Case, "Kansas City," 112; Laura Coates Reed, ed., *In Memoriam: Sarah Walter Chandler Coates,* 62, 92.
7. "Society." Mounted Clippings File, MVR-KCPL.

population, mostly Irish and black, occupied East Kansas—an area so tough that the police gave it up to its vice lords to control.[8]

Some of the Knob Hill refugees moved to Quality Hill, a neighborhood of fine homes overlooking the West Bottoms along the Kansas River. Kersey Coates had developed the area in the mid-1860s, building his own home there as well as the town's first luxury hotel and opera house. But Coates's developments attracted commercial establishments southward, too. The city's business center consequently shifted several blocks south by 1880, turning the old town center into a haunt for sports, bawds, and transients that came to be called the North End. Meanwhile, the new commercial center pressed on the flank of Quality Hill, and rail yards, packing houses, and soap factories filled the bottomland below it. Clouds of stinking vapor and the shanty houses of workers rose together toward the hilltop. By 1910, Quality Hill's mansions had been converted to private hospitals or rooming houses for penniless clerks and transient craftsmen. Development overtook other pockets of wealthy homes, too. Southern-born refugees from Knob Hill, who preferred not to settle among the Yankees who predominated on Quality Hill, had settled on Independence Avenue east of the business center, only to see blocks of flats for the middle class cluster around their mansions after new streetcar lines reached the avenue. The southerners escaped south to a new development along Troost Avenue in the 1880s. Within twenty years, they were driven out of that enclave when new streetcar lines brought hordes more middle-class straphangers to live beside them.[9]

Even more unsettling was a real estate boom that swept the city between 1880 and 1887. Kansas City's population increased by 240 percent in the decade of the eighties, and speculators rushed to capitalize on that amazing growth. Properties sometimes changed hands two or three times in a day as building contractors, carpenters, and men with more ambition than construction skills erected houses and apartment blocks. Together they took out more than $10.5 million in building permits in 1886. Even after the bubble in real estate trades broke in 1888, builders continued to put up cheap two-story frame houses and garish three-story frame apartment blocks. Sometimes lacking paved sidewalks, sewer connections, and adequate streetcar service, these hasty subdivisions, which abutted many stable, more affluent neighborhoods, jeopardized property values. By the end of the decade,

8. George Ehrlich, *Kansas City, Missouri: An Architectural History*, 9; A. Theodore Brown and Lyle W. Dorsett, *K.C.: A History of Kansas City, Missouri*, 45.

9. Clifford Naysmith, "Quality Hill: The History of a Neighborhood"; "Structural Kansas City, Topography, and Annexations," Native Sons Archives, MVR-KCPL.

Kansas City, 1897 and 1909

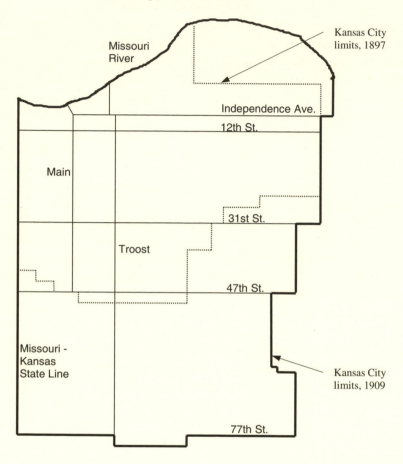

Figure 1.1

seven thousand such houses stood vacant. Out-of-town investors, who had supplied most of the capital for the boom, foreclosed on mortgagees for the unoccupied properties, leaving the city short of capital and scarred by weed-choked, semivacant subdivisions.[10]

Clearly, some sort of controls over the uses of the city's space were needed if its homes were to provide secure financial investments and unmistakable

10. Cowherd, "Experiences and Observations," 6–7; Chamber of Commerce of Kansas City, "Kansas City on Parade: The Real Estate Industry," Vertical File, MVR-KCPL; Brown and Dorsett, *K.C.*, 53–54.

signals of their owners' status. The first to invent some control measures were developers of neighborhoods for the well-to-do, but their innovations would later be used by the middle class both to secure and to segregate their own subdivisions. Near the end of the real estate boom in 1886, two new subdivisions called Hyde Park and Kenwood were designed to remove the uncertainties in the real estate market that plagued the rich. Both included deed restrictions that required high standards of quality in home construction and placement, but what truly distinguished them was the developers' foresight regarding a deep ravine that separated Hyde Park and Kenwood. Similar gullies dotted the topography elsewhere in Kansas City, attracting shanty-dwellers because the land was too irregular for proper homesites. Where shanty hollows sprouted near high-class residential areas like Quality Hill, they eroded land value. As a preventive measure, Hyde Park's developers, Samuel Jarvis and C. C. Conklin, hired George Kessler, a young landscape architect who had apprenticed briefly with Frederick Law Olmsted. Kessler's task was to guard the ravine against use by undesirables. Retaining much of the ravine's natural beauty, he transformed it into the median of a rambling roadway, where residents could take the air or stage athletic contests. Affluent refugees from deteriorating neighborhoods snapped up the lots and built homes that retained their cachet long after other such enclaves had lost their prestige.[11]

Hyde Park might have been beautiful, but it was just one pocket surrounded by what remained an ugly city. Almost none of the city's 89 miles of street were paved in 1880. Fewer than a third of its houses were connected to the sewer system, which was in itself inadequate, while the rest relied on leaking vaults, cesspools, and gutters to dispose of wastes. Rains converted streets to quagmires and leached offal into many residents' sources for drinking water; billboards scarred the hillsides or concealed muddy vacant lots in the center of downtown. No one, regardless of income, escaped the obnoxious sights and smells. Compounding the problem, city leaders believed, Kansas City's ugliness hampered growth. In the 1890s, the local economy still depended on outside investors for much of its capital, largely in eastern and British money invested in agricultural mortgages, local real estate, and the wholesale trade that dominated the local economy. City fathers hoped to expand a slender industrial base by attracting manufacturers, but the city functioned largely as a broker marketing and distributing agricultural

11. Kansas City Landmarks Commission, "Hyde Park Historic District," 1; William S. Worley, *J. C. Nichols and the Shaping of Kansas City: Innovation in Planned Residential Communities*, 52–53; Lyle Kennedy, "The First Flight to the Suburbs," 6–7; William H. Wilson, *The City Beautiful Movement in Kansas City*, 45–46.

commodities, linking rural tradesmen to eastern suppliers, and wholesaling money.[12] In any case, Kansas City depended on its ability to impress outsiders as a prime location in which to live or do business—an impression the city's shabby appearance contradicted.

A movement to dress up the city with public parks sputtered briefly in the 1870s, then regained vigor in the late 1880s by claiming that urban beautification would spark economic growth. Once the city acquired legal authority, it created a Board of Park and Boulevard Commissioners, which in turn hired George Kessler to design and construct the most ambitious system of parks and boulevards in the country. Kessler completed his plans in 1893. By 1915, work was largely finished on a network of gracious boulevards that threaded the city and linked its carefully planned parks to each other and to Swope Park, a huge acreage given to the city by real estate magnate Thomas Swope.[13] To benefit the working population, the park plan scattered smaller green spaces and playgrounds around the city. But the arguments Kessler made in defense of his design indicated who he believed would be the real beneficiaries of the park and boulevard system. His system, Kessler promised, would give "a permanent residence character to certain sections of the city, and will determine and fix for a long time to come, if not permanently, the best and most valuable residence property."[14] Builders of fine homes would seek out the boulevards, Kessler predicted, because boulevards retained the value of adjacent properties. Stable middle-class neighborhoods would develop at a slightly greater distance from the new thoroughfares. In the absence of zoning ordinances, Kessler proposed that his planned land use would naturally divide the city into industrial, mercantile, and residential areas and prevent the blighting encroachment of small shops and businesses upon districts of quality homes. In short, his project aimed to raise values of select properties and keep them elevated.

Park construction also targeted "blight." West Terrace Park replaced the shacks and signboards that crept up the bluffs from the industrial West Bottoms toward Quality Hill. Penn Valley Park evicted shanty dwellers from a ravine that lay between Kansas City and the fine suburbs of Westport—a separate municipality until Kansas City voters elected to annex it in 1897. Modest homes, many of them occupied by African Americans, gave way to

12. Wilson, *City Beautiful,* 15–16, 73; Research Department, *Economic Growth in Kansas City.*

13. William H. Wilson, "Beginning of the Park and Boulevard Movement in Frontier Kansas City, 1872–1882," 255–73.

14. *Report of the Board of Park and Boulevard Commissioners of Kansas City, Missouri,* 14.

the Paseo, Kessler's loveliest and most ornamented boulevard. While the landscape architect tacitly acknowledged that evicted families were forced to swell other, overcrowded slums, he was content so long as the displaced poor did not spawn new slums elsewhere in the city. Energized by their success with parks and boulevards, city leaders convinced the railroad companies to abandon old Union Depot in the West Bottoms, where the sounds and smells of the stockyards assaulted arriving passengers and resident plug-uglies relieved them of their wallets. The new Union Station, an enormous building in the Beaux Arts Classical style, sat atop the bluffs southeast of the Bottoms, where its construction ousted yet another settlement of African American and white squatters along O.K. Creek. A station park prevented dives and gaming parlors from infesting the new terminal site. In all, the project gave newcomers and potential investors a sanitized first glimpse of the city.[15]

Despite these examples of slum clearance, the wealthy remained uneasy enough about property values to attract the attention of a young real estate developer named J. C. Nichols. The lessons of Hyde Park and Kessler's plan registered with Nichols, who shifted his real estate interests from Kansas City, Kansas, to the Missouri side of the state line. Between 1905 and 1908, the young Nichols assembled a large parcel adjacent to the Kansas City Country Club. With the help of George Kessler, Nichols incorporated boulevards and curving roadways into his subdivision and preserved some of the natural topography's rugged beauty in its layout. Borrowing the cachet of the nearby links, he called his the Country Club District to entice affluent buyers. What truly distinguished Nichols's district from similar developments in Kansas City and elsewhere was the rigor with which he restricted buyers' use of their property. He included the typical requirements concerning minimum size and cost of homes, along with strictures against selling or renting to blacks. Unlike other developers, however, Nichols added a legal safeguard by filing the initial restrictions with the plat map and attaching them to the home buyer's deed. To buttress the property restrictions, Nichols organized an association of home owners to enforce them. Membership and dues were mandatory for property owners in the Country Club District. Thus, Nichols's realty company, abetted by the homes association, ensured that successive owners met fairly high standards in maintaining their property and that they complied with the restrictions that bound present and future deed holders. The developer advertised his restrictions aggressively to high-income buyers, who

15. Wilson, *City Beautiful,* 85, 91–99; Naysmith, "Population," folder 4, 74; Ehrlich, *An Architectural History,* 77; *Kansas City: A Place in Time,* 148.

quickly purchased lots and erected expensive homes in the Country Club District.[16]

By 1908, Kansas City's notables had secured their own social and physical niches. They proclaimed their status with lavish displays, private entertainments, and public spectacles. The Country Club District and other planned developments insulated them from urban squalor and guaranteed their investments in their homes against rapid changes in land use and occupancy. One now could choose an address of lasting noblesse. And they had tidied up an unsightly town. At least, those areas of blight that were most likely to strike the eye of an affluent resident or a potential investor had given way to beautiful parks, winding boulevards, or civic monuments. But none of this did a Clarence Burton much good, for horrendous slums remained where visitors were not likely to see them, and commerce and light industry continued to encroach on humbler neighborhoods. The Burtons of Kansas City had to keep their households on the move to stay ahead of it all. While the elite had managed to articulate for the middle class an obsession with ugliness and untidy spaces, they had succeeded in controlling and beautifying only the spaces germane to their own interests.

■ ■ Urban Space and the Middle-Class Home

In fact, it only became *more* difficult for the likes of Clarence Burton to distance their families from the squalid side of urban life. Decorum, respectability, the chance to associate only with people of similar rectitude— these were difficult to preserve when residents were exposed to the morally corrosive influences of the city. Crises involving saloons and brothels illustrated just how difficult in 1913. Eight years earlier, progressive governor Joseph Folk had tried to provide some protection for the middle class when he ordered Kansas City police to keep saloons out of the so-called "residential districts." Having the power to appoint two out of the three members of the Kansas City Board of Police Commissioners, Folk and the like-minded governors who succeeded him kept the quarantine in place. Unfortunately for respectable householders, however, the quarantine ended in 1913. Newly appointed police commissioners abandoned the policy by issuing licenses to twenty-six saloons in residential areas and school zones and by discharging the police officers who had been the most zealous in enforcing the earlier ban. In their place commissioners hired "men who are notoriously identified

16. Worley, *J. C. Nichols,* 65–71; Ehrlich, *Architectural History,* 64, 72.

with the most vicious elements of society," protested the Good Government League in its open letter to the governor.[17]

Alarmed by this reversal, church men and women trained their sights on a greater social menace—the city's red-light district. Ironically, Kansas City owed its tenderloin to the election of a reform-minded Republican governor, Herbert Hadley, in 1908. Determined to cleanse the state's big cities of vice, Hadley appointed Republican attorney Thomas Marks to Kansas City's Board of Police Commissioners. Rather than attempt to eradicate prostitution, however, Marks adopted a European scheme to confine it to a regulated red-light district in the city's North End. According to the so-called Marks plan, police officers quietly collected fines of thirty dollars per month from each bawdy house (twenty dollars additional from houses where spirits were served) in exchange for the resort keeper's promise to run an "orderly" disorderly house and to remain within the boundaries of the North End. While prostitution survived under his so-called segregation system, Marks believed that the plan achieved his most important purpose by keeping the business away from decent neighborhoods. "Vice cannot be suppressed and cannot be scattered like measles along our boulevards," he argued. "So we must reduce the evil to the minimum."[18]

Public satisfaction with Marks's system eroded in 1911, when the Board of Public Welfare commissioned New York social worker Maud Miner to survey prostitution in the city. Miner "challenged the credulity of leading society and clubwomen" when she informed them that 460 white girls worked in 99 resorts in the city. In particular, the social worker condemned the city's fines system for licensing immorality. Horrified by the city's compromise with vice, the Church Federation of Kansas City raised objections of its own. Segregation did not protect respectable folk from contact with the social evil, the federation argued, because men and women alike had to venture into the North End to transact their affairs at the city hall and courthouse. Moreover, segregation perpetuated the white slave trade, a menace to daughters of even the best homes, and it propagated venereal diseases that "cripple the mechanical efficiency of production." Just as ominous, by allowing the police to wink at prostitution, segregation encouraged lax prosecution of all crimes and destroyed the ordinary citizen's respect for law and order.[19] In short, the civic order that safeguarded middle-class proprieties was at risk.

17. *Kansas City Times,* September [missing date] 1913.
18. William M. Reddig, *Tom's Town: Kansas City and the Pendergast Legend,* 69. See also, *Social Improvement News,* October 1943.
19. *Kansas City Post,* May 25, 1911, May 28, 1911; *Kansas City Times,* September 20, 1913.

Demands to extinguish the red-light district intensified in October 1913, when the Church Federation's vice committee reorganized as the Society for the Suppression of Commercialized Vice. That month, the society staged a mass meeting to protest the fines system. Police commissioners found themselves in an embarrassing position. Only a month before, the commission had outraged middle-class householders by abandoning the eight-year-old policy that kept saloons out of the residential wards. Now they faced calls for appointment of a new police board because of the red-light issue. Consequently, the commissioners closed down the red-light district, sending officers to evict four hundred women from the North End's brothels in a few nights of raids. The city's leading madam, Annie Chambers, warned the society that its tactics would only scatter the "girls" throughout the city. Within a few weeks, it was clear that Chambers was correct, for the society began receiving evidence that streetwalkers were operating in formerly chaste residential neighborhoods. Meanwhile, the society brought suits demanding the removal of bawdy houses as public nuisances, only to be balked by a Missouri Supreme Court ruling that a brothel was not "a public nuisance in any sense of the term."[20] For the remainder of the decade, the society tried in vain to secure a state abatement law with which to enjoin the use of private property for immoral purposes.

Without injunctions to wield, the society watched helplessly as prostitution spread outside the North End. Streetwalkers, most of whom now lacked the protection they had received from the madams of the old brothel district, took their clients to the rooming houses that clustered between Twelfth and Nineteenth Streets. The northern end of the Paseo, the grandest of the city's new boulevards, acquired an unsavory reputation. In the central business district itself, employees in the hotels along the principal western thoroughfares procured women, liquor, and narcotics for guests, while drug peddlers followed the brothel keepers back into the wide-open North End. If anything, prostitution was now more open and brazen, more aggressive in claiming territory, and more closely linked to the illicit trade in narcotics. Having aimed to suppress commercialized vice altogether, the society had to settle for decontamination of the better neighborhoods. Consequently, the society's officers announced plans for a vice census to "protect the residence districts of the city from an invasion of the evicted women of the

20. Quoted in reports of the Society for the Suppression of Commercialized Vice in "Prostitution," Vertical File, MVR-KCPL. See also, *Kansas City Star,* October 12, 1913; *Kansas City Journal,* November 12, 1913; *Kansas City Times,* September 1913, in "Prostitution," Mounted Clippings File, MVR-KCPL.

red light zone," and they called on householders to report to the society any immoral enterprises that located in their neighborhoods.[21] In effect, the word *segregation*—which was originally applied to the enclosure of vice within bounds—now came to describe more limited, defensive measures for excluding undesirable occupants only from selected zones.

In 1917, complacent politicians found this proliferation of prostitution difficult to ignore. That year, the U.S. Army discovered an unusually large outbreak of venereal disease in Kansas military encampments. When the army traced the source to Kansas City, which an army survey found to be riddled with vice, the U.S. Attorney General ordered the city council to enact an ordinance providing medical inspections and isolation of diseased prostitutes. Otherwise, the military would post sentries at Union Station to prevent soldiers from venturing into Kansas City proper. City fathers, who would be hard-pressed to explain to visitors why doughboys required armed protectors in their city, hastened to pass the ordinance. After another army survey found no improvement in the notorious city by early 1918. Locals learned that if Kansas City did not clean up its own vice problem, the War Department intended to do it. Confessing its own impotence, the Society for the Suppression of Commercialized Vice applauded a federal plan that established a vice-free zone within a five-mile radius of an army encampment in the city.[22] Once the fines system had confined vice to a single district, but the opponents of vice had destroyed that system. Now, the best they could do to repair the damage was to establish a few islands of morality. They had lost considerable ground. And, if middle-class families like the Burtons wanted to make their homes in one of those islands, they had to be prepared to call the moving van.

■ ■ Ward Politics and Moral Order

As in other cities, attempts to clean up urban vice in Kansas City foundered in machine politics. From 1892 until his death in 1911, Jim Pendergast controlled the Democratic First Ward, which encompassed the West Bottoms. From there he "guided" upward of one-half the votes cast in the city as a whole. Tom Pendergast inherited his brother's First Ward satrapy and his rivalry with Democratic boss Joseph Shannon when Jim died in 1911. Tom

21. *Kansas City Star,* October 12, 1913; *Kansas City Times,* February 2, 1918.
22. *Kansas City Times,* January 31, 1918, February 5, 1918; *Kansas City Post,* May 16, 1918.

proved to be an even better organizer. Until the younger Pendergast's imprisonment in 1939, Kansas City would be known as "Tom's Town."[23]

Yet, the Pendergast machine offered middle-class voters like Clarence Burton some help in making their neighborhoods wholesome and secure, for the Pendergasts showed considerable ingenuity in how they maneuvered local politics. For the most part, their methods were the proven ones. The down-and-out obtained food, fuel, jobs, or shelter from the politicos. Profits on sin paid for the handouts: Jim Pendergast owned a saloon, and his brother owned both a liquor wholesaling company and the Jefferson Hotel, the special target of antivice crusaders who regarded it as the most infamous resort in town. Lesser men in the Pendergast and Shannon factions pocketed a share of the illicit trades in the form of graft, kickbacks, or sales revenues. It was no surprise that Kansas City's two state senators played the deciding part in defeating the abatement and injunction law against prostitution in successive legislatures.[24] Kansas City's peculiar demographics, however, required a certain amount of versatility on the part of its bosses. Numerically speaking, Kansas City was a middle-class town. Despite growth in the city's manufacturing sector in the twentieth century, growth of the tertiary sector of the local economy outpaced growth in heavy industry. Insurance and financial services employed an army of clerical and sales personnel. Wholesalers, railways, and manufacturers hired a similar phalanx of bookkeepers, timekeepers, and shipping clerks. Together, the white-collar employees in manufacturing, trade, transportation, and clerical services accounted for nearly 40 percent of those employed in 1919. Altogether, wage earners in manufacturing accounted for just 27 percent of employed persons in the city in that same year. Lack of heavy industry meant that the city's immigrant population also hovered at a comparatively low 15 percent in the late nineteenth and early twentieth centuries.[25]

Given the small number of ethnic voters and a preponderance of office workers and petty entrepreneurs in the population, the Pendergasts had to

23. Lyle W. Dorsett, *The Pendergast Machine*.

24. *Kansas City Times*, February 7, 1918; Society for the Suppression of Commercialized Vice, "Secretary's Annual Report," October 15, 1920, in "Prostitution," Vertical File, MVR-KCPL.

25. By comparison, in Milwaukee, a city of similar size and age, only 29 percent of the employed population held lower level white-collar jobs. Wage earners in manufacturing represented 38.0 percent of Chicago's employed population and 50.1 percent of Milwaukee's labor force in 1920. *Fourteenth Census of the United States: Occupations*, vol. 4, 168–85, and vol. 9, 806–8. Occupations were categorized as "middle class" according to Stephan Thernstrom's occupational rankings in *The Other Bostonians: Poverty and Progress in the American Metropolis, 1880–1970*, Appendix B.

look beyond the usual electoral base of the urban machine for support. When it was expedient, Boss Jim formed strategic alliances with the business elite. He gave critical support to the proposal to build parks and boulevards and to the plan to move Union Station, which won him support from the middle class for his statesmanlike conduct. Boss Tom would improve upon that tactic by sending lieutenants into the eastside middle-class neighborhoods to organize residents into Democratic Clubs, which provided those householders with personalized access to the seats of power. One of the rewards Boss Tom offered middle-class voters was a promise to keep vice out of their neighborhoods. A vote for the machine might not eradicate immorality—the machine depended too heavily on vice profits to do that—but it could keep vice out of your own backyard if your backyard lay in the right neighborhood. This meant, ironically, that the machine shared some of the middle- and upper-class interest in purifying selected urban spaces.

■ ■ Spatial Order and Social Reform

If voting the machine ticket struck one as unethical or ineffective, another tool emerged in the early twentieth century for imposing some order on Kansas City's spaces. A new kind of civic leader aimed to domesticate the city. Fired by innovative ideas for bettering society, these men and women established new kinds of organizations, some with unprecedented statutory powers. The new leadership represented a shifting coalition of upper-class and upper-middle-class activists—"civic housekeepers"—who aimed to make the city as clean, orderly, and attractive as the housewife strove to make her home.[26] They understood that exclusive clubs and neighborhoods offered no protection to those like the Burtons who could not afford them. The machine's compromise with the devil appalled them. Instead, civic housekeepers proposed wholly new ways to quell the urban disorder that plagued employers and family heads like Burton.

One of these housekeeping coalitions established the nation's first municipal welfare bureau in Kansas City in 1910. William Volker, a wealthy

26. William J. Reese has coined the term *municipal housekeepers* to refer specifically to female progressives who applied the values of the cult of domesticity to the reform of urban schools and other social and political institutions in the late nineteenth and early twentieth centuries. I have amended his term to describe a largely male coalition that seemed to me to share a housekeeper's interest in neatness, order, and loveliness. See Reese, *Power and the Promise of School Reform: Grassroots Movements during the Progressive Era,* 30–49.

manufacturer and irrepressible philanthropist, headed the drive for a public welfare department and provided a good deal of its early funds from his own pocket. Jacob Billikopf, who aided Volker, was superintendent of United Jewish Charities. Prominent lawyer and political figure Frank Walsh had a hand in numerous reform activities, in addition to his participation on the Board of Public Welfare. As its first secretary, the welfare board hired Leroy Halbert, who had been schooled in the Social Gospel as an assistant to the Rev. Charles Sheldon. Until it was severely weakened by machine politics in 1917, the welfare department provided factory inspections, legal aid, emergency relief and loans, job placement, and mothers' allowances.[27] Much of the department's early effort went into gathering research for a report to the public on social conditions in 1913. That report, titled *Social Prospectus of Kansas City,* demonstrated that civic housekeepers were preoccupied with spatial environment. The report paid scant attention to wage or employment problems, but detailed instead the sanitary conditions and state of building repair in slum areas and the degree to which slum residents were subject to the corrosive temptations of saloons, vice dens, gaming parlors, and candy stores. If social ills had social cures, as Frank Walsh promised, then both the ills and the cures could be found in the uses of urban space. In Paul Boyer's words, these were optimistic environmentalists who aimed "to create in the city the kind of physical environment that would gently but irresistibly mold a population of cultivated, moral, and socially responsible city dwellers."[28]

■ ■ Conclusion

As the nineteenth century closed, only the upper class had established social and physical distance between itself and "undesirables"—whether land uses or people—with green spaces, manicured boulevards, civic monuments, and restricted subdivisions. Spatial distance and social seclusion were more difficult for members of the middle class to attain, since middle-class social life still exposed its members to varied social contacts. After all, membership in the Businessmen's Bible Class, with two thousand men enrolled, did not distinguish one nearly so well as membership in the Kansas City Club. Recreation drew the middle class to the theaters and amusement parks where the working class also gathered, not to the sequestered club rooms and ballrooms where the rich relaxed. Men and women of the middling ranks rode

27. Department of Superintendence, *Kansas City and Its Schools,* 93–94; Brown and Dorsett, *K.C.,* 155–56.
28. Paul Boyer, *Urban Masses and Moral Order in America, 1820–1920,* 190.

the streetcars with the lower class, sent their children to public schools, and shopped or worked in a business center where harlots inveigled customers and dope dealers canvassed their routes. Middle-class anxieties over vice and crime multiplied, in part because its members could not distance themselves from evil as thoroughly as the elite had done. Their vehemence in the struggles over saloon licensing and prostitution showed how precarious their protection from vice really was. Just as worrisome, a heavier proportion of their income went to the purchase of housing that lacked the safeguards of value that the affluent enjoyed. And just about anyone could be their neighbor.

Still, the elite had provided some models for how to create social distance that a middle class might imitate. Rivalry between bosses and reformers only intensified the attention paid to urban space, since they bid for the allegiance of middle-class constituents by offering opposite methods for sprucing up the urban landscape. Perhaps because their city had looked so wretched at the start, many Kansas Citians developed an intense preoccupation with their city's appearance and an abiding faith in beauty and cleanliness as a social palliative.

2

Setting Boundaries

The Emergence of Jim Crow, 1900–1920

■ ■ ■

IN 1900, WHEN Joseph Johnson ended his day as a pressman, he came home to the 1000 block of Vine Street in Kansas City's eastside, a still-young suburb of roomy frame and shirtwaist houses on tree-lined streets. Johnson might exchange a wave or a friendly word with his nearest neighbor, Judge John Wofford, or with one of the adult Wofford children, who still lived with their parents while holding down jobs as clerk, stenographer, and surveyor. Across the street, Johnson could see the homes of a day laborer and a tobacco cutter—like himself and Judge Wofford, both white and native born. Directly opposite Johnson, however, lived Mrs. Stokes, an African American widow and washerwoman who shared her home with her adult daughter and niece, yet still found room to take in eight black youngsters under age ten. The neighborhood in the 1100 block just south of Johnson's home lacked some of the diversity of his own block. Its residents were all white; nearly all their households included young children. But some of those households also afforded live-in servants, and the household heads' occupations included a grocery store owner, a newspaperman, and a wholesale liquor salesman among its white-collar residents, along with a rich assortment of blue-collar trades that included carpenter, hairdresser, hat trimmer, and jewel worker.

A decade later, not much had changed in the 1000 block of Vine. One of Judge Wofford's sons, now an attorney, still occupied the Wofford home, along with two of his adult sisters. Across the street, the widow Stokes had changed her name to Ray and her job to servant "working out," and she no longer housed young children, but she remained in her former home, and hers remained the only African American household on the block. While none of the other residents of the 1000 block in 1900 still lived there in 1910, they had been replaced by a nearly identical cohort of whites employed in a mixture of blue-collar building trades and white-collar, largely clerical, jobs. By contrast, the 1100 block of Vine had undergone a dramatic transformation. In 1910, only one white household containing a wholesale dry goods clerk and his wife, a Christian Science practitioner, remained. All other residents of the block were African Americans, almost all toiling as waiters, porters, and servants.

By the end of yet another decade, both blocks housed an entirely African American population. But it had taken twenty years for those blocks to "turn black," even though they lay at the heart of what was becoming a black ghetto. The Jim Crow that emerged along Vine Street was a patchy affair with irregular borders. Just as surprising, the transformation, along with the animosity it triggered, occurred in one of the city's "nicest" neighborhoods peopled by solid citizens of both races. Examining the dynamics of change on Vine Street and elsewhere—the timing, the location, the participants—helps account for those surprises. It reveals as well the ways in which concerns about space and social status entwined to shape both a city and its racial hierarchy in the twentieth century's first two decades.

■ ■ Beginnings of Kansas City's African American Community

Kansas City's African American population developed from a tiny core of just 166 slaves and 24 free blacks who resided in the city in 1860. Within ten years, the black population had risen to more than 3,700.[1] As Table 2.1 shows, it continued to expand steadily throughout the nineteenth century. The most visible group of African American newcomers reached Kansas City in 1879, when the first "Exodusters" appeared at the city's wharves. Hoping to escape the violence and political repression that the white south inflicted on emancipated blacks after Reconstruction, these southern black emigrants had sold their meager goods for river passage and headed to Kansas, where they expected to find free land and just treatment. Instead, many of the Exodusters (perhaps a third of the fifteen thousand to twenty thousand who made the journey) found themselves stranded in Kansas City, Missouri, and Kansas City, Kansas, when their travel funds ran out. Relief funds raised by African Americans and by the mayors of the two cities enabled many of them

---

1. *Eighth Census of the United States: Population,* vol. 1, 281; *Ninth Census of the United States: Population,* vol. 1, 190.

to reach their destinations in Kansas, but other emigrant families stayed behind to establish permanent homes in the two Kansas Cities.

A less dramatic but steady migration brought hundreds more African American families from the rural south to Kansas City in following years. More important to the city's growth, large numbers of African Americans abandoned rural Missouri in favor of life in the city, where jobs and schooling were more readily available. Consequently, Kansas City's African American population increased by 68 percent in the 1880s while the African American population of surrounding Jackson County shrank by 40 percent. In the period 1880 to 1910, when the total black population in Missouri rose by a scant 8 percent, Kansas City's African American population nearly tripled. And the city achieved that growth in spite of a high rate of out-migration of African Americans from Kansas City.[2]

■ ■ Race Relations in the Latter Nineteenth Century

Relations between black and white Kansas Citians in the latter nineteenth century were shaped in part by Missouri law. One of four slaveholding states that remained in the Union during the Civil War, Missouri waited until 1865 to abolish slavery within its borders. Thereafter, the state's lawmakers imposed comparatively few legal disabilities upon black citizens, in part because the Radical Republicans who controlled state politics after the Civil War reckoned that their schemes for economic and social progress would be difficult to carry out if black Missourians were kept an "ignorant and degraded class."[3] Consequently, the state's new constitution in 1865 granted most civil rights to African Americans, except the capacity to vote or hold public office, and it included a provision that permitted local school districts to educate black children. Both provisions, however, fell far short of the full citizenship that Missouri freedmen sought. In 1865, black activists formed the Missouri Equal Rights League to petition for voting rights. Although the state legislature withstood freedmen's demands for seven years, ratification of the Fifteenth Amendment to the United States Constitution enabled

2. Nell Irvin Painter, *Exodusters: Black Migration to Kansas after Reconstruction;* Dwayne Martin, "The Hidden Community: The Black Community of Kansas City, Missouri, during the 1870s and 1880s," 23–29, 43, 58, 70–71; Susan D. Greenbaum, *The Afro-American Community in Kansas City, Kansas: A History,* 24–29; Lorenzo J. Greene, Gary R. Kremer, and Antonio F. Holland, *Missouri's Black Heritage,* 114. By 1900, 55 percent of black Missourians lived in cities.

3. Speech of an unnamed delegate to Missouri's constitutional convention in 1865, quoted in Virginia Louise Glover, "Negro Education in Missouri, 1865–1900," 7–8.

Population of Kansas City, Missouri
1870-1920

Year	Total* Population	WHITE			FOREIGN			BLACK		
		Census Count	% Total	% Chg.	Census Count	% Total	% Chg.	Census Count	% Total	% Chg.
1870	32,260	28,484	88		7,679	24		3,764	12	
1880	55,785	46,484	83	+63	9,301	17	+21	8,143	15	+116
1890	132,716	119,016	90	+156	20,858	16	+124	13,700	10	+68
1900	163,752	146,090	89	+23	18,410	11	-12	17,567	11	+28
1910	248,381	224,677	90	+54	23,327	9	+27	23,566	10	+34
1920	324,410	293,517	90	+31	27,320	8	+17	30,719	10	+30

Source: U.S. Census   *Total includes other categories of residents not listed in the table.

Table 2.1

Radicals to overcome conservative opposition and to enfranchise black men in 1872. Meanwhile, black activists publicized the lack of adequate education for black Missourians and campaigned for an increase in both the number and the quality of black schools. African Americans' objectives suited the Radical Republicans, who insisted that black Missourians must have enough schooling to enable them to vote judiciously. Consequently, a revision of the constitution in 1875 required that districts containing at least fifteen school-aged black children must provide separate schools for black pupils.[4]

After Radical ascendancy began disintegrating in the late 1860s, Missouri state lawmakers sought to further separate the races. To keep African Americans from demanding complete desegregation of schools, the legislature approved a law in 1889 making it illegal to educate children of different races in the same schools. Having prohibited the marriage of whites to blacks or to mulattos of one-fourth black ancestry in 1869, the state's legislature revised the marriage statute in 1879 to prohibit marriage between whites and persons of one-eighth black ancestry. Except for strengthening the color line in education and marriage, however, the state enacted no other segregationist laws in the nineteenth century.[5]

4. Note also that Missouri enacted no "black codes" like those imposed in Confederate states immediately following the Civil War. C. A. Phillips, "A Century of Education in Missouri"; Glover, "Negro Education," 6–8; William E. Parrish, *A History of Missouri, 1860–1875*, 9, 123–24, 151, 254; Greene, et al., *Missouri's Black Heritage*, 93–95, 95–102; "State Auditor's Report," in *Senate Journal of the Twenty-Fourth General Assembly*, 186; W. Sherman Savage, "The Legal Provisions for Negro Schools in Missouri from 1865–1890."

5. Greene et al., *Missouri's Black Heritage*, 107; "Examples of Missouri Statutory and Constitutional Provisions Relating to Racial Segregation Other Than in Education,"

Nor did Kansas Citians enact local segregation ordinances before 1913. Perhaps because the black population never exceeded 15 percent of the total, white Kansas Citians were content to keep black Kansas Citians in their allotted place with a combination of custom, paternalism, and patronage. The way local white businessmen reacted to passage of the Civil Rights Act of 1875 showed how confident whites were that existing patterns of custom and deference would keep blacks subordinate. When the *Kansas City Times* asked whether proprietors intended to alter customary segregation practices to comply with the new legislation, reporters discovered that businessmen were, as one put it, "of the opinion that everything will go on as before." Theater managers expected to continue seating black patrons in the balconies and hotel captains to turn black lodgers away. Saloon keepers, on the other hand, declared themselves willing as ever to serve any man who could pay for his drink, regardless of skin color. None of the proprietors anticipated pressure from would-be black patrons. The *Times* concluded with some satisfaction that Kansas City could afford to dispense with the more rigid forms of segregation because, in Kansas City, "the colored people evidently know their place and are possessed of too much common sense to attempt to force themselves on the white people."[6]

Apparently, the *Times* did not believe that African Americans' common sense extended to moral or ethical matters, however. Described by journalists as "the voice of the southern Democracy and a latter-day champion of the unrepentant Confederacy," the *Times* portrayed African Americans who committed crimes as childish objects of fun and reported their misdemeanors in mocking, playful tones, as in the case of the jilted bride who assaulted her fiancé because she "loved, and loved too well."[7] A mixed race couple who demanded that a judge marry them featured in several articles that made fun of their passion for each other and of the judge's comic struggle to convince the couple that the law forbid them to marry.[8] Apparently, the *Times* and its readers found their black fellow citizens amusing but harmless. Even the Exodusters' appearance in Kansas City failed to disturb whites' satis-

---

folder 1, Box 301, Benson Papers; Bernard D. Reams, Jr., and Paul E. Wilson, eds., *Segregation and the Fourteenth Amendment in the States: A Survey of State Segregation Laws, 1865–1953*, 354–57. According to Howard Rabinowitz, it was the near majority of black residents in southern cities that induced the white residents to impose segregation in order to ensure for their own physical safety and political mastery. Howard N. Rabinowitz, *Race Relations in the Urban South, 1864–1890*, 26.

6. *Kansas City Times*, March 20, 1875.

7. *Ibid.*, October 10, 1871. The characterization of the *Times* appeared in *The First 100 Years: A Man, a Newspaper and a City*, 4.

8. See for example, *Kansas City Times*, June 22, 1872.

faction with customary relations between the races. The *Times* did worry about the sudden influx, but its concern rose not from the refugees' skin color, but from their "feeble, filthy, and destitute" condition, which made them potential carriers of deadly disease. Whether they were moved by the Exodusters' need or by their own desire to rid the city of paupers, ordinary white residents contributed food, clothing, and money to help emigrants on their way, and white philanthropists organized the Provident Association to coordinate the charitable activities required to relieve want among both stranded Exodusters and impoverished whites.[9]

Although black Kansas Citians were never as acquiescent as the *Times* reported in 1875, even their collective acts of protest failed to alarm whites. In the late nineteenth century, those protests usually targeted the police for mistreating black citizens. When angry crowds of African Americans occasionally gathered to denounce a police shooting, the Democratic *Times* blamed the protests on whites who, the *Times* claimed, "incite and encourage the colored people of Kansas City to riot." Except in these rare outbursts, the *Times* reassured readers, local black residents were too wise to be led into mischief by "would-be leaders and advisors."[10] The *Evening Star-Mail*, on the other hand, condemned the "criminal recklessness" of police officers and the tendency to excuse an officer if "he has 'only killed a nigger.'"[11] When hundreds of angry black residents formed a Protective League in 1882 to defend themselves against police abuses, the white press greeted the action without a qualm.[12]

When African Americans demanded better service from tax-supported institutions, the Kansas City Board of Education was somewhat more responsive than the police force. In fact, the desire for education seems to have been a significant inducement for African American families to move to Kansas City in the late nineteenth and early twentieth centuries. In 1885, for example, two-thirds of the eligible black children were enrolled in Kansas City schools, compared to fewer than half of the eligible white children.

9. *Kansas City Times,* April 9, 1879, April 12, 1879. Suzanna M. Grenz, "The Exodusters of 1879: St. Louis and Kansas City Response"; *Kansas City Evening Star-Mail,* October 11, 1880, October 21, 1880, October 27, 1880, October 28, 1880, November 11, 1880; Theodore A. Brown and Lyle W. Dorsett, *K.C.: A History of Kansas City, Missouri.* 77.

10. *Kansas City Times,* July 13, 1876.

11. *Kansas City Evening Star-Mail,* December 31, 1881. Established in 1880 by William Rockhill Nelson, the *Evening Star-Mail* was later called simply the *Star.* Little more than a century later, the *Star* was the only mass circulation daily to survive in Kansas City.

12. *Kansas City Evening Star-Mail,* January 31, 1882; February 1, 1882.

Two decades later the percentage of eligible black children who attended city schools had slipped to just over one-half, but that still exceeded the percentage of school-aged white youngsters who were enrolled. Consequently in 1869, two years after its organization, the school board opened Lincoln School for black youngsters. The school district created five more elementary schools for black pupils between 1880 and 1899 and converted Lincoln into a secondary school in 1887. Still, the district barely kept pace with the level of demand among African American parents. Classrooms remained crowded, with a pupil to teacher ratio of 65:1 in 1898, or one-quarter higher than the ratio in white schools. Rather than a source of disquiet for whites, black Kansas Citians constituted a "hidden community" whose presence their fellow white citizens chose more often to ignore and whose needs to neglect.[13]

■ ■ Locations of Black Population

Geographic dispersion of African Americans helped to hide their presence in the city. In 1880, blacks constituted at least 10 percent of the population in sixteen of the twenty-one census enumeration districts in the city. As late as 1890, at least one thousand blacks could be found in eight of Kansas City's ten most populous wards. Typically, these eight wards each contained about 10 percent of the total number of blacks residing in the city.[14] Despite that fairly even distribution, however, a few noticeable concentrations of African Americans emerged in the latter 1880s, as indicated on the accompanying map, Figure 2.1.

Overt racial discrimination appeared to have little to do with the emergence of these enclaves. Kansas City's black press did not mention open attempts by whites to exclude blacks from residential areas before 1903. Furthermore, these black enclaves also housed a significant number of whites. At the turn of the century, the city had yet to sort itself into homogeneous

13. *Annual Report of the Board of Education of the Kansas City Public Schools.* 1898–1899 and 1907; Carrie Westlake Whitney, *Kansas City, Missouri: Its History and Its People, 1808–1908,* 325, 337–41. The term *hidden community* is borrowed from Dwayne Martin's study.

14. Martin, "Hidden Community," 9–11; *Eleventh Census of the United States: Population,* vol. 1, pt. 1, 466. The remaining four wards on the city's periphery reported from 37 to 310 black residents. Such wide distributions of blacks were characteristic of other cities in the mid-nineteenth century. See, for example, Kenneth Kusmer, *A Ghetto Takes Shape: Black Cleveland, 1870–1930,* 41–42; Allan H. Spear, *Black Chicago: The Making of a Negro Ghetto, 1890–1920,* 14–15.

Black Enclaves – 1900

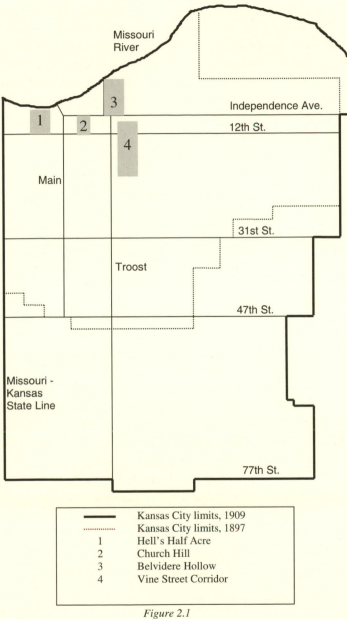

Figure 2.1

districts by class, ethnicity, or race. Instead, aggregations of African Americans seem to have developed out of a variety of decisions that black Kansas Citians made about where to live. Based on demographic studies and interviews with longtime black residents, Clifford Naysmith concluded that those decisions were shaped largely by income levels, the need to live within walking distance of employment, and the desire to live in proximity to black cultural institutions. Naysmith could not find either a pattern of residential segregation before 1900 nor any evidence of open, purposeful acts of hostility by whites toward black neighbors—real or potential—anywhere in the city.[15] Manuscript census data from four of those enclaves corresponds with Naysmith's findings. More important, the data reveal something of the place that blacks occupied in the spatial organization of the city at the turn of the century and provide a benchmark for measuring change in residential patterns after 1900.

One such enclave, located in a section of the West Bottoms called Hell's Half Acre, originated in the late 1860s as a housing site for black workers employed in building Hannibal Bridge. Around 1880, the enclave expanded when Exodusters moved from riverside refugee camps into shacks and shanties in the river bottoms. Stretching from Ninth Street north to the Missouri River's banks, the shanty slum offered cheap housing near the rail yards, packing houses, and warehouses where unskilled migrants found their first jobs as laborers and porters. The high transiency rate in the area indicated that black families left the slum as soon as they could afford better lodgings, for Hell's Half Acre deserved its nickname. A sanctuary for the thugs and grifters who infested the city's nearby train depot and for the barflies and prostitutes who inhabited the area's numerous saloons, its lack of clean water, sanitation, and paving further justified its moniker.[16]

By the turn of the century, only a fragment of the black population of Hell's Half Acre were southern migrants. In 1900, the census enumeration district that included Hell's Half Acre housed 535 black residents, two-thirds of whom were Missouri born (see Table 2.2). Almost 80 percent of the black residents who were employed earned a meager living at unskilled labor. Blacks by no means monopolized the mean accommodations of Hell's Half

15. Naysmith, "Population in Kansas City, Missouri," folder 5, 171–72. Naysmith's population study was done as part of the "History of Kansas City Project," a massive and ambitious effort initiated in 1958 by the University of Chicago and funded by the Rockefeller Foundation. The project assembled a cadre of senior scholars and young researchers to compile a detailed history of community organization and leadership within a single city.

16. Martin, "Hidden Community," 11, 32, 60; Naysmith, "Population," folder 4, 52–53.

Hell's Half Acre,
Population Profile, 1900

BLACK POPULATION		BLACK NATIVITY				
Number	535	Missouri	Midwest	Deep So.	Border So.	
% of Total	33%	66%	2%	15%	17%	
No. of Households	108					
% of Total	44%	BLACK OCCUPATIONS				
Persons/Household	5.0	White Collar	Skilled	Semiskilled	Unskilled	
Workers/Household	2.5	4%	3%	14%	79%	

WHITE POPULATION		WHITE NATIVITY				
Number	1,094	US	Ireland	Germany	Other	
% of Total	67%	79%	8%	5%	9%	
No. of Households	136					
% of Total	56%	WHITE OCCUPATIONS				
Persons/Household	8.0	White Collar	Skilled	Semiskilled	Unskilled	
Workers/Household	5.7	17%	28%	19%	36%	

Source: Twelfth Census of the U.S., Manuscript Census,
Ward 1, Enumeration District 12
Enumeration District 12, which included Hell's Half Acre, extended from the Missouri River south to Twelfth Street between Bluff and Hickory Streets.

Table 2.2

Acre, however, for the enumeration district that incorporated the slum was decidedly heterogeneous. While the heaviest concentrations of black occupants were found along Freight and Eighth Streets, black households were scattered throughout the district among their white neighbors, who made up more than two-thirds of the enumeration district's total population. Those whites were, themselves, a heterogeneous assortment. A third of them were immigrants or the children of immigrants, largely from Ireland and Germany. Although slightly more than half of the district's employed whites toiled at semiskilled or unskilled labor, nearly a fifth of them were proprietors of saloons, stores, peddling enterprises, and other small businesses. The remainder worked in white-collar clerical and sales positions or skilled trades attached to the railroads, stockyards, and farm supply houses located in the West Bottoms.[17]

17. Much of the white-collar population of the district resided in the lodging houses and hotels located in or near Hell's Half Acre. For many of them, these were probably temporary residences that they chose to be near the industries with which they did busi-

Church Hill,
Population Profile, 1900

BLACK POPULATION	
Number	372
% of Total	15%
No. of Households	114
% of Total	21%
Persons/Household	3.3
Workers/Household	1.9

BLACK NATIVITY				
Missouri	Midwest	Deep So.	Border So.	
60%	12%	10%	17%	

BLACK OCCUPATIONS			
White Collar	Skilled	Semiskilled	Unskilled
7%	8%	60%	25%

WHITE POPULATION	
Number	2,132
% of Total	85%
No. of Households	437
% of Total	79%
Persons/Household	4.9
Workers/Household	2.8

WHITE NATIVITY				
US	Ireland	Germany	Other	
90%	2%	2%	6%	

WHITE OCCUPATIONS			
White Collar	Skilled	Semiskilled	Unskilled
59%	22%	17%	2%

Source: Twelfth Census of the U.S., Manuscript Census,
Ward 8, Enumeration Districts 77 & 78
Enumeration Districts 77 and 78 extended from Ninth to Eleventh Streets between Campbell and Grand Avenue.

Table 2.3

A second black enclave, called Church Hill, offered more comfortable surroundings. Located just southeast of the city's commercial center, Church
Hill took its name from two prestigious black churches, Allen Chapel A.M.E.
and Second Baptist, whose sanctuaries stood on a summit at Tenth and
Charlotte Streets. In 1880, 15 percent of Kansas City's black population
lived within the census enumeration district containing Church Hill. Among
them were families who chose to make their homes there because the two
churches served as community centers, offering social events and recreation
as well as worship for adults and youth. Employment patterns influenced
others' preference for a Church Hill home. Many of the enclave's black residents worked as servants in the nearby homes of the city's southern elite,
or they performed domestic and laundry chores for middle-class households

---

ness. Yet the fact remains that, whatever disquiet these members of the middle class may
have felt at lodging among assorted race, ethnic, and class groups, it was not enough to
outweigh their desire for simple convenience.

in adjacent McGee's Addition.[18] By 1900, domestics outnumbered all other workers among blacks living in the Church Hill area (see Table 2.3). Two census enumeration districts encompassed Church Hill in 1900. Out of the black residents of the two districts, more than 60 percent lived at the intersections of Tenth Street with Charlotte and McGee Streets, on the hill that gave the enclave its name. But the remaining 40 percent of the enumeration districts' black population was scattered along streets where whites were a decided majority. Moreover, whites formed a near majority on Church Hill itself. Along the three intersecting blocks that comprised Church Hill proper, 46 percent of the total population and 52 percent of the households were white. Nearly half of the employed whites in the two districts held jobs in clerical, sales, or other white-collar positions; another 15 percent were professionals or proprietors of businesses, while nearly a fifth worked in skilled manual labor. In short, Church Hill was integrated in terms of both race and class.

A third African American enclave developed along two ravines located in a section of the North End that lay east of the city's old commercial center. Dubbed Belvidere and Hicks Hollows, the ravines first served as disembarkation points and encampments for Exodusters. But the hollows grew appreciably in population in the 1890s by attracting black householders who had escaped the dreary West Bottoms. While a number of black professionals owned comfortable homes overlooking the hollows, most black residents of the ravines toiled as day laborers, teamsters, and domestics. The hollows' location near the central business district and the central streetcar lines suggests that the North End ravines were an attractive location for men and women whose employment required that they move often from job site to job site within the center of heaviest population and commerce. Moreover, housing in the hollows was cheap, an important consideration for ill-paid and underemployed laborers. Unfortunately, it was also ramshackle. Landlords jammed flimsy frame structures onto the hollows' unpaved streets and alleyways. Sanitation facilities were scant, and just a fifth of the buildings were connected to city water mains, so that householders often drew their water from contaminated cisterns or carried it home from nearby saloons. Inevitably, mortality rates in the hollows far exceeded rates for the city as a whole.[19]

18. Martin, "Hidden Community," 9; Naysmith, "Population," folder 4, 53–54; folder 5, 173.
19. Martin, "Hidden Community," 32; Naysmith, "Population," folder 4, 63; folder 5, 172, 200–203; Asa Martin, *Our Negro Population: A Sociological Study of the Negroes of Kansas City, Missouri,* 96. Belvidere Hollow stretched along Lydia Avenue between

Belvidere Hollow,
Population Profile, 1900

BLACK POPULATION		BLACK NATIVITY				
Number	1,710	Missouri	Midwest	Deep So.	Border So.	
% of Total	38%	65%	13%	7%	15%	
No. of Households	446					
% of Total	43%	BLACK OCCUPATIONS				
Persons/Household	3.8	White Collar	Skilled	Semiskilled	Unskilled	
Workers/Household	2.0	2%	6%	45%	46%	

WHITE POPULATION		WHITE NATIVITY				
Number	2,821	US	Ireland	Germany	Other	
% of Total	62%	86%	5%	4%	5%	
No. of Households	581					
% of Total	57%	WHITE OCCUPATIONS				
Persons/Household	4.9	White Collar	Skilled	Semiskilled	Unskilled	
Workers/Household	1.9	29%	24%	28%	18%	

Source: Twelfth Census of the U.S., Manuscript Census,
Wards 6 & 7, Enumeration Districts 59, 60 & 61
Enumeration Districts 59, 60, & 61 extended between Troost Avenue and Highland from
Independence Avenue northward to Front Street along the Missouri River.

Table 2.4

By 1900, certain streets in the hollows were segregated, with populations as much as 90 percent black (see Table 2.4). Yet the hollows represented mere islands in a larger North End neighborhood that was at least as heterogeneous as the Church Hill vicinity. In addition to the residents of the hollows themselves, African Americans were also scattered throughout the four census enumeration districts that contained Belvidere Hollow, living on all but the northern- and southernmost streets that lay within the four enumeration districts. Of the more than 4,500 residents of those four enumeration districts, just over a third were black. Wage earners among these black men and women were virtually evenly divided between unskilled and semiskilled labor—the latter category comprised largely of teamsters and domestics. While just 14 percent of white residents were foreign born, more

---

Pacific and Belvidere Streets; Hicks Hollow was centered at the intersection of Independence and Highland Avenues. The hollows closely resembled in these characteristics the black enclaves in Pittsburgh. John Bodnar, Roger Simon, and Michael P. Weber, *Lives of Their Own: Blacks, Italians, and Poles in Pittsburgh, 1900–1960*, 68–71.

than 40 percent were the children of immigrants from Ireland, Germany, and Italy. Their occupations displayed still greater variety. Three-quarters of the employed white population was evenly divided among lower level white-collar jobs, the skilled trades, and semiskilled occupations, but members both of the professions and of unskilled labor's ranks resided in these districts. In fact, members of both white- and blue-collar ranks could be found living in neighborly proximity on nearly every city block within these four enumeration districts.

A fourth African American enclave emerged in the 1890s on the city's eastside, where builders had erected hundreds of spacious two-story homes during the real estate boom of the late 1880s. The boom's collapse left developers, contractors, and mortgage lenders with lots of modestly priced vacant houses on their hands. Anxious to move those properties in a flat market, owners gladly sold or leased homes when they could, regardless of the purchaser's skin color. Thus, a growing number of African American households came to locate between Troost and Woodland Avenues from Twelfth to Twenty-Fifth Streets, including the block of Vine Street where Judge Wofford and the widow Stokes resided. Here, certain sections earned the names Negro Quality Hill and Negro Hyde Park for their handsome homes and manicured lawns.[20] Within a decade, a corridor along Vine Street in this eastside black settlement would form the nucleus of the black ghetto in Kansas City. In 1900, however, only a patchwork of black households dotted this corridor, and a mere one-quarter of its population was African American (see Table 2.5). Those black households were somewhat more affluent than the residents of the hollows to the north, as more than half of employed blacks in the eastside Vine Street enclave reported semiskilled occupations. Another 12 percent worked at skilled labor, largely as Pullman porters, while 6 percent held white-collar or professional positions. Their white neighbors on the eastside ranked still higher on the occupational scale, since 43 percent of employed whites reported white-collar positions as professionals, proprietors of small businesses, or sales or clerical workers. More than 90 percent of white eastsiders were American born.

After 1900, however, the city's beautification projects, together with the dynamics of its real estate market, began to reconfigure African Americans' residential patterns. Kansas City's black population grew more concentrated and hence more visible, making the African American community seem more threatening to a white population whose anxieties over the occupancy of urban space were also mounting. In fact, the tendency toward a greater

20. Naysmith, "Population," folder 4, 64, 69–70; folder 5, 205–6.

Vine Street Corridor, Population Profile, 1900

BLACK POPULATION	
Number	1,331
% of Total	29%
No. of Households	336
% of Total	30%
Persons/Household	4.0
Workers/Household	2.0

BLACK NATIVITY				
Missouri	Midwest	Deep So.	Border So.	
68%	8%	8%	16%	

BLACK OCCUPATIONS				
White Collar	Skilled	Semiskilled	Unskilled	
6%	12%	51%	31%	

WHITE POPULATION	
Number	3,203
% of Total	71%
No. of Households	779
% of Total	70%
Persons/Household	4.1
Workers/Household	1.7

WHITE NATIVITY				
US	Ireland	Germany	Other	
90%	1%	4%	5%	

WHITE OCCUPATIONS				
White Collar	Skilled	Semiskilled	Unskilled	
43%	26%	26%	6%	

Source: Twelfth Census of the U.S., Manuscript Census,
Ward 9, Enumeration Districts 83, 89, 103, & 104
Enumeration Districts 83, 89, 103, & 104 were bounded on the west by Lydia Avenue and on the
east by Woodland Avenue as far as Seventeenth Street and Euclid Avenue to Twentieth Street,
with the northern boundary at Eleventh Street and the southern boundary at Twentieth Street.

Table 2.5

geographic concentration of black Kansas Citians was, initially, a by-product of both the emerging differentiation of land use in Kansas City and of white Kansas Citians' efforts to impose some order on the city's physical aspect. Specifically, the development of distinctly industrial and commercial districts, together with the construction of the park systems and of Union Station, dislodged formerly integrated neighborhoods. Prior to 1890, for example, the West Bottoms sheltered nearly an equal mix of industrial enterprises and private residences in racially integrated neighborhoods. But the expansion of rail yards, stockyards, packing houses, and warehouse facilities steadily encroached on private living space, converting the West Bottoms into a largely industrial district and uprooting householders. By 1900, the black enclave in Hell's Half Acre had shrunk to just a fragment of the West Bottom's previous black population. The encroachment of light industry continued to uproot black families from the bottoms after 1900. Meanwhile, the city's park and boulevard project led to the demolition of houses in an integrated neighborhood along the bluffs above the West Bottoms to make way for West Terrace Park. During the next decade, the new Union Station replaced the shanty homes of black and Irish laborers along O.K. Creek. Uprooted from the bottoms and bluffs, some black and Irish households found homes in a settlement along Southwest Boulevard, but commercial development there restricted the capacity of that increasingly blighted neighborhood to absorb a new population.[21] Thus, black residents and newcomers alike found their housing choices narrowed somewhat by these early examples of urban renewal.

Still, there were alternative neighborhoods from which black households might choose a homesite, depending upon the household's preferences. The old enclave at Church Hill also lay in the path of commercial expansion by the central business district, but a black enclave in nearby McGee's Addition expanded eastward across Troost Avenue in the early twentieth century. Families who wished to augment their wage incomes by growing produce sought out settlements in the Blue River Valley or at Roundtop, located on the city's far east side. Whether newcomer or longtime residents, however, most black Kansas Citians who needed to find new accommodations after 1900 preferred to locate in one of two enclaves, the North End hollows or the eastside community on Vine Street.[22]

Negro Quality Hill and its vicinity appealed more strongly to black residents who could afford to rent or purchase quarters there. With its paved and lighted streets, its access to city water and sewer lines, and its array of apartment buildings and single-family dwellings, this area made a very pleasing alternative to the North End. Equally compelling, the Vine Street corridor developed a social and economic infrastructure for communal life. A commercial district serving a largely black clientele and owned by black as well as white proprietors emerged along Vine Street. More than a dozen black churches opened their doors in or near this corridor between 1900 and 1915, most of them having moved from their original sanctuaries located in the North End or on the city's west side. Construction of new schools provided another incentive to locate in the Vine Street corridor. First opened at Eighteenth and Brooklyn in 1893, Attucks School for black pupils grew so rapidly that the school had to be moved to larger quarters at Nineteenth and Woodland in 1907. Construction of the new Lincoln High School at Nineteenth and Tracy in 1906 attracted black parents who could afford secondary schooling for their offspring. By 1912, a sociological survey estimated, some

21. Naysmith, "Population," folder 4, 55, 63; folder 5, 199.
22. *Ibid.*, folder 4, 204; folder 5, 206.

700 to 800 African American home-owners and 1,900 black renters lived in this eastside black community.[23]

■ ■ Emergence of Residential Segregation

Where once African Americans had considered communal life, commuting distances, and housing costs in selecting a homesite, locating in the Vine Street corridor or in the North End became a matter of necessity rather than choice for black Kansas Citians. As the twentieth century proceeded, housing alternatives for African Americans constricted. The local black press reported in 1907 that white realtors were increasingly reluctant to sell or rent homes to blacks in so-called respectable neighborhoods. Other real estate agents worked to dislodge black householders from otherwise white-occupied areas. According to the African American newspaper the *Rising Son,* those black purchasers who could afford comfortable homes outside the existing black enclaves were turned away by real estate agencies so often that they gave up, some of them forced to house their families in the unwholesome hollows. Where realtors failed to steer blacks away from white-occupied areas, death threats or the torching of black occupied houses succeeded. Thanks to a handful of bombings, the receipt of a letter signed "Dynamite" was usually sufficient to dislodge a new black resident. Six explosions that occurred in 1910 and 1911 on Montgall, on the disputed eastern flank of the black eastside, made dynamite letters doubly menacing.[24]

At the same time, African Americans found themselves increasingly isolated on other fronts as race relations in Kansas City made a perceptible shift toward Jim Crow. In 1904, black teachers who attended the Kansas City School District's teachers' meetings were assigned seats in a separate section.[25] Previously, black educators had mingled freely with their white colleagues at these meetings and had sat on the panels that presented scholarly papers. That same year, owners of meeting halls began to refuse to rent their facilities to blacks. By 1907, white-owned cemeteries refused to bury

23. Olive L. Hoggins, "A History of Kansas City Churches," Items 15.3 to 57.3; Martin, *Our Negro Population,* 93.

24. Naysmith, "Population," folder 5, 218–20; Martin, *Our Negro Population,* 35.

25. Race relations in Kansas City, Kansas, began to deteriorate at roughly the same time, owing in part to a 1904 incident in which a black teenager shot and killed a white boy who had been harassing him. A black vigilance committee prevented a lynching, but racial antagonisms increased, and a faction of local whites used the incidents to convince the governor to exempt Kansas City, Kansas, from a state law prohibiting segregation of public high schools. Greenbaum, *Afro-American Community,* 64–67.

the black dead, and 90 percent of black Kansas Citians who received medical care were treated by black physicians because white doctors were turning away their black patients.[26] At the state level, opponents barely managed in 1903 to beat back the Crisp bill requiring common carriers in Missouri to segregate passengers. Nonetheless, proponents introduced the bill again in 1907 and 1917.[27]

While whites tightened the boundaries that confined blacks to established zones of residence, the effects were not uniform everywhere in the city. Based on manuscript census data, the accompanying maps and figures reveal something of the dynamics of change in the two largest black enclaves between 1900 and 1920. One of those areas was Belvidere Hollow, centered at Belvidere Street and Lydia Avenue (see Figures 2.2–2.4 and Table 2.6). Census data for an area roughly two blocks by six blocks, and incorporating the core of Belvidere Hollow, shows remarkably little change in occupancy over those twenty years. Black population remained roughly a third of the total throughout the period. Owing to the smaller average size of black households, nearly half the total number of households had black occupants. Meanwhile, the streets along the eastern flank of the sampled area developed a heavier concentration of black residents between 1900 and 1910. Surprisingly, however, Lydia Avenue became more integrated in the following decade due to a 50 percent increase in the number of whites living on Lydia and a 17 percent decrease in black residents. Similarly, the appearance of black residents on the 600 block of Troost in 1910 did not touch off white flight, for the number of whites living on the block remained stable between 1910 and 1920, while the number of resident blacks returned nearly to zero. Thus, Belvidere Hollow was no more a black ghetto in 1920 than it was in 1900.

At the same time, the character of the white population altered. Where natives dominated in 1900, by 1920 some 40 percent of the area's white residents were Italians or Russian-born Jews. Furthermore, the area's population became slightly more working class. The portion of whites employed

26. *Annual Report of the Board of Education,* 1901–1902; Naysmith, "Population," folder 5, 217–18.

27. Credit for defeating the bill on each occasion was owed to a variety of interests. African Americans, including the Negro Protective League of Kansas City, lobbied strenuously to beat back the measure. See *Rising Son,* February 20, 1903; *Kansas City Sun,* March 10, 1917, March 17, 1917. Machine Democrats also opposed it in hopes of building black constituencies in St. Louis and Kansas City. See Larry Grothaus, "The Negro in Missouri Politics, 1890–1941," 34, 47. According to the *Rising Son,* Bernard Corrigan, president of Kansas City's Metropolitan Street Railway, also proved decisive in defeating the Crisp bill in 1903 because separate accommodations would increase carriers' costs.

Belvidere Hollow
Population Profile

1900

BLACK POPULATION	
Number	1,191
% of Total	36%
No. of Households	325
% of Total	42%
Persons/Household	3.7
Workers/Household	2.0

BLACK NATIVITY				
Missouri	Midwest	Deep So.	Border So.	
63%	12%	7%	16%	

BLACK OCCUPATIONS				
High Wht.Collar	White Collar	Skilled	Semiskilled	Unskilled
2%	1%	4%	46%	48%

WHITE POPULATION	
Number	2,139
% of Total	64%
No. of Households	458
% of Total	58%
Persons/Household	4.7
Workers/Household	1.9

WHITE NATIVITY				
US	Ire. & Gr.	Italy	Russia	Other
87%	8%	1%	1%	3%

WHITE OCCUPATIONS				
High Wht.Collar	White Collar	Skilled	Semiskilled	Unskilled
9%	25	23%	29%	15%

1910

BLACK POPULATION	
Number	1,132
% of Total	32%
No. of Households	380
% of Total	41%
Persons/Household	3.0
Workers/Household	2.0

BLACK NATIVITY				
Missouri	Midwest	Deep So.	Border So.	
71%	10%	10%	9%	

BLACK OCCUPATIONS				
High Wht.Collar	White Collar	Skilled	Semiskilled	Unskilled
3%	1%	6%	52%	38%

WHITE POPULATION	
Number	2,406
% of Total	68%
No. of Households	537
% of Total	59%
Persons/Household	4.5
Workers/Household	1.8

WHITE NATIVITY				
US	Ire. & Gr.	Italy	Russia	Other
61%	2%	17%	18%	1%

WHITE OCCUPATIONS				
High Wht.Collar	White Collar	Skilled	Semiskilled	Unskilled
20%	21%	17%	26%	16%

1920 Belvidere Hollow (continued)

BLACK POPULATION		BLACK NATIVITY				
Number	1,083	Missouri	Midwest	Deep So.	Border So.	
% of Total	34%	57%	17%	17%	9%	
No. of Households	347					
% of Total	44%	BLACK OCCUPATIONS				
Persons/Household	3.1	High Wht.Collar	White Collar	Skilled	Semiskilled	Unskilled
Workers/Household	1.8	2%	2%	3%	50%	43%

WHITE POPULATION		WHITE NATIVITY				
Number	2,132	US	Ire. & Gr.	Italy	Russia	Other
% of Total	66%	57%	1%	28%	12%	2%
No. of Households	448					
% of Total	56%	WHITE OCCUPATIONS				
Persons/Household	4.8	High Wht.Collar	White Collar	Skilled	Semiskilled	Unskilled
Workers/Household	1.4	25%	16%	12%	17%	30%

Source: Twelfth, Thirteenth, & Fourteenth Census of the U.S., Manuscript Census

Table 2.6

at unskilled labor doubled between 1900 and 1920. Although the portion employed in white-collar ranks increased in the same period, hucksters, peddlers, secondhand dealers, and proprietors of small businesses—most of them Italians and Jews—accounted for the increase. Linked by trade to a working-class clientele, many with resident kin in working-class occupations, these blue-collar entrepreneurs were still closely connected to working-class life.

By contrast, the Vine Street Corridor developed many of the earmarks of a ghetto in the same period. A sample portion of the corridor, shown in Figures 2.5–2.7 and Table 2.7, extended from Tenth to Nineteenth Streets and included the oldest section of black occupancy, as well as the black commercial district. Between 1900 and 1920, the area's black population more than tripled, raising blacks' share of the population from a quarter to almost three-quarters of the total. Meanwhile, white population shrank to little more than a third of its former numbers, and occupancy on block after block turned from white to black, particularly after 1910. By 1920, the newly built Paseo, with its elegant apartment buildings, stood out as a ribbon of white in an otherwise black village. Nearly half the whites who lived in the area in 1920 had a Paseo address. Among the employed white residents of the Paseo, almost half worked in lower level white-collar positions, and another 13 percent were professionals or owners of businesses. But the northernmost

Belvidere Hollow, 1900

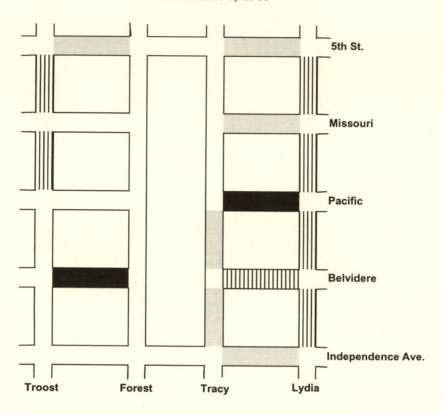

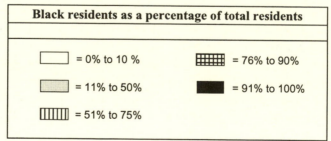

Figure 2.2

Belvidere Hollow, 1910

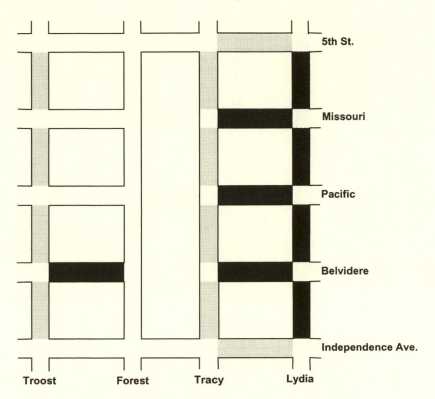

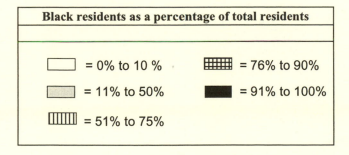

Figure 2.3

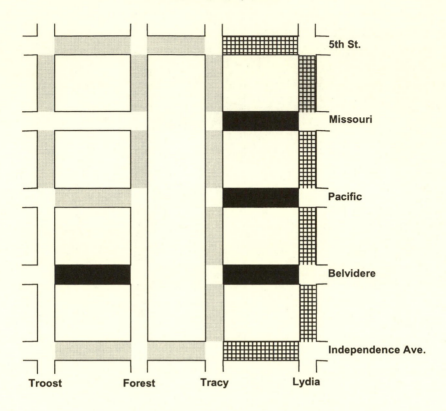

Figure 2.4

blocks of Lydia Avenue also retained a white population, of which white-collar employees formed the majority. In fact, the proportion of white-collar residents increased.

Several factors may explain the occurrence of a dramatic racial turnover in one enclave and not the other. For one, the Vine Street Corridor had decidedly more attractions for black residents than Belvidere Hollow, whose black population declined slightly in this period and declined most precipitously on Belvidere Street and Lydia Avenue, the most congested and noisome streets in the hollows. Families who could afford to leave the hollow itself had little to gain by moving onto nearby "white" streets in the North End, where the housing stock was little better than what they had left behind. But the Vine Street Corridor offered, at least initially, comfortable homes on well-kept streets and the proximity of cultural and commercial institutions. Thus blacks' preferences help explain why the Belvidere area did not "turn black." Moreover, white residents near Belvidere proved to be more tenacious occupants than the whites living near Vine Street, for the Belvidere area offered several attractions to certain groups of whites. The Orthodox synagogue Tefares Israel served as the anchor to a settlement of Russian Jews that radiated from the synagogue's location at Admiral Boulevard and Tracy Avenue, immediately south of Belvidere Street. Just west of Belvidere Hollow were Holy Rosary Catholic Church and the communal center of Italian life in the city. Both immigrant groups made ample use of Karnes Elementary School in the North End, which served almost as a settlement house providing both social services and programs to preserve the culture of its largely Italian and Jewish pupils.[28]

If cultural institutions encouraged Jews and Italians to remain in the North End, so too did land use patterns. Kansas City's North End followed a sequence found in other U.S. cities as well.[29] Abandoned first by its elite residents and then by commerce when the central business district shifted southward, the North End languished as a commercial site. Increasingly unattractive to middle-class natives as well, the area offered material inducements to immigrants: easy commuting distances to the business center, to the West Bottoms, and to the rail yards along the Missouri River at the city's northern boundary. Moreover, the North End had retained one of its original foci of commerce—the City Market, where produce and cheap

28. John W. Briggs, *An Italian Passage: Immigrants to Three Cities, 1890–1930,* 205–6; Department of Superintendence, *Kansas City and Its Schools,* 62–63; Naysmith, "Population," folder 4, 109.

29. David Ward, "The Emergence of Central Immigrant Ghettos in American Cities, 1840–1920," 171.

Vine Street Corridor
Population Profile

1900

BLACK POPULATION	
Number	1,634
% of Total	23%
No. of Households	403
% of Total	24%
Persons/Household	4.1
Workers/Household	1.9

BLACK NATIVITY				
Missouri	Midwest	Deep So.	Border So.	
67%	10%	8%	14%	

BLACK OCCUPATIONS				
High Wht.Collar	White Collar	Skilled	Semiskilled	Unskilled
3%	2%	13%	56%	25%

WHITE POPULATION	
Number	5,441
% of Total	77%
No. of Households	1,293
% of Total	76%
Persons/Household	4.2
Workers/Household	1.8

WHITE NATIVITY				
US	Ire. & Gr.	Italy	Russia	Other
87%	8%	1%	1%	3%

WHITE OCCUPATIONS				
High Wht.Collar	White Collar	Skilled	Semiskilled	Unskilled
13%	32	25%	25%	6%

1910

BLACK POPULATION	
Number	3,358
% of Total	46%
No. of Households	948
% of Total	48%
Persons/Household	3.5
Workers/Household	2.2

BLACK NATIVITY				
Missouri	Midwest	Deep So.	Border So.	
56%	12%	17%	12%	

BLACK OCCUPATIONS				
High Wht.Collar	White Collar	Skilled	Semiskilled	Unskilled
4%	5%	8%	55%	27%

WHITE POPULATION	
Number	3,902
% of Total	54%
No. of Households	1,028
% of Total	52%
Persons/Household	3.8
Workers/Household	1.9

WHITE NATIVITY				
US	Ire. & Gr.	Italy	Russia	Other
61%	2%	17%	18%	1%

WHITE OCCUPATIONS				
High Wht.Collar	White Collar	Skilled	Semiskilled	Unskilled
16%	39%	17%	23%	5%

1920 Vine Street Corridor (continued)

BLACK POPULATION		BLACK NATIVITY				
Number	5,423	Missouri	Midwest	Deep So.	Border So.	
% of Total	73%	57%	17%	17%	9%	
No. of Households	1,556					
% of Total	74%	**BLACK OCCUPATIONS**				
Persons/Household	3.5	High Wht.Collar	White Collar	Skilled	Semiskilled	Unskilled
Workers/Household	2.1	5%	3%	7%	48%	36%

WHITE POPULATION		WHITE NATIVITY				
Number	1,980	US	Ire. & Gr.	Italy	Russia	Other
% of Total	28%	90%			4%	5%
No. of Households	546					
% of Total	26%	**WHITE OCCUPATIONS**				
Persons/Household	3.6	High Wht.Collar	White Collar	Skilled	Semiskilled	Unskilled
Workers/Household	1.9	14%	47%	14%	19%	5%

Source: Twelfth, Thirteenth, & Fourteenth Census of the U.S., Manuscript Census

Table 2.7

goods were sold—and it saw the development of small pasta making plants. It was an ideal location both for the produce distributors' labor force and for the hucksters who obtained their inventory at the City Market. However much North End whites may have disliked having black neighbors, the presence of a large number of blacks seems not to have outweighed these advantages. In fact, North End blacks and whites appear to have reached a sort of modus vivendi. In the 1910s and 1920s, when overt acts of racial hostility erupted over housing, only one such incident occurred in the North End.[30] Otherwise, the North End remained a peaceable, partially integrated district.

Not so the Vine Street Corridor and its environs. First developed during the boom of the 1880s, the area was dedicated to a single land use—housing the middling ranks of Kansas Citians in suburban comfort. Construction of the Paseo aimed to anchor that land use pattern. When the area no longer met white residents' expectations for comfortable suburban living, as apparently happened when large numbers of blacks moved in, they evacuated it. In the 1910s and 1920s, when black residents of the corridor tried to penetrate

30. These incidents are examined in later chapters.

Vine Street Corridor, 1900

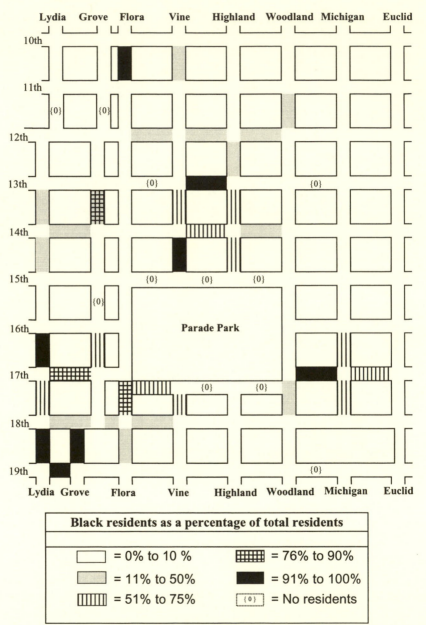

Figure 2.5

Vine Street Corridor, 1910

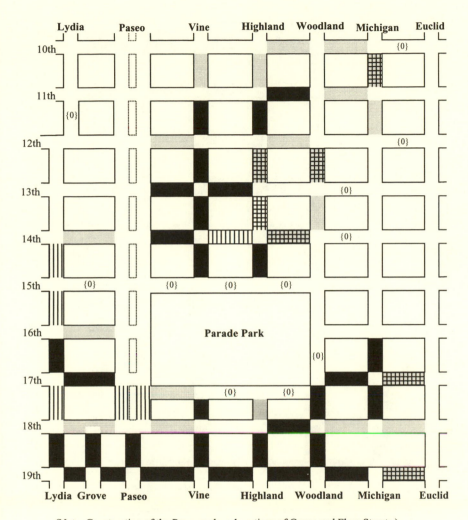

(Note: Construction of the Paseo replaced portions of Grove and Flora Streets.)

Black residents as a percentage of total residents		
= 0% to 10 %		= 76% to 90%
= 11% to 50%		= 91% to 100%
= 51% to 75%		= No residents

Figure 2.6

Vine Street Corridor, 1920

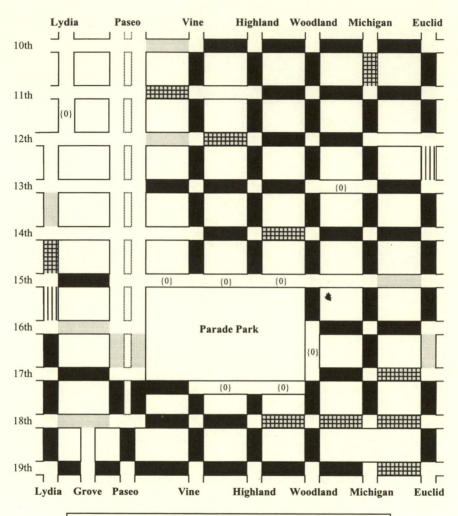

Figure 2.7

its unofficial boundaries, whites tried to repel them with dynamite, statutes, and covenants. In the decade before and after the First World War, nearly all the racial troubles over housing in the city occurred in the volatile fringes of the Vine Street corridor.

One of the consequences of these residential patterns was the rapid deterioration of the entire black eastside. Kansas City's African American population rose by six thousand between 1900 and 1910, and grew by another seven thousand over the following decade.[31] While some newly arrived families were able to find space in the North End or in small outlying enclaves like Roundtop, most newcomers and former hollows-dwellers made their way to the black eastside. Some moved into a section of apartment buildings that came to be called the Bowery. This twenty-two block zone housed more than four thousand people by 1912. Once the apartment buildings were filled, landowners began crowding families into basement flats. Cheaply built lodgings sprouted along alleys and then were subdivided to meet yet more demand. Then, the Bowery having filled beyond its capacity, home seekers pushed farther into the eastside black community, an area no longer deserving the title Quality Hill. A survey taken in 1912 by H. O. Cook, principal of Lincoln High, revealed the effects when multiple families jammed into structures intended for single households, and property owners crowded jerry-built dwellings into available space. Canvassing the south-central sector of the black eastside, Cook discovered living quarters so cramped that half the rooms were used for sleeping. Twenty percent of houses lacked a water supply, while half of the number of households had no sink. The number of bathtubs averaged one for every twenty-two persons. Typical apartment buildings provided water to all their occupants from a single hydrant in a hallway.[32]

The inescapable result of such conditions, combined with the worsening state of the black North End, was a mortality rate for blacks that was twice that for whites in 1912. Rates for tuberculosis, pneumonia, and urinary tract diseases—the maladies of overcrowding and poor sanitation—far exceeded the rates for whites and accounted for much premature death. What local sociologist Asa Martin called constitutional diseases—ailments brought on by inadequate diet, hard labor, and poor living conditions—afflicted others with high rates of heart disease and infirmities of the nervous system.

31. *Twelfth Census of the United States: Population,* vol. 1, 663; *Thirteenth Census of the United States: Population,* vol. 2, 1122; *Fourteenth Census of the United States: Population,* vol. 2, 53.
32. Martin, *Our Negro Population,* 90, 102–3. The boundaries of the Bowery in 1912 were Seventeenth to Twenty-Fifth Streets, between Troost and Woodland Avenues.

Meager employment opportunities contributed to the decline in living standards as well. Among the 8,100 black men Asa Martin surveyed in 1912, three-quarters worked at unskilled labor. A scant 1 percent worked in white-collar positions or the professions. Black women fared just slightly better, for 3 percent of the 3,100 women Martin surveyed held white-collar positions, largely as teachers and nurses. But nearly all the remainder toiled as domestics or laundresses. Consequently, employed black males averaged only $470 in yearly income—considerably below the estimated $600 per year considered adequate for maintaining a family in decency—and black women earned still less. Owning just .0112 percent of realty in the city and .0175 percent of personal property, blacks had $80.61 per capita of wealth compared to $667.96 for whites.[33]

A number of factors help to explain why white Kansas Citians tried harder to separate themselves from African Americans in the early twentieth century. For one, black population increased by 72 percent between 1900 and 1920. As historians of race relations in other cities have noted, sizable increases in local black populations helped to excite whites' animosities and to spur ghettoization. If population increase were enough to explain Jim Crow's new vitality in Kansas City, however, the phenomenon would have occurred in the 1870s, when black population more than doubled, or in the 1880s, when the number of African Americans enlarged by another two-thirds. Unlike northern cities, where sudden leaps in the black portion of the population sparked racial tensions in the early twentieth century, blacks' share of Kansas City's population remained essentially constant from 1890 through 1920.[34]

Of course, race acquired a new saliency in Kansas City at a time when racism infected the whole of American politics and culture more virulently. On the heels of the *Plessy* decision legitimating segregation in 1896, southern states and localities disenfranchised and segregated African Americans more completely, and numerous interest groups tried to restrict foreign immigration. Scholars and pseudoscholars, from Madison Grant to the fathers of the Stanford-Binet intelligence test, gave intellectual respectability to racism while southern politicians like James K. Vardaman of Mississippi and "Pitchfork" Ben Tillman of South Carolina translated the scholarly racism

---

33. Martin, *Our Negro Population*, 32–33, 50, 56, 107–22.

34. See for example, Kusmer, *A Ghetto Takes Shape*, 157–73; Spear, *Black Chicago*, 11–27; Gilbert Osofsky, *Harlem: The Making of a Ghetto, Negro New York, 1890–1930*, 40–43. For a comparison of growth rates for black populations in border cities, see George C. Wright, *Life behind a Veil: Blacks in Louisville, Kentucky, 1865–1930*, 44–46.

into more flamboyant hate-mongering.[35] In Missouri, would-be Democratic Party leaders from small towns and rural communities published di-
atribes on Negro inferiority and launched a campaign for de jure segregation and the disenfranchisement of black Missourians.[36] Yet, if white Kansas
Citians accepted any of these theories, it was most likely because the theories
could be made to fit their own experiences nearer to home; the theories
seemed, in other words, to make sense of incidents and circumstances in
their lives.[37]

■ ■ Conclusion

The day-to-day experiences that verified a racist ideology in Kansas City
were rooted in the struggle by the local middle class to establish a status
identity in an environment that venerated middle-class domesticity. Kansas
City's African American population grew not only in size but in visibility, as
both a physical entity and a political group, in a city beset by tensions over
the differentiation and control of urban space. Geographic concentration
of blacks—propelled initially by beautification and cleanup projects that destroyed scattered, integrated neighborhoods—gathered African Americans
into noticeable agglomerations on the urban landscape. At the same time,
the middle class grew more apprehensive about urban blight and moral disorder, features that crowding and low incomes guaranteed would blight black
neighborhoods more than others. In fact, African Americans would come to
personify the most threatening aspects of urban life—the very features the
middle class longed to escape.

35. Thomas F. Gossett, *Race: The History of an Idea in America*, 271, 353–401.
36. Grothaus, "The Negro in Missouri Politics," 31–65.
37. Concerning the ideology of race, Barbara Fields notes, "a vocabulary stays alive
only to the degree that it names things people know, and . . . these things are ritually
verified in day-to-day social practice." Barbara J. Fields, "Ideology and Race in American
History," 153.

3

The Webwork of Race, Status, and Gender, 1900–1920

■ ■ ■

B ETWEEN 1900 AND 1920, a variety of factors conspired to make African Americans a more visible element in Kansas City's urban landscape. An ever larger black population was increasingly concentrated—and so its size more noticeable—in the North End and Vine Street corridor. But, though circumstances of social geography made whites more aware of blacks as a (potentially hazardous) aggregation, so also did black Kansas Citians' self-assertive acts. When they moved their families out of the compacted black enclaves into predominantly white neighborhoods, or struck for better wages and working conditions, or demanded a share in political decision-making, African Americans attested that they were not only present in Kansas City but claimed the same prerogatives as whites to shape an urban environment that would meet their expectations for decency and honor. And some white Kansas Citians reacted to black assertiveness with varying degrees of dread and dismay.

■ ■ Class, Race, and Labor Activism

For African Americans, few actions were as assertive as a labor strike. Before 1900, labor unions in Kansas City had a checkered history where black workers were concerned, often excluding them from membership, yet sometimes supporting their organizations in trades like hod carrying, where black workers were the majority.[1] In the first two decades of the century, blacks not

1. In 1899, for example, the federated Building Trades Council called a general work stoppage on construction sites to support a strike by the black Hod Carriers Union, and

only engaged in strikes but helped to instigate them. The hack drivers' local that struck against transfer companies in 1904, for example, included blacks among its highest officers, and black drivers cast the most votes in favor of the strike. But the job action had the support of white drivers and the white-dominated Teamsters council. Instead, it was employers who drew the color lines when they promised to rehire only striking white drivers, not the black "disorganizers" who launched the strike. White union men protested hotly to the *Kansas City Star* that transfer-company owners were injecting race into the contest. "The union men are bitter over this question," the *Star* noted. "They assert that the transfer men are exciting a dangerous race feeling. They assert that while the negroes [*sic*] are the backbone of the strike that nevertheless it was the companies that first brought the negroes into the business and put them in competition with the whites."[2]

Later that same year, meat packers used roughly similar tactics to crush a strike that the Amalgamated Meat Cutters called in Kansas City and eight other cities in an attempt to win pay increases and union recognition. Packers kept their Kansas City plants in operation by hiring hundreds of nonunion workers and housing them in the heavily guarded plants.[3] The scab labor force included African Americans from Kansas City and elsewhere, some of whom the packers commissioned as private detectives and issued revolvers. Interestingly, there were no reports of white strikebreakers having been given weapons by the meat companies. In a strike-torn city with a southern heritage, arming black workers was an unusual tactic and one the white citizenry in general and white strikers in particular were likely to regard with apprehension. In fact, the *Kansas City World* reported, "This action has infuriated the strikers. . . . The strikers are threatening to procure guns if the negroes are allowed to carry them."[4] Even after the police promised to strip black

the council pressured the American Federation of Labor into granting the hod carriers an AFL charter. "Patricia Wagner Papers," folder 3, 71; folder 6, 93; folder 7, 129; folder 10, 66–71; A. Theodore Brown Collection, KC 37, WHMC; Naysmith, "Population," folder 5, 221.

2. *Kansas City Star,* March 3, 1904. For accounts of strike action, see *Kansas City World,* February 11, 1904, March 3, 1904, March 5, 1904; *Kansas City Star,* March 2, 1904, March 3, 1904; *Kansas City Times,* February 8, 1904; *Kansas City Labor Herald,* February 19, 1904.

3. *Kansas City Labor Herald,* July 15, 1904, July 29, 1904, August 26, 1904; *Kansas City Star,* July 22, 1904; *Kansas City Journal,* July 23, 1904, July 29, 1904; *Kansas City World,* July 24, 1904.

4. *Kansas City World,* July 29, 1904. See also, *Kansas City Star,* July 26, 1904, July 28, 1904, July 29, 1904, July 30, 1904, August 7, 1904, August 10, 1904; *Kansas City Journal,* July 29, 1904, August 7, 1904, August 10, 1904; *Kansas City World,* July 25, 1904, July 29, 1904, August 7, 1904.

strikebreakers of their special police commissions, they continued to carry the private detective badges and pistols issued to them by the packinghouses, and union officials were hard-pressed to curb violent assaults on African American strikebreakers as a result. Intending to provoke strikers into violent acts that would discredit them among the public, the packers were willing to risk a race riot in order to incite racial antipathies between strikers and scabs.

But black workers were prominent on both sides of the picket line. Several years before the strike, the meat cutters' union had aimed to make scab labor harder to procure by organizing African American and East European laborers in the city's packinghouses. Consequently, black workers and recently employed immigrants numbered among the strikers and the scabs. Ultimately, the strike failed in Kansas City for reasons having little to do with race, for meager strike benefits, coupled with the financial losses from a recent flood, forced many strikers to return to work without a victory. In September, Amalgamated Meat Cutters declared the strike over in Kansas City and elsewhere. For another thirteen years there would be no union in Kansas City's packing plants, and Amalgamated's membership dropped so sharply in every meatpacking city that the labor force in the packinghouses was largely unorganized after 1904.[5] During those years, the number of African Americans working in meatpacking climbed to 16 percent of the Kansas City packers' labor force in 1909 and nearly 20 percent in 1917. Although local packers reported that they liked to hire African Americans because blacks were disinclined either to join unions or go out on strike, they discovered their error in 1917. That year, African American women and men helped precipitate a wildcat strike of momentous proportions in local packinghouses.[6]

The spontaneous walkout began in Kansas City on September 4, when some sixty black and white women canners at Cudahy walked off the job demanding a living wage for the women in the cannery. By midafternoon,

5. *Kansas City World,* July 28, 1904; *Kansas City Star,* July 29, 1904, July 30, 1904; *Kansas City Labor Herald,* September 9, 1904; *Kansas City Journal,* August 7, 1904; *Kansas City Times,* September 7, 1917. Organized in 1897, the Amalgamated Meat Cutters and Butcher Workmen of North America adapted to mechanization of meat processing by admitting unskilled as well as skilled workers. The international also admitted African American members. Notes David Brody, "There was a real effort to develop a sense of solidarity." David Brody, *The Butcher Workmen: A Study of Unionization,* 25, 38–41.

6. A similar wildcat strike in Omaha had idled more than four thousand packinghouse workers on September 1, 1917. *Kansas City Labor Herald,* September 14, 1917; *Kansas City Journal,* February 15, 1918; Brody, *Butcher Workmen,* 75. See also, Roger Horowitz, "The Path not Taken: A Social History of Industrial Unionism in Meatpacking, 1930–1960," 290.

all but sixty of Cudahy's personnel had joined a procession of six hundred to seven hundred strikers, who made the rounds of the other packinghouses shouting at workers inside to come out for an eight-hour day. According to the *Kansas City Journal,* "Many in the procession were women, and nearly half the number negroes."[7] When strikers asked Amalgamated Meat Cutters and Butcher Workmen's International to organize the strike, an African American employee at the Wilson plant assured demonstrators that black workers in the packinghouses were in sympathy with the strike. "All we ask is that when you divide up the pie, do not forget your colored brother."[8] Within a week of its start, freight handlers and workers in local soap factories had joined the spontaneous walkout, while five meatpacking plants were crippled by the "strike epidemic"—something of a crisis in wartime. By the time federal mediator Patrick C. Gill arrived to negotiate a settlement, a general strike was in the offing. Luckily for America's soiled and hungry doughboys, Gill ended the strike with management's promise to increase pay and rehire all striking employees.

Attention then shifted to Chicago, where a similar strike led to federal arbitration by Federal Judge Samuel B. Alschuler, whose decisions would affect Amalgamated's members in Kansas City as well. During the arbitration hearings, Amalgamated's Kansas City organizer, T. A. McCreash, took particular pains to protect the interests of white males by advancing the welfare of African American and female workers in the Kansas City plants. Over the previous two years, McCreash testified in early 1918, Kansas City's packers had substituted female workers for better-paid males in hundreds of positions. Most of those women, McCreash asserted, were African American. Instead of demanding work rules or arbitration decisions that reduced the number of black or female workers, McCreash asked Alschuler to erase the wage differential that made those workers more attractive to employers by establishing equal wages for men and women of both races. In fact, Alschuler's mediation decisions in March 1918 provided a partial victory for Amalgamated and its members. The judge granted an eight-hour day, equal pay for men and women, and time and a quarter for overtime. Unfortunately, he

7. *Kansas City Journal,* September 7, 1917. See also, *Kansas City Times,* September 5, 1917, September 6, 1917, September 7, 1917; *Kansas City Star,* September 7, 1917.

8. *Kansas City Times,* September 8, 1917; *Kansas City Journal,* September 9, 1917. See also, *Kansas City Times,* September 14, 1917; *Kansas City Labor Herald,* September 14, 1917; Letter of Patrick Gill to Assistant Secretary of Labor Hugh L. Kirwin, October 19, 1917, and "Preliminary Report of Commissioner of Conciliation," October 31, 1917, in *Black Workers in the Era of the Great Migration, 1916–1929,* microfilm reel 1, entry 14.

refused to order union recognition in the packinghouses—an omission that eventually proved disastrous for Amalgamated.[9] But Kansas City's unorganized workers had at least witnessed the short-term effectiveness of federal mediation in improving working conditions.

A few months after the packinghouse strike, black and white workers once again launched a wildcat labor dispute, this time igniting a general strike. That job action began with the unorganized workers in the city's commercial laundries, where working conditions were among the worst in the city. While black women dominated the ranks of independent washerwomen, fewer than a third of commercial laundresses were African Americans. Nonetheless, the commercial laundries represented a significant entry into industrial labor for black women for, outside of the packing plants and two bag factories, no other industrial employers in Kansas City hired them. Attempts to unionize the laundries in the decade before the First World War foundered, and the Laundry Owners' Association was determined to maintain open shops. On February 14, 1918, however, some three hundred laundry women walked out demanding a union.

Just as in the packinghouse strike, "crowds of men, women and girls, both negroes and white, were loaded into trucks and went from laundry to laundry in an attempt to get those who had remained to join them."[10] By February 19, an estimated one thousand workers were on the picket lines or hurling stones at the scab laundry drivers, and the laundries were hard-pressed to meet customers' demands. Consequently, federal mediator Gill and Sarah Green of the Women's Trade Union League came to Kansas City to try to negotiate a settlement, but their attempts to hold a hearing into the causes of the strike failed because the Hotel Muehlebach, where the hearings were to be held, refused to allow striking black workers into the building. The white strikers refused to testify in segregated hearings. According to the *Kansas City Journal,* "The white workers said if the negroes were to be excluded, they would not remain."[11] Soon after, the laundry strike became

9. *Kansas City Journal,* February 15, 1918; Brody, *Butcher Workmen,* 82–96. The federal government intervened in December 1917 and ordered mediation because, four days before the mediated settlement was reached in Kansas City, a drive began to enroll Chicago's black and white packinghouse employees in Amalgamated locals. That made a nationwide strike possible. Rick Halpern, "Race, Ethnicity, and Union in the Chicago Stockyards, 1917–1922," 32–39; Brody, *Butcher Workmen,* 78–80.

10. *Kansas City Star,* February 18, 1918.

11. *Ibid.,* February 28, 1918. See also, Board of Public Welfare, *Report on the Wage-Earning Women of Kansas City,* 8–9, 27; *Kansas City Journal,* February 20, 1918, February 21, 1918, February 24, 1918, February 26, 1918; *Kansas City Labor Herald,* May 19, 1911, July 3, 1914. In 1904, fifty-four black women organized a local of the Federal Labor Union for Working Women and received an AFL charter. Despite its intention

a general strike, idling fifteen thousand unionists and, in the midst of war, tying up streetcar service, bakeries, restaurants, building sites, breweries, and buildings with elevator service. Even the arrival of the Seventh Regiment of the Missouri National Guard failed to end the strike, which lasted six days before union leaders accepted a wage offer from the laundry owners.[12]

These strikes were remarkable in part because unions and management approached the race issue so differently. While the white press made much of the race of the strikers in its reporting, the weekly *Labor Herald*, published by the Industrial Trades Council, made almost no mention of race in its lengthy coverage, portraying the events as a collective action by an undifferentiated mass of workers. Presumably, working-class blacks and whites had reason for hostility to each other because they competed for shabby housing, low-paid jobs, and slivers of political influence. And conventional wisdom has so often blamed lower-class whites for stirring racial troubles that it has earned its own nickname, the "redneck thesis." In Kansas City, however, the white employers paid more attention to race than workers did and fostered racial friction to their own advantage.[13] The circumstances that seemed to make natural adversaries of lower-class blacks and whites—the very meagerness of the pickings they had to share—helped to lower the potential for racial animosity. In fact, job actions and union activities in the early decades of the twentieth century even revealed some tentative stabs at cooperation across race lines. Having organized the National Council of Colored Workers during the packinghouse strike in Kansas City, local barber Rucker Smith urged other African Americans "not to be a scab, remember you belong to the working class, and if the unions offer to be fair with you,

────

to unionize black washerwomen and office scrubwomen, the local was apparently short-lived. *Kansas City Labor Herald*, June 3, 1904.

12. *Kansas City Journal*, March 6, 1918, March 8, 1918, March 19, 1918, March 27, 1918, March 29, 1918, March 30, 1918, March 31, 1918, April 3, 1918; *Kansas City Star*, March 28, 1918; *Kansas City Labor Herald*, April 5, 1918.

13. A significant number of historians have refuted the so-called redneck thesis, finding instead that upper- and/or middle-class whites were both more hostile to African Americans and more effective than the working class in turning their hostilities into public policy—often hiding behind a facade of redneck racism. See for example, Ronald P. Formisano, *Boston against Busing: Race, Class, and Ethnicity in the 1960s and 1970s*, 233; Joel Williamson, *The Crucible of Race: Black-White Relations in the American South since Emancipation*, 292; Bill Cecil-Fronsman, *Common Whites: Class and Culture in Antebellum North Carolina*, 74–90; and J. Morgan Kousser, *Shaping of Southern Politics: Suffrage Restriction and the Establishment of the One-Party South, 1880–1910*, 238–52. The instances when working-class whites were most responsible for racism were race riots. See for example, William M. Tuttle, Jr., *Race Riot: Chicago in the Red Summer of 1919*; Elliott M. Rudwick, *Race Riot at East St. Louis, July 2, 1917*; and Roberta Senechal, *The Sociogenesis of a Race Riot: Springfield, Illinois, in 1908*.

join hands with them in the struggle, capital against labor."[14] In the end, Kansas City's working class failed to establish truly interracial unionism. But segments of the black and white labor force did try to bridge the racial gulf, on terms of relative equality that the "better element" of whites scarcely approximated.[15]

■ ■ Race, Sex, and Political Activism

Like labor actions, political activism drew whites' attention to the African American community, sometimes in curious ways. In particular, racism took on a sexual tinge when it entered the political debate in the early twentieth century. Thus, when a faction of silk-stocking Democrats tried to attract white voters by characterizing black political influence as a sexual menace, the tactic scored meager political gains; yet, it contributed to a process that was giving a gendered quality to race relations in Kansas City.

In the latter nineteenth century, not surprisingly, the great majority of African American voters in Kansas City were Republicans. From time to time, black politicians bolted from the GOP whenever its white leadership was more oblivious of black voters' interests than usual. By joining third-party coalitions or threatening to withhold the black vote, black tacticians were able to bargain for increased patronage from the GOP and to publicize African American demands for equitable law enforcement. The most vocal black political activists used the tactic more frequently in the early 1900s. Periodically, Lewis Woods, editor of the *Rising Son,* and Nelson Crews, foremost black Republican leader and later editor of the *Kansas City Sun,* acted alone or in tandem to withhold the black vote from an inattentive Republican Party.[16] Their efforts produced few material gains, however. White Repub-

14. *Kansas City Sun,* September 22, 1917.

15. Rick Halpern discovered a similar direction among Chicago packinghouse workers in 1917, where "a dynamic working-class movement sought to overcome the barriers imposed by a hierarchical job structure and reinforced by divisions of ethnicity and race." Halpern, "Race, Ethnicity, and Union," 27. Joe William Trotter, among other historians, maintains, in fact, that the central dynamic shaping the black urban experience and black migration in the twentieth century was the proletarianization of black laboring people and their development of an identity that was both race and class conscious. See Joe William Trotter, Jr., *Black Milwaukee: The Making of an Industrial Proletariat, 1915–45,* and Trotter, *Coal, Class, and Color: Blacks in Southern West Virginia, 1915–32.* See also, Earl Lewis, *In Their Own Interests: Race, Class, and Power in Twentieth-Century Norfolk, Virginia,* and Dennis Dickerson, *Out of the Crucible: Black Steelworkers in Western Pennsylvania, 1875–1980.*

16. The *Rising Son* was published in Kansas City from 1896 to 1918, but the paper saw its circulation and influence decline sharply in 1911. The *Kansas City Sun* began

licans usually short-circuited them by luring the insurgents back into the fold with promises of more patronage—promises that were seldom kept in full. For example, the election of a Republican mayor in 1904 netted a city clerkship for Nelson Crews; yet, even a Democratic newspaper could find no more than forty black appointees on the city payroll after two years of Republican control of city patronage.[17]

Dissatisfied with the way the Republican Party neglected its black constituency, a small but growing number of black voters opted for the Democratic machine. Democratic ward bosses Jim Pendergast and Joseph Shannon began expanding their existing political bases by appealing to black voters. Although a sizable portion of black Democrats were gamblers, saloon keepers, and "sports" from the North End, the organization of a Negro Central League in 1900 helped attract more "respectable" black voters, and Dr. William J. Thompkins's arrival in Kansas City in 1906 provided an able and prestigious leader for the black Democracy. Consequently, the Democratic machine tried to offer more to the black electorate than just protection for the rackets. In 1903, for example, urban Democratic factions from Kansas City and St. Louis played a decisive role in defeating the Crisp bill to segregate railroad coaches in Missouri.

By 1906, however, local Democrats were in considerable disarray. In a hard-fought primary campaign prior to the municipal elections in April, independent Democrats tried to wrest control of the party from machine Democrats, whom the Democratic blue bloods accused of pandering to the black vote. Although Robert Gregory, the mayoral candidate preferred by bosses Pendergast and Shannon, won in the primary, and the independents rallied round their party's candidate, the independents continued to inject the race issue into the ensuing campaign. When its first issue came out in mid-March, the brand new *Kansas City Post* gave the independents a voice that was unabashedly Democratic and antiboss.[18]

Unfortunately for Democrats, they hoped to regain control of City Hall in a spring election campaign that promised to be a dull debate over cheap gas, clean streets, and the extension of a street railway's franchise. Democrats

---

publication in 1913 and lasted through 1921. George Everett Slavins, "A History of the Missouri Negro Press," 28–33.

17. Naysmith, "Population," folder 5, 179–81; *Kansas City Post*, March 27, 1906; *Rising Son*, January 5, 1907, June 15, 1907.

18. Grothaus, "The Negro in Missouri Politics," 22–34, 43. Leaders among the Democratic independents were William S. Cowherd, Thomas T. Crittenden, and William T. Kemper, prosperous business and professional men. The *Labor Herald* reported that the *Post* was established as a "campaign sheet" for Democrats. *Kansas City Labor Herald*, March 9, 1906.

needed an issue that would galvanize voter interest and compensate for the disharmony between bosses and independents. Elsewhere in the state, rural Democrats had been urging since 1904 that the state party should hobble the GOP by charging that it was Negro dominated. Debate over state party strategy, together with blacks' increasingly vocal political activism in Kansas City, suggested that race might provide local Democratic independents the issue they needed. Trying to whip up voter alarm over black influence within the local GOP, the *Post* warned that "the white Republicans of Kansas City seemingly have abandoned the conduct of the city to Nelson Crews, the noted negro politician and leader of the entire Republican Party."[19] Moreover, "it is a real and not a fancied condition which confronts us," the *Post* warned; "negroes are now in the saddle in the Republican councils and city offices; they are demanding and being promised ten times more pie than they now receive and Nelson Crews is the actual leader and brains of the Republican party in this, the second city in the great state of Missouri."[20] A vote for the Democratic ticket would be a "vote against Negro influence."[21]

Of course these claims were ludicrous. As the *Post* itself reported, black and white Republicans were at loggerheads once again, and Crews and Woods were organizing independent ward clubs of black Republicans in hopes of winning a greater share of Republican patronage. Thus, early in the campaign, the *Post* seized on other, more electrifying evidence that Republicans were "Negro-dominated." That evidence came from the so-called workhouse scandal. The *Kansas City World* first uncovered the scandal in late 1905 when it reported that John Allen, a black guard at the city workhouse, had beaten a white female inmate with a hose. "The people of Missouri, Republican and Democratic, are not in the habit of seeing white women beaten by negroes or of standing idly by while such things are done," said a *World* editorial.[22] The discovery led to an investigation by a committee of the Women's Christian Temperance Union, whose members were dismayed that white women were sometimes forced to bathe in the presence of black guards and that black and white women inmates were housed in

19. *Kansas City Post*, March 27, 1906.
20. *Ibid.*, March 31, 1906.
21. *Ibid.*, March 16, 1906, March 20, 1906, March 21, 1906, March 29, 1906, April 2, 1906. The *Post*'s tactic mirrored an effort led by Democrats from Missouri's bootheel to weaken the state GOP, both by appealing to race prejudice to win votes and by reducing the effects of the Republican black electorate through various disenfranchisement and segregation measures. See Grothaus, "The Negro in Missouri Politics," 31–40.
22. *Kansas City World*, December 22, 1905.

the same cells. A subsequent city council investigation discovered that T. C. Unthank, a black physician in the city health department, treated work-house inmates and examined its white female prisoners. Distressed by its findings, the investigating committee recommended building a new prison facility solely for white women prisoners and organizing a board of pardons to reduce overcrowding by releasing only the most deserving prisoners, but the recommendations were not enough to protect the city government from criticism. With city elections approaching, Alderman S. C. Woodson, sole Democrat on the investigating committee, used every opportunity to express his outrage over workhouse conditions and to blame a Republican city administration for them. Most horrifying, he said, were the intimate or violent contacts between black male warders and white women prisoners. "This is just about 1,000 years too late for negro brutes to whip white women," Woodson pronounced.[23] Likewise, the "huddling together" of "white women and negresses occupying the same cells" enraged him. "This is unnatural," he stated, "and the committee is going to insist that there be a segregation of the races without further delay."[24]

When the Republican-controlled city council failed to enact the proposed reforms of the workhouse or to censure its administrators, the *Post* seized on the workhouse outrages as a demonstration of what black Republican pa-tronage meant. "No self-respecting white man can or will endorse such out-rageous brutality or condone such horrible violation of all racial instincts," its editor protested.[25] Will the "better class of white Republicans" permit "this magnificent city [to be] the stronghold of negro equality in the whole United States?" asked a *Post* editorial. "This city can be turned over to negroes, who have shown at the workhouse what they will do when clothed with a little brief authority, and then such a reign of debauchery and iniquity will take place here as was never seen in civilized communities." To emphasize its point, the paper published cartoons showing a black behemoth clubbing a prostrate white woman and the Democratic mule kicking a Republican elephant with a whip-wielding black man astraddle it. An unnamed source

23. *Ibid.*, December 22, 1905, December 23, 1905, December 27, 1905, December 29, 1905, January 1, 1906, January 4, 1905. While the *World,* moderately Democratic in its leanings, gave extravagant coverage to the scandal and its racial overtones, both the *Journal* and the *Star,* two Republican dailies, disclaimed any responsibility for the scandal on the part of the Republican administration and even omitted the word *negro* where it appeared in investigators' quoted statements. See for example, *Kansas City Journal,* December 26, 1905, December 27, 1905, January 4, 1906; *Kansas City Star,* December 21, 1905, December 27, 1905, December 28, 1905, April 2, 1906.
24. *Kansas City Journal,* January 5, 1906.
25. *Kansas City Post,* March 30, 1906.

also mailed copies of the cartoon to Kansas City voters.[26] While Democratic leaders James A. Reed and Frank Walsh appeared at citywide rallies to hammer the Republicans for encouraging "negro atrocities," the ward bosses' mayoral candidate Gregory spoke somewhat halfheartedly on the topic, preferring to focus his campaign on his opposition to extending the street railway franchise.[27] The Republican *Star*, in fact, saluted Gregory for refusing to embrace the racial demagoguery of the Democratic platform.

Ultimately, however, neither issue profited Gregory, who ran reasonably well in the white-collar southern wards but drew disappointing returns from the working-class river wards. Assessing Gregory's loss, the *Post* blamed the Democratic bosses for sullying their party's reputation. Making it clear that the *Post* represented the ideas and interests of Democratic respectability, the paper claimed that decent voters naturally avoided a party "in which men not socially recognized are wittingly or unwittingly permitted to have potent voice in the party councils."[28] The Republicans swept the local elections in April, and the *Post* returned to its earlier theme in the wake of its loss, describing lines of Crews cronies waiting for their appointments at GOP headquarters and parading downtown streets "to let the white women of the city see the kind of clerks that will transact their business at the city hall after the new administration goes into office."[29] In fact, both the waiting lines and the added appointments for blacks proved to be imaginary, for the GOP failed to live up to its pledges of patronage for its black constituents. Nonetheless, local Democrats returned to the race issue in the election of 1908.

Independent Democrats took control of local party leadership, electing Thomas Crittenden mayor in spring elections and placing one of their own, William Cowherd, at the head of the party's autumn ticket as gubernatorial candidate. Faced with the lackluster William Jennings Bryan at the head of their national slate and a numbing debate over tariffs dominating the national campaign, the independents and the *Post* tried once more to excite interest in the state ticket by charging Republicans with "negro domination." Yet, Democrats were hard-put to define what Negro domination

26. *Ibid.*, April 2, 1906; *Kansas City World*, March 26, 1906. Enraged by this cartoon, the editor of the *Rising Son* accused the Democrats of inciting race hatred. *Rising Son*, March 22, 1906, March 29, 1906.

27. *Kansas City Post*, April 2, 1906. While loosely aligned with bosses Pendergast and Shannon, Walsh and Reed came of a more privileged class than either ward boss. Both were successful attorneys and former county prosecutors, and both were destined for more eminent careers—Reed as U.S. Senator and Walsh as a member of Woodrow Wilson's administration.

28. *Kansas City Star*, April 4, 1906; *Kansas City Post*, April 4, 1906.

29. *Kansas City Post*, April 5, 1906.

would mean in terms that might impress the voters. They accused Republican gubernatorial candidate Herbert Hadley of advocating the desegregation of Missouri schools, but the charge lacked the desired note of menace because it was based solely on the fact that Hadley had attended an integrated public grammar school and state university in his native Kansas. Luckily for the *Post*, however, Charles Zueblin unwittingly came to the aid of the Democratic Party. In October, Zueblin, whom the *Post* dubbed "the freak sociologist from Chicago," gave a series of lectures in Kansas City school auditoriums. Among his various observations about American society, Zueblin condemned racial prejudice and suggested that intermarriage would elevate humankind by erasing harmful social divisions. Zueblin later denied that he had advocated the marriage of white and black, but the *Post* ignored his denials and demanded instead that the board of education close schoolhouse doors to anyone who might utter "further damnable theories of social equality." Democratic mayor Thomas Crittenden likewise condemned a doctrine "so abhorrent to the fine sensibilities of the white and dominant race, its mere mention is nauseating."[30]

In fact, *Post* editors and independent Democrats may have been delighted by the speech, for it allowed them to link Republican candidates with "Zueblinism" and to define Republican-sponsored Negro domination as the sure road to social equality and miscegenation. "Hadleyism and Zueblinism is [*sic*] abroad in the land," intoned the *Post*. "With the wives, the mothers, and daughters of Missouri pleading with those who are near and dear to them to avert the curse of Hadleyism, the result is not in doubt."[31] In case any reader missed the point, the paper printed a cartoon in several issues showing five figures standing atop a map of the state. The central figure, a huge black man, faced a portly white man labeled "political corruptionist," with whom he exchanged cash for his vote before turning to assault his victims, a young white family standing near Kansas City's location on the map. Father clutched the hand of his cherubic daughter and, with his other arm, sheltered Mother, who stood with hands clasped to her breast in confusion and terror. Below the cartoon, the *Post* asked, "Shall Missouri be a white man's state and a white woman's home?"[32]

Others worried about social equality, too. Having downplayed the racial overtones of the workhouse scandal in the 1906 election, the Republican

---

30. Grothaus, "The Negro in Missouri Politics," 47; *Kansas City Journal*, October 23, 1908, October 26, 1908, October 29, 1908; *Kansas City Post*, October 30, 1908, November 1, 1908.

31. *Kansas City Post*, October 27, 1908.

32. *Ibid.*, November 2, 1908.

Journal printed the first outraged reports of Zueblin's speech and called on the school board to bar from school platforms any speaker advocating "degrading theories affecting women" or "any scheme of miscegenation." Republican leaders and the *Star* engaged in some race baiting of their own by noting that Democratic presidential candidate Bryan sent his own children to the racially integrated University of Nebraska and was thus as guilty of Hadleyism as Hadley was. Hadley himself lambasted Cowherd for appointing "criminal negroes" to city jobs during his tenure as Kansas City mayor. In fact, the only political luminaries to remain silent on the race issue were Jim Pendergast and Joe Shannon, who nonetheless gave the Democratic state and county tickets their support.[33]

The combination of party reunification and race baiting netted a spectacular local victory for the Democrats, who won every county office in Jackson County in 1908. Crittenden, one of the authors of the local party's race tactics, received lukewarm support in the working-class North End in earlier municipal elections, but factional harmony netted gubernatorial candidate Cowherd a sizable majority in Kansas City in the fall. More surprising, though Cowherd lost in the governor's race statewide, he managed to carry eleven of fourteen Kansas City wards, including all but one of the southside residential wards where machine influence was minimal and Democratic victories were rare.[34] A considerable portion of the middle-class electorate that populated those wards either agreed with the *Post* that black political assertiveness represented sexual aggression against white women, or they found the *Post*'s stance inoffensive enough that it did not prevent them casting a Democratic ballot.

So, as happened in the labor wrangles, expediency led an upper-middle-class faction of Democrats to emphasize race by raising anxieties about morality and social distance. Even the Republican *Journal* began to worry that the mere suggestion of sexual intimacy between black and white threatened the "refinement and wholesome morality of a community of home-loving and women-respecting citizens."[35] According to the *Post,* the participation of black men at the ballot box and in political office did more than suggest such intimacy. That participation, they predicted, would require white women to pay their utility bills directly into the hands of black clerks, would place black

33. *Kansas City Journal,* October 24, 1908; *Kansas City Star,* October 28, 1908, October 29, 1908; Grothaus, "The Negro in Missouri Politics," 52, 55.
34. In fact, Grothaus calls Crittenden's election "a triumph of the middle class vote of Kansas City's south side." Grothaus, "The Negro in Missouri Politics," 52. *Kansas City Star,* November 4, 1908; *Kansas City Times,* November 5, 1908.
35. *Kansas City Journal,* October 24, 1908.

children in school desks beside white children, and would encourage the marital union of white women and black men. It would, in short, eliminate the physical distances that separated African Americans from intimate contact with members of the white middle-class family. By the time the commotion over licensed prostitution and closure of the red-light district raised middle-class anxieties over the moral sanctity of the home and the uses of urban space in 1913, the political campaigns of 1906 and 1908 had provided the symbolism and language for thinking about those apprehensions in terms of race. After 1908, Democratic race baiting diminished, in large part because of the revived influence of Democratic urban machines, whose chieftains still hoped to add black voters to their coalitions.[36] Nevertheless, sexual morality remained a compelling political issue among the "home-loving and women-respecting citizens" of Kansas City.

■ ■ Race, Sex, and Real Estate

At the same time that politics and labor activism raised blacks' visibility in Kansas City, social investigators alerted white residents to the presence of a growing black community. In so doing, sociologists identified the black population with the deterioration of urban space. Consequently, deteriorating living standards in their neighborhoods proved a double misfortune for African Americans in Kansas City, for the quality of life in the hollows and in the Vine Street corridor came to represent the very nature of black people to many whites. Ironically, a good deal of the credit for associating African Americans with urban squalor belonged to white members of the so-called "helping professions."

In 1908, the city council finally responded to the workhouse scandal by organizing a Board of Paroles and Pardons. Two years later, the pardons board was replaced by the Bureau of Public Welfare, the first municipal welfare agency in the nation. The bureau published its *Report on Housing* in 1912 and, in 1913, issued the *Social Prospectus of Kansas City*. Both studies reflected the social environmentalist's conviction that character and physical environment were intimately linked. So did *Our Negro Population*, the master's thesis that local civics teacher Asa Martin published in 1913. His study, Martin claimed, would demonstrate to Kansas Citians "that cleanliness, sense

36. In Kansas City, for example, Jim Pendergast halted Mayor Crittenden's attempt to segregate streetcars, and Joe Shannon engineered a state Democratic platform that renounced discriminatory legislation in 1910. Grothaus, "The Negro in Missouri Politics," 60–65.

of security, modesty, health, and good citizenship all depend upon the kind of houses in which people live, regardless of race or color."[37] All three publications aimed to eradicate the conditions they described, but their immediate effect was to publicize the fact that neighborhoods where black residents predominated were the most squalid in the city. Worse, the surveys' authors identified race as one of the causes of urban squalor. The *Social Prospectus,* for example, consistently singled out blacks as a "negative social force." Its data on housing and family life implied that black occupancy created neighborhoods of "low civilization," and its special sections on Negro crime reinforced perceptions of blacks as "steeped in crime, with lost virtue, and without purpose and without hope." The hollows were sordid and filthy, Asa Martin proposed, because "the occupants are the most ignorant and shiftless type of Negroes."[38]

Martin further told his readers, "Social workers say that no class of people with whom they have to deal is so shiftless, indolent, and lazy as the Negro; that he has very little self-pride, and hence will lie and misrepresent the facts in order to get any assistance whatever." His chapter on morality claimed that moral laxity accounted for a fair portion of ill health among blacks, while his ample statistics on crime demonstrated that the tenth of the population who were black supplied one-quarter of the arrests in the city for state offenses. At times Martin acknowledged prejudice, poverty, and the inequitable enforcement of moral and legal codes as causes for the conditions he described, but more often he attributed blacks' misery to an innately vicious character. Although their circumstances might be tragic, "hundreds of Negroes . . . seem perfectly satisfied, not only with their accommodations, but also with their station in life."[39] Failing to distinguish between character and environment, these surveys of Kansas City's nascent ghettos provided seemingly scientific data that equated black Kansas Citians with disorderly conduct and criminality, unclean habits, immorality, and the deterioration of property.

The sociological examination of the city, strike actions involving blacks, the political campaigns of 1906 and 1908, and the proliferation of vice that followed the closure of the red-light district—these events provided historical experiences from which the white middle class began to construct its perceptual framework about race. Prominent people, using their access to public media, raised issues that touched deep and fundamental sentiments,

37. Martin, *Our Negro Population,* 87.
38. *Social Prospectus,* 31; Martin, *Our Negro Population,* 93.
39. Martin, *Our Negro Population,* 106, 97, 131.

then linked them to race in the public arena. They portrayed black men as sexual aggressors, warned that immorality could penetrate to the very doorstep of the home, and claimed to show how badly a neighborhood could deteriorate with the admixture of blacks. Together, these four phenomena raised alarms about the potential for moral and physical degradation of residential neighborhoods and connected race to the quality of a homesite as both an investment and a domestic sanctuary. These were not only issues of deep personal significance to middle-class Kansas Citians, however. By classifying African Americans as a threat to domestic virtue and wholesome neighborhoods—both the hallmarks and the rewards of middle-class status—middle-class whites began the collective image making that defined their racial as well as social group position. Since these issues also connected to questions of urban space and land use, it is not surprising that in this context white, middle-class Kansas Citians launched their first attempts to segregate their neighborhoods by race.

■ ■ Residential Segregation

Initially, anonymous whites relied on death threats or arson to remove black residents from predominantly white neighborhoods. A particularly terrifying outbreak occurred in 1910 and 1911 when a series of six explosions rocked the area of Twenty-Fifth Street and Montgall Avenue on the eastern flank of the Vine Street corridor. According to letters sent by black residents to the National Association for the Advancement of Colored People and reprinted in the *Crisis,* black families had lived on those streets since 1903, when the area was newly developed. Approximately twenty-four black families were living peacefully in the area in 1908, when their white neighbors began meeting to agitate for their removal. Three years later, a black family purchased a house on a nearby all-white street, and the Montgall bombings began. On the surface, the area seemed an unlikely spot for such outbreaks. The manuscript census for 1910 showed eighty-eight blacks residing in nineteen households clustered in the 2400 block of Montgall. More than half the employed persons living in those households held semiskilled jobs, but more than a third were business owners or professionals. Their white neighbors included 267 persons living in sixty-four households distributed along Montgall from Twenty-Fourth to Twenty-Seventh Streets. The white residents were overwhelmingly native born, and white collars outnumbered

blue among white residents, although the neighborhood housed a fairly heterogeneous mix of classes.[40]

According to the state's governor, the *Crisis* reported, Kansas City police
operated on the assumption that these respectable white residents had either
done the dynamiting or hired it done. But police made no arrests for nearly
two years. Said one white correspondent to the *Crisis,* "I am inclined to
suspect that on account of race prejudice here detectives have not shown the
energy which they should have shown."[41] Ultimately, only one person was
arrested and sentenced for the explosions—a black man who, police claimed,
had aimed to reduce property values in the area on behalf of prospective
black buyers. As white and black correspondents pointed out, the theory
was absurd.

Yet, effective as dynamite and arson were in terrorizing individual home
owners, they did not offer blanket protections to white neighborhoods. Nor
did fire-blackened houses add to the value of adjacent property, with or
without black occupants. Searching for a device that would replace ad hoc
vigilantism with a consistent and pervasive policy of residential exclusion,
Alderman C. J. Gilman introduced an ordinance in early 1911 that would
prohibit blacks from living in areas occupied by whites. In February, however, a committee of the lower house of the city council decided not to report the bill favorably because the Maryland courts had recently overturned
a Baltimore, Maryland, ordinance on which the Kansas City bill was based.
Under the circumstances, a similar law was unlikely to withstand challenge
in the Missouri courts.[42]

A few months later, attention turned to the Kansas City Board of Education. In May, residents along the southern border of the Vine Street
black corridor gathered in indignation meetings to protest the movement
of black families into adjacent neighborhoods. Tension mounted after a rash
of bombings and confrontations greeted black families who had moved onto
formerly all-white streets between Prospect Avenue and Benton Boulevard
from Twenty-Fourth to Twenty-Sixth Streets. Because a good number of
these black families included teachers in the public schools, aroused mem-

40. Of the white residents who were employed, 13 percent were professionals or business owners, and another 43 percent held lower level white-collar jobs; the remainder
were evenly divided between the skilled and semiskilled trades. Manuscript Schedules of
the *Thirteenth Census of the United States.*

41. *Crisis* (February 1912), 162.

42. The Baltimore plan designated city blocks for all-black or all-white occupancy.
Despite the law's ultimate failure, eleven other cities, including St. Louis, Missouri, and
Louisville, Kentucky, passed similar legislation between 1911 and 1916. Roger L. Rice,
"Residential Segregation by Law, 1910–1917," 180–82.

bers of the Tenth Ward Citizens' Association demanded action from the school district. Colonel Milton Moore, president of the board of education, promptly introduced a resolution to the board requiring the dismissal of any black school employee who lived in a predominantly white neighborhood. Fortunately for black faculty members, board member Frank A. Faxon scotched the measure by arguing that the board had no jurisdiction over where its employees chose to live.[43]

Whites who lived near the borders of the Vine Street corridor continued to dispute the boundaries, but without the benefit of official sanctions. Instead, it was residents living far to the south of predominantly black neighborhoods who succeeded in winning the only Jim Crow ordinance the city enacted. The ordinance originated in 1913 in tensions over a proposal by Western College, a Bible school for black students, to move from its quarters in Macon, Missouri, to a vacant mansion at Thirty-Third Street and Jackson Avenue in Kansas City. Protest meetings among the middle- and upper-middle-class property owners in the vicinity led college officials to declare that the college would not occupy the site if neighbors granted them time to find a buyer for the property. When residents learned that the college did intend to occupy the mansion, protest meetings resumed in the summer of 1914, complete with uniformed drummers and a "call to arms."

Instigating the meetings were the officers of the Greenwood School Parent Teachers Association, whose school was located near the mansion, and the East Thirty-First Street Civic and Improvement Association. A clutch of similar organizations later joined the fight in one of the earliest instances in the city in which whites used so-called improvement associations to impose segregation. While similar improvement associations in Chicago included violence and intimidation among the tactics they employed, the Kansas City organizations aimed for legalistic solutions. They failed to convince the park board to convert the mansion site into a playground, but a petition campaign began in August that won an ordinance from the city council banning the use of nonfireproofed buildings for schools. Not satisfied that this weak measure would keep the black college out, the improvement associations continued their pressure on the city council for another year. Early in 1915, both houses of the city council passed an ordinance forbidding a school for pupils "of African descent" to locate within twenty-four hundred feet of a public or private school for whites. Since Central High School and Milton Moore Elementary School had recently opened near the disputed mansion,

43. *Kansas City Journal,* February 6, 1911, May 25, 1911, May 28, 1911, June 16, 1911.

proponents hoped that this bill would not only remove the threatened college but help other neighborhoods turn back similar invasions. Democratic Mayor Henry Jost vetoed the measure, but he was overridden in both chambers of the city council, and the Jim Crow measure became law in August 1915. Kansas City whites attempted no further segregation ordinances.[44]

Most Kansas Citians who took part in these efforts remained anonymous, at least so far as the printed record was concerned. However, twenty-eight individuals appeared by name in the press, either as officers of improvement associations or as speakers at indignation meetings, or they affixed their names to petitions opposing the relocation of Western College. The city directory reported occupations for twenty-five of them. A few held blue-collar jobs. Three of the men who spoke at an indignation meeting about Western College worked in the construction trades, and another performed casual labor. A fifth man, whose occupation was listed as driver, headed the East Thirty-First Street Civic and Improvement Association. But the remainder held white-collar positions—twelve as clerical workers, teachers, or managers, and eight as professionals or business owners. Redneck thesis to the contrary, whether in labor disputes, local politics, or the campaign for residential segregation, middle- and upper-middle-class whites played the greater part in seeking color lines.

■ ■ Whites' Thinking about Race—What Whites Had to Say

Neighborhood activists like these left a fairly meager record of their motives. When white Kansas Citians spoke publicly at all about housing segregation ordinances, a code of civility governed their discussions, for the bombings on Montgall had demonstrated that whites' racial animosities could erupt into lawlessness and disorder.[45] Kansas City could ill afford the raw-boned race baiting of a Vardaman or Tillman. Thus, the *Journal* complimented the lack of "incendiarism" at a meeting of whites who gathered in 1911

44. Spear, *Black Chicago*, 22–23; Tuttle, *Race Riot*, 174–78; *Kansas City Star*, July 24, 1914, July 25, 1914, July 26, 1914; *Kansas City Times*, August 8, 1914, August 28, 1915, August 30, 1915. In fact, the U.S. Supreme Court struck down all such ordinances in 1917 in its ruling on a similar Louisville ordinance in *Buchanan v. Warley*. Rice, "Residential Segregation by Law," 189–94.

45. Indeed, bombings recurred in 1918 even as a bomb victim's sons fought in France. The outbreaks followed the pattern of the Montgall and Linwood area occurrences: black home-owners had lived in the target neighborhood without incident for a number of years before the violence. All but one of the target areas were essentially middle-class neighborhoods. *Kansas City Sun*, September 28, 1918.

to protest the movement of blacks into their neighborhood, and the paper chided one exceptional individual for using the offensive term *burrheads*. After all, the *Journal* noted, whites had resorted to "illegal methods" to repel black neighbors in the past. An overtly racist public debate might inflame similar, dangerous passions among hotheaded Caucasians. In any case, there was apparently enough consensus about racial matters among the whites who combated blacks' residential encroachment that they could dispense with plain speaking, confident that they comprehended each other's veiled and decorous language. While the meeting in 1911 was clearly "anti-negro," a reporter observed, it was conducted in "obscure" words which "clearly were understood by those who were in attendance, and they were received with expressions of pleasure."[46]

Occasionally, however, whites discussed the "Negro problem" in public or in print, revealing how they believed race affected their social environment and uncovering their reasons for making race an increasingly salient factor in their community. Among the first to do so were a group of churchmen who gathered at St. George's Episcopal Church in 1910 to debate the "Negro problem." The difficulty, several speakers agreed, was Negro criminality—a problem they could easily solve by added vigilance and better policing. After all, one man observed, black men comprised just two and one-half percent of the entire state's population. "This is about one negro to forty white men, a long shot to raise a panic over. The other forty of us ought to be able to attend to that one man—that 2 ½ per cent." But the problem was not only the black criminal. More alarming were the whites who might be goaded into lawlessness in reaction to black crime. Thus, if the better classes of both races failed to solve the problem of black criminality, "some day a mob will wreak vengeance and the decent, law-abiding negro will be the sufferer, the criminal will escape." Others at the meeting saw a sexual threat in the mixing of black and white residences, claiming that white women refused to go out at night for fear of assault by black men living in their vicinity. Several speakers agreed that a "reign of terror existed in their neighborhoods." According to a reporter, a man who lived near the black eastside, "spoke of his wife at home, with a baby at her breast, afraid to go to sleep while her husband was absent, for the fear in her heart that the home might be invaded."[47] Defined by these men as sexually aggressive and disinclined to keep their place, black males endangered the authority by which they maintained property rights in both a home and in its female occupants.

46. *Kansas City Journal,* May 28, 1911.
47. *Ibid.,* March 15, 1910.

For other whites, African Americans represented an economic threat. Whether they lived in residential districts where turnover of a heterogeneous population jeopardized their investments in a home, or they had moved to neighborhoods that they hoped would remain stable, they were preoccupied by property values. An assistant city prosecutor, who spoke at a meeting demanding that the school board force black teachers out of his neighborhood, concluded by assuring, "I do not say this because of race prejudice or of social prejudice, but it is a question of economics." Housing segregation measures simply promised investment security, he claimed, because he believed that "there is no deterioration of property as we know it" in the segregated South.[48] Beneath these discussions lay a shared understanding of the link between financial security and race. A speaker at a meeting to protest the location of Western College drew on a familiar theme when he described his unfortunate search for a secure homesite: "Two weeks ago I wrote to my sister in Los Angeles and told her one of the finest high schools in Kansas City was being built within two blocks of property I own. I can imagine what she will say when I write her a negro college is to be established an equal distance from my property. She will hold up her hands and say, 'Oliver always did have hard luck.'"[49] Likewise, white residents who petitioned the city council for an ordinance to keep Western College out of their district swore that they did not object to college education or home ownership for blacks. They simply demanded what they believed was due them as home owners in the so-called residence districts. That a black presence in their neighborhood denied them their just due needed no explanation. As a petition reminded the city council, "It is a matter of common knowledge that the occupation of property by negroes, even though lawful, in the midst of or in close proximity to property owned or occupied by white people, especially in the residence districts, tends to depreciate the value of property belonging to white people, and greatly restricts the sale and use thereof."[50]

When protesters' attention did stray from their economic interests, it fastened once more on sex. The *Star* reported that feeling against Western College was strongest in the area where a letter had circulated purporting to have been written by a black man. The letter "contained threats against the women of the neighborhood and was so vile in character it was turned over to the postal inspector's office."[51] Apparently no one believed that a

48. *Ibid.*, May 28, 1911.
49. *Kansas City Star*, July 26, 1914.
50. Petitions contained in Box 301, folder 2, Benson Papers.
51. *Kansas City Star*, July 24, 1914.

black man truly had written the thing, but it served as a potent reminder that occupying space together implied social equality of blacks and whites, and social equality implied sexual access to white women by black men.

An incident in 1914 further revealed the way in which white observers linked race, gender, and the maintenance of property in their perceptions of city life. That year, a young white nurse was seized by a black man while on her way from church to her residence at Children's Mercy Hospital. The man dragged her behind a billboard, where he raped her in a weed-choked vacant lot. There were the expected lamentations in the press about "the mean nigger," the "black Minotaur which draws into its foul clutches its tribute of innocent womanhood." Hospital founder Dr. Katherine Berry Richardson publicly regretted the hospital's location on the heights above Hicks Hollow, and she complained of police failure to arrest black men who leered in hospital windows at nurses or shouted insults to them from nearby vacant houses. But Richardson and the white press directed most of their animus against the property owners who permitted a wilderness of weeds and billboards to provide concealment for such attacks, and they upbraided city officials for the inadequacy of street lighting. In their analysis, a well-kept urban landscape was a prerequisite to preserving the sanctity of womanhood; ill-kempt thoroughfares endangered the female chastity on which social order rested. The very essence of civilization lay in a society's ability to maintain its moral precepts and to safeguard female virtue, or so the *Journal* argued when it condemned derelict property owners. That "a woman on her way from church, with a prayer-book and a rosary in her hand" should fall victim to assault profaned both religion and womanhood. "There is something troglodytic in the horror of this shameful sacrilege which makes a mockery of civilization itself in its atavistic barbarism."[52] If Kansas Citians more scrupulously maintained their cityscape, they might prevent further violations of racial and gender boundaries. Instead, urban blight produced social atavism.

Few in number, sometimes oblique in their discussions, those whites who spoke at all about race in the early twentieth century nonetheless exhibited certain shared perceptions. Blacks embodied those qualities of urban life that were coming to bedevil them so: crime, immorality, and the precarious status

52. *Kansas City Times,* July 29, 1914; *Kansas City Star,* July 23, 1914; *Kansas City Journal,* July 24, 1914, July 26, 1914. In this respect, the *Journal* merely articulated a commonplace of Victorian culture, namely that a liberal society, with its weak institutions of religious and social authority, depended on the family, and hence on women, to instill and maintain moral, cultural, and civic responsibility. Consequently, that purity must be safeguarded if the fabric of social order were to be preserved intact. Steven Mintz, *A Prison of Expectations: The Family in Victorian Culture,* 28–33; Elaine Tyler May, *Great Expectations: Marriage and Divorce in Post-Victorian America,* 15–22.

of the middle-class home. Where these whites differed among themselves was not in the meaning of race but in the means by which their shared understanding of race should structure Kansas City society. The *Journal*, for one, hoped that coercive ordinances to separate the races would be unnecessary. To deny decent housing as a reward for ambitious blacks' accomplishments was to threaten the very ethos of social mobility that held society together. Herein lay one more danger that an African American population posed to white Kansas Citians. In their attempts to contain the "Negro problem," whites might sacrifice their own liberties—might weaken the individual's right to buy and sell property, or foster excessive police powers, or incite a lawless mob. They could be tempted to "monstrous abrogation of the commonest rights of citizenship." Yet the *Journal* asserted that blacks and whites must live apart. Articulating what Alan Anderson and George Pickering call an "ethic of racist realism," an editor for the *Journal* wrote that "the existence of race prejudice which prevents negro and white people of good conduct and morals living in proximity under conditions of toleration, if not amity, is an indisputable fact, and one may go farther and admit that the segregation of the races is eminently desirable in view of the existence of this prejudice."[53] The fairest solution, the *Journal* concluded, would be to designate a high-class residence district solely for enterprising and respectable blacks.

In 1919, Kansas Citians returned to the *Journal*'s proposal. Amid rumors of coming mob action to dislodge black families from southeastern residential districts, an editorial writer for the *Post*, now under new management, warned that Kansas City must either dampen racial tensions over housing or face the horrors of a race riot like that which had prostrated East St. Louis the previous year. Not only was Kansas City's black population certain to expand, the paper predicted, but that population was entitled to "sanitary homes, healthful homes, safe homes." The danger to the community rose, not from blacks, but from whites who threatened to resist expansion of black settlement by Klan tactics or dynamite. Thus the *Post* directed most of its scolding to whites: "The public sentiment of this town will not stand for the use of dynamite nor lawless procedure of any kind in connection with this

53. *Kansas City Journal*, February 8, 1911, June 16, 1911. Anderson and Pickering define "racist realism" as the contention that, because it is an undeniable (though unsubstantiated) "fact" that whites do not like blacks, and nothing can be done to change that, the responsible thing to do is to separate the races to prevent racial conflict. The unspoken assumption among race realists is that whites are the potential danger point; whites will instigate racial disorder. Therefore, separation will help whites control their disruptive impulses. Alan B. Anderson and George W. Pickering, *Confronting the Color Line: The Broken Promise of the Civil Rights Movement in Chicago*, 4, 10.

question any more than it will in the matter of strikes. This town wants to be law abiding, and it will be law abiding. Any man who takes the law into his own hands, whether striker, Ku Klux, or bolshevist, will run slap bang up against the machine gun of public opinion."[54]

At the *Post*'s urging, Mayor James Cowgill called a special committee of prominent black and white Kansas Citians to confer on these disputes over housing. Condemning race violence and the regulation of black residence by "arbitrary bounds," the committee promised full protection of the law to black residents. Instead, the committee offered to meet regularly to identify areas of the city where blacks could purchase homes without meeting resistance. Meanwhile, committee members acted swiftly to calm fears and squelch inflammatory rumors among both races.[55] Although the committee's plans to designate a safe area for black residential expansion never materialized, its preemptive rumor-control measures, along with modest in-migration by black southerners, may have had some effect. While race riots tormented Chicago and Omaha that summer, Kansas City escaped the terrors of mob violence. It was a close call, however. Only a short time before this latest crisis over housing, two black homes were burned and a church was dynamited following the local screening of *Birth of a Nation*.[56]

■ ■ Whites' Thinking about Race—What Blacks Had to Say

If whites spoke sparingly about race, a growing number of African Americans examined whites' perceptions in the black press and calculated how those perceptions affected black Kansas City. They provided useful insights into

54. Editorial reprinted in the *Kansas City Sun*, April 26, 1919. Sale of the *Post* in 1909 to the publishers of the *Denver Post* gave the *Kansas City Post* a more judicious editorial stance on race than it had displayed in 1906–1908.

55. *Kansas City Sun*, May 3, 1919. The committee was composed of luminaries from both races. White members were C. W. Armour of the meatpacking family; Judge Ralph S. Latshaw; W. T. Kemper, prominent banker; Rev. Burris A. Jenkins, clergyman and editor of the *Post*; and lumber magnate R. A. Long. Black members were Dr. William J. Thompkins, physician and Democratic leader; T. B. Watkins, funeral director and Republican leader; Rev. William H. Thomas, pastor of Allen Chapel A.M.E. Church; C. H. Calloway, an attorney; Dr. Dibble, a physician; and T. C. Chapman, a dentist. *Kansas City Star*, April 24, 1919.

56. Letter of Myrtle F. Cook to John R. Shillady, May 7, 1919; "The Negroes of Greater Kansas City Present for Consideration of the General Public, Facts of Their Side of the East Side Residential Controversy," open letter published in the *Kansas City Post*, April 27, 1919, copy with handwritten notes in Group C, Box 404, Branch Records of the NAACP Papers, Collections of the Manuscript Division, Library of Congress (hereafter LOC).

white mentality. They also revealed a striking agreement between white-collar blacks and whites about the social functions of home ownership, morality, and gender roles. Historians have sometimes dismissed those ideological similarities as the attempts of a black bourgeoisie to win bourgeois whites' good will by mimicking their values.[57] In Kansas City, however, those points of agreement served a more radical purpose, for domesticity, morality, and gender provided a framework by which race-conscious African Americans critiqued racial injustice and challenged whites' racist beliefs.[58]

Since the 1890s, black editors and clergy had advocated home ownership by African Americans as a way of guaranteeing economic security, thrift, and wholesome living standards. As an editorial in the *Rising Son* noted in 1903, however, home ownership served a political purpose as well. Like his middle-class white counterparts, the editorial writer believed the health and vitality of a community required that the greatest number of its members possess property. Thus a black community in which property ownership was widely dispersed would be best equipped to advance its own interests. Moreover, home ownership was an assertion of dignity in the face of a white society that denied blacks' dignity. By 1914, Charles Starks saw still more radical political consequences of home ownership. An advertising copywriter and officer of the local NAACP chapter, Starks reckoned home ownership to be among the basic rights and privileges of American citizenship. Specifically, the purchase of a home represented a vital step in the citizen's pursuit of happiness, while his right to life required that the home be in a healthful environment. Although critics of the NAACP "objected to the association on the ground that it makes us appear to want to 'get away from the race,'" Starks urged blacks to purchase homes in the healthful surroundings of white neighborhoods as a pure exercise of liberty and an assertion of civil rights. Whites who objected, Starks concluded, were moved by a pernicious desire to abridge all rights of citizenship for the black race.[59]

Also a frequent contributor to the *Sun*, W. E. Griffen saw another motivation behind segregated housing. "Race prejudice in the United States

57. See for example, E. Franklin Frazier, *Black Bourgeoisie*, 195–212.

58. In Norfolk, Virginia, Earl Lewis believes, African Americans sought social empowerment by stressing industrious but remunerative work, capital accumulation, health, and maintenance of strong, vital family institutions, a strategy Lewis calls the "home sphere." Lewis, *In Their Own Interests*, 5–6, 25, 80–84. Dollard termed the black bourgeoisie's behavior "caste aggression." By stressing the similarity of values, ability, and rectitude between themselves and the white middle class, the black middle class espoused revolutionary values in a society that held those norms to be the sole preserve of whites. Dollard, *Caste and Class in a Southern Town*, 420–21.

59. *Rising Son*, September 12, 1903; *Kansas City Sun*, November 28, 1914.

is almost wholly an economic question," Griffen offered. "When [whites] denounce 'social equality' they unwittingly mean economic equality." Thus, when blacks purchased homes in comfortable, middle-class neighborhoods, they signaled their achievement of an economic status equivalent to their white neighbors' standing, engendering a "terrifying fear" that whites' status was thereby diminished. After all, what merit lay in possessing a house on a given street if a presumably inferior black man obtained an adjacent address? "The great middle class of white people are by no means convinced of the Negro's inferiority. In fact, they are keenly alive to the fact that Negroes cannot be held down and in that they sense grave danger to themselves."[60]

Despite this commonality of values between the "better classes" of both races, Nelson Crews recognized that blacks most often suffered discrimination at the hands of middle-class whites. Commenting wryly on the opposition to Western College, Crews wrote, "Our people are constantly being urged to lead intelligent, religious lives, yet when decent facilities for such progress are being sought, opposition rises and the unchristian spirit of race hatred bursts into flame." Crews had not far to look for the source. "So-called refined, fair, [C]hristian people have met and solemnly vowed that the school must not come near them and that they will keep it away at any cost. . . . We know what 'any cost' means to Negro haters. We knew what it meant out on Montgall Avenue and in other parts of the city."[61]

Nor did whites' code of civility in racial matters really benefit blacks. Charles Starks warned the *Sun*'s readers, "The enemies of the race are sitting up at night scheming how to 'politely' and 'graciously' enslave us." The result was the kind of misdirection of the eye that magicians practiced. Proprietors and public officials began to defuse potential conflict over segregation by denying their own responsibility for it. In 1918, for example, park watchmen ejected Mrs. Julia Morrison from the Paseo Parkway adjacent to the black commercial center, informing her, "You Niggers are not going to light in this Parkway between Ninth and Twelfth streets." Members of the park board denied that they had ordered segregation of the park and refused to take corrective action on that account. When Jenkins Music Store barred black patrons from the store's listening rooms, management blamed the prejudice of white customers and the obnoxious behavior of two unnamed black

60. *Kansas City Sun*, November 11, 1914. William Tuttle reaches a similar conclusion concerning white motivations in Chicago prior to the First World War, where white property-owners "inevitably linked aspirations of social equality to the blacks' quest for better housing." William M. Tuttle, Jr., "Contested Neighborhoods and Racial Violence: Chicago in 1919, a Case Study," 240.

61. *Kansas City Sun*, August 8, 1914.

patrons. The *Sun* noted, "These two men are always handy when wanted. It will be remembered that they broke up the attendance of Colored people at Electric Park, caused the alley entrance at the Orpheum and brought about 'jimcrowism' in many other public places."[62]

Like their white peers, African American commentators were dismayed by what they considered to be high rates of crime, alcohol use, and sexual promiscuity among blacks. Some evinced class resentment of the "bad Negroes" who sullied the race's image, or of the flashy arrivistes, whose earnings from illicit businesses gave them entry into African American high society, despite their lack of cultural attainments. More often, however, editors and contributors to the black press condemned black-on-black crime and immorality as political liabilities. So long as blacks preyed upon each other in assaults and robberies, they inquired, what were the chances of uniting the African American community in solidary activism? How much race pride and race loyalty might one expect from a man who squandered his health, savings, and self-esteem on liquor and craps or sold his vote for a dram of whiskey? Unlike whites, however, these observers denied that criminality and vice were inherent flaws in the black character. Rather, they believed that whites encouraged antisocial behavior among blacks as a means of oppressing the race as a whole. "Some of the most vicious and notorious dives that ever infested the city are run by WHITE MEN for the debauchery and degradation of Negroes," a *Sun* editorial thundered.[63]

According to some African American observers, whites in positions of authority were most responsible for blacks' antisocial behavior, particularly whites who worked in the justice system. Protesting in 1903 that Democratic judges gave lenient sentences to black criminals in order to curry favor with black voters, Lewis Woods warned, "The fact that the democracy of this community refuses to punish [N]egroes for crime is a very dangerous condition of affairs so far as the Negro race is concerned." Black crime would decline "if the courts were to punish [N]egroes who commit crimes and who run hell joints the operation of which is calculated to make criminals of the worst type." Scoring a local city attorney, the *Rising Son* protested that the prosecutor had done law-abiding blacks no favors by turning criminals of color loose to prey upon them. If white judges were lenient, several black political and civic leaders believed, ordinary white citizens encouraged the police to use excessive force in policing black citizens. Referring to the case of

62. *Ibid.*, November 28, 1914, August 17, 1918, December 15, 1917.
63. See for example, letters to the *Rising Son*, January 16, 1903, and the *Kansas City Sun*, January 20, 1917, March 24, 1917.

a patrolman who was judged to have been overzealous, the *Rising Son* commented, "Officer Parks, who was so dull of understanding as to not know that it makes a great deal of difference as to whose head is clubbed, must stand trial for murder because he lightly tapped a Swede upon the cranium, incidentally causing death. Now, if the officer had been wise, he would have cracked a Negro's head and stood for promotion."[64]

Worse, Charles Starks asserted, the behavior of the police and police administrators discouraged respect for the law among even the most upright black citizens. Black Kansas Citians displayed a "positive horror and antipathy" toward the police because of "the exercise of an unwarrantable tyranny on the part of White Policem[e]n whose ignorance overlap[s] their duty and discretion and who imagine that Cruelty instead of intelligence is the watchword in handling and adjusting cases coming under their care." But African Americans held the few black officers who patrolled their streets in equal disrespect with the white officers. According to Starks, even law-abiding black citizens tended to sympathize with wrongdoers and to condemn black officers as "biggety" when they made arrests. If the black community were given more black officers, and if the community gave those patrolmen cooperation, neither black nor white criminals would so easily victimize the African American population. Nor would the community be infested with enterprises that whites typically barred from their own neighborhoods:

> If the Good Colored People would interest themselves more in having the Law upheld a "Buffet Flat" would not be so Brazen; vice could not encroach upon us with impudence; thieves and gamblers would not be so bold and thrive so easily; Hoodlums would not be so manifestly boisterous and a White Drug Store on 18th street would not sell Liquor with such abandon to inebriates, derelicts and fiends on the beautiful Sabbath—when the legitimate saloons are closed.[65]

For Starks, vice was not victimless crime, because it vented underclass black people's frustrations in ways that dissipated their health and energy without really challenging the racial system that caused their frustrations. At the same time, it divided the race against itself. Moreover, by permitting or

64. *Rising Son*, October 16, 1903, February 15, 1906, October 2, 1903.
65. *Kansas City Sun*, February 16, 1918. In his study of black life in Washington, D.C., alleys, James Borchert misses the point when he dismisses such petty crime and prostitution as recreational folkways that relieved frustration and provided income opportunities. James Borchert, *Alley Life in Washington: Family, Community, Religion, and Folklife in the City, 1850–1970*, 193.

encouraging vice and crime to flourish throughout the black community, these black writers believed that whites created a categorical racial disability by which *all* blacks were denied the safeguards from crime and immorality that the white "establishment" considered fundamental to civility. In short, these African American men sought "respectability." Rarely, however, did they suggest that moral repute would win them whites' approval. Nor did they appear to want acceptance or social intimacy with whites. Rather, they understood respectability to be an assertion of one's personal worth, a demand that one's honor and integrity be acknowledged. Whether that acknowledgment led to approval or personal liking between individuals was immaterial. At the same time, they regarded the bourgeois code of respectable behavior as empowering, for thrift, moral continence, diligent labor, and purposeful application of one's energies gave one a measure of control or mastery of one's fortunes. Collectively, respectable behavior enhanced communal autonomy. That whites were repulsed by African Americans' presumed amorality mattered less than these men's perception that whites created a social environment in which black men and women could not easily live respectably if they chose.[66]

In particular, female respectability was the linchpin of strong family life and acknowledged moral excellence, these writers believed. Therein lay their problem. It was harder for black women to keep virtue intact than for white women, and it was almost impossible for them to be acknowledged for their victory when they succeeded. In important ways, this was nothing new. The sexual exploitation of black women by white men undergirded slavery; the putative amorality of slave women that white men claimed as justification for the abuse reinforced the slaveholders' ideology of racial inferiority. After emancipation, rape served as powerfully as lynching to oppress the freed people in the Deep South. Like lynching, rape worked on more than one level. It punished the victim for uppityness, at the same time traumatizing every other black woman by reminding her that she was likewise vulnerable to assault and demeaning every black man who could not protect her. Because rape was always accompanied by the suspicion that the victim had invited the attack or cooperated in it, "rape law" put black women in a double bind: the incidence of rape proved that black women lacked moral virtue, while their presumed lack of virtue made it impossible to prove rape or claim protection

66. In his study of black crime, historian Roger Lane reaches strikingly similar conclusions. He finds that the prevalence of crime and vice in the ghetto made it difficult for parents to transmit alternative values to their children, encouraged conspicuous consumption, obstructed the achievement of economic security through self-denial, and weakened the family structure. Roger Lane, *Roots of Violence in Black Philadelphia, 1860–1900.*

from attack. Consequently, taking a place on the pedestal of female chastity might enhance a white woman's prestige; for a black woman it could mean protection from nightmarish attacks and the racial domination those attacks helped to legitimate.[67]

According to numerous African American observers in Kansas City, the moral disorder that whites encouraged in the black community operated as a subtler alternative to rape to produce much the same results. These commentators clearly understood that race was a social construction—an arbitrary and artificial contrivance to support inequitable balances of power—in which gender played a critical role in demarcating difference.[68] According to several of them, the most debilitating effect of moral disorder was the degradation of black women, who were central to the maintenance of strong family life and moral excellence. In 1890, Kansas Citian Moria Morris acknowledged the pivotal role women played. In her "Plea for the Negro Race," published in the *Kansas City Times,* Morris claimed that moral advancement held the key to improving blacks' status. But morality depended, in turn, on female chastity, and black women found the path of virtue full of impediments that few white women encountered:

> The negro woman is subject to the double trials of temptation from her own race and from the immoral men of the white race. The poverty and menial condition of the negro woman renders her liable to temptation and insult at the hands of the base and depraved of the white race, who seeks to spoil the virtue of a people inferior to his own. Such a man should or ought to be tabooed among respectable white people and subjected to punishment at the hands of the law.[69]

67. Darlene Clark Hine, "Rape and the Inner Lives of Black Women," 912–14; Patricia Morton, *Disfigured Images: The Historical Assault on Afro-American Women,* 22; Angela Y. Davis, *Women, Culture, and Politics,* 44; Jacqueline Dowd Hall, "'The Mind That Burns in Each Body': Women, Rape, and Racial Violence," 337–40; Angela Y. Davis, "Reflections on the Black Woman's Role in the Community of Slaves," 12–13; Nell Irvin Painter, "'Social Equality,' Miscegenation, Labor, and Power," 63; Nellie Y. McKay, "Alice Walker's 'Advancing Luna—and Ida B. Wells': A Struggle toward Sisterhood," 249; Greer Litton Fox, "'Nice Girl': Social Control of Women through a Value Construct"; Glenda Elizabeth Gilmore, *Gender and Jim Crow: Women and the Politics of White Supremacy in North Carolina, 1896–1920,* 95–99; Jacquelyn Dowd Hall, *Revolt against Chivalry: Jessie Daniel Ames and the Women's Campaign against Lynching.*

68. There is a rich body of literature exploring the role of gender in the social construction of race. Among the most useful works are Henry Louis Gates, Jr., "Introduction: Writing 'Race' and the Difference It Makes"; Evelyn Brooks Higginbotham, "African-American Women's History and the Metalanguage of Race"; Barbara J. Fields, "Ideology and Race in American History."

69. *Kansas City Times,* August 3, 1890.

A double standard defined gender roles for black and white women, Lewis Woods believed. In a patriarchal society, he thought, "the moral status of a people is reckoned from the standpoint of the female."[70] Consequently, when whites insulted black women on the streets, or consorted with the most degraded of them in vice dens, they discounted the moral worth of every black person and every black family. So long as a black woman could not expect the same protection of her virtue that gender automatically afforded white women, the black home itself stood outside the guardianship of organized society—a society ostensibly pledged to the sanctity of the home.

Unfortunately, Woods protested, the white authorities and institutions charged with guarding the home and family life failed to safeguard black families. Thus, Woods objected repeatedly to the school board's habit of ignoring charges of moral unfitness that black patrons lodged against black teachers. If black families struggled to inculcate sound values in their children, if a disproportionate number of blacks were to be found in jail, Woods reckoned that white schoolmen had only themselves to blame, for the poor examples they set before black youths in the classrooms revealed how low they valued African American morality. Later, the *Rising Son*'s publisher vowed to destroy a white judge who dismissed charges against a man who raped a little black girl. Commenting on the double standard by which lynch law and the justice system defended the sexual integrity of white women while permitting moral corruption or sexual assault of black women and children, Woods lamented, "The white men impose upon our women and we cannot protect them because the whites are in majority and they administer the law to suit themselves and we have to take whatever they put upon us."[71]

The faulty exercise of authority discounted the moral worth of African American women. Laws against intermarriage actually codified their debasement, in the view of many race-conscious African Americans. Missouri's legislature first banned the intermarriage of whites with Negroes or mulattos in 1865. In 1879, the statutes redefined a mulatto as a person of one-eighth rather than one-fourth "Negro blood." Black Missourians did not mount a campaign to overturn the law. Indeed, the state legislature strengthened

70. *Rising Son*, March 3, 1905.

71. *Ibid.*, May 19, 1905. A similar refusal to discharge a black principal on immorality charges in 1881 had sparked indignation meetings among black Kansas Citians. According to one of their resolutions of protest, "If the charges had been made against any white teacher the school board would not have dared to ignore them." *Kansas City Evening Mail*, January 31, 1882. Letters to the *Rising Son* indicated that angry parents shared Woods's frustration with the school board on this issue. See for example, *Rising Son*, February 13, 1903, May 12, 1905, May 26, 1905, June 6, 1906, April 6, 1907.

the intermarriage ban to include "Mongolians" among the proscribed races in 1909. But anti-intermarriage laws nonetheless figured in local discussion when the legislature in neighboring Kansas considered enactment of a simi- lar statute in 1913. The Kansas City, Missouri, chapter of the NAACP gave moral support to the national body and to the Kansas City, Kansas, chapter in their opposition to the bill. When the bill passed in the Kansas House but died in the state's Senate, the *Crisis* gave much of the credit for its defeat to the Kansas City, Kansas, chapter. Meanwhile, the NAACP's national journal kept a close watch on the fortunes of similar bills in other states and reiterated its pleas to readers to combat what it called "concubinage laws."[72]

Despite its eventual defeat, the Kansas bill sparked a hot dispute on the Missouri side of the state line. Shortly after the bill was introduced, J. Silas Harris, a teacher in Kansas City, Missouri, and head of the National Negro Education Council, wrote a letter to the bill's sponsor praising the proposed legislation. The *Crisis* dismissed his organization as a fake and excoriated Harris for race treason. Bans on intermarriage implied that black blood was a biological taint, a *Crisis* editorial charged. Worse, black women were "left helpless before the lusts of white men," who were excused by such laws from providing the financial or moral protection of marriage to the black women whom they used sexually. Moreover, "concubinage" laws devalued African American women, "the ownership of whose bodies no white man is bound to respect." Acknowledging that a sexual double standard governed relations between whites and blacks, the *Crisis* later charged that intermarriage bans "deprive colored girls and women of much of the legal protection against immoral men that others have."[73]

Harris countered the attack by the *Crisis* in 1914 by giving a long state- ment to the *Kansas City Post* in which he condemned the NAACP for stir- ring racial animosities. In particular, Harris attacked the NAACP's stance on marriage law:

> The most contemptible of all of the questions propounded is that which pertains to the anti-intermarriage laws; only the negro who is endeav- oring to get away from his race opposes the passage of such a law. The principal contenders against such legislation are to be found among the negro school teachers, many of whom are colored only to the extent of

72. See for example, *Crisis* (March 1913), 220; (May 1913), 15; (June 1913), 79, 91; (June 1914), 72. *Revised Statutes of Missouri*, 1866, 458; 1879, 268; *1909 Missouri Laws*, 662. The intermarriage ban remained on the Missouri statute books until it was removed by the legislature in 1969. *1969 Missouri Laws*, 545.

73. *Crisis* (March 1913), 234–35; (February 1913), 180; (June 1914), 72.

drawing salary for misinstructing the negro youth, and who are, in the main, responsible for the restless condition of the race.[74]

Among the rebuttals that local NAACP members offered, Kansas City, Missouri, branch president Woody Jacobs denied that local NAACP members wished to marry into the other race. Instead, they opposed marriage bans because the statutes created legal differences based on color that opened the door to other discriminatory legislation. H. O. Cook, principal of Lincoln High School, objected to any attempt "to deny the protection of marriage laws to our women, who, despite the abuses of men both white and black, have survived the terrible trials and burdens of slavery as well as supplied inspiration and ambition for fifty years of progress."[75]

According to these men, issues revolving around morality and womanly honor had political implications. If, as they assumed, a healthy, dynamic community depended upon the rearing of productive citizens in stable, virtuous homes, then the whites who obstructed blacks' ability to maintain such homes condemned African Americans to communal misrule by individuals who lacked personal and ethical standards. People like those could not act on behalf of the race or take the collective welfare of the race as a personal responsibility. How could such a community act purposefully for its own good under those conditions? Through personal honesty, mutual respect between husbands and wives, and devotion to home life, Lewis Woods believed, "we must learn to combine our forces and work for the good of the race."[76] Those whites who assumed that family decency and womanly virtue were beyond blacks' natural capacities also assumed that there was a fundamental inferiority that justified excluding blacks from respectable suburbs, stores, restaurants, and theaters. Indeed, a white man wrote to the *St. Louis Post-Dispatch* in 1915 arguing that the state's ban on interracial marriage proved the wisdom of that city's residential segregation ordinance: "Miscegenation is unlawful in this county. Thus by law the Negro is declared to be inferior to the white. Socially, the law should draw the same distinction."[77]

While black men chose the public outlets of newsprint and political pressure to demand equal protection of black women, African American women in Kansas City marshaled resources of their own. Middle- and upper-class women established numerous social organizations devoted to needlework,

74. Statement reprinted in the *Kansas City Sun*, November 14, 1914.

75. *Kansas City Sun*, November 21, 1914.

76. See for example, *Rising Son*, September 12, 1903, for a statement of this ideological position.

77. Quoted in the *Crisis* (July 1915), 125.

art, music, and benevolence. Membership in these clubs required a rock-ribbed respectability—a display of personal propriety that served, in part, to rebut whites' assumptions that all black women were equally degenerate by virtue of skin color.[78] The Colored YWCA, organized in 1907, and the Women's League's home for young working women, opened in 1913, tried to counter the social and economic pressures that led to promiscuity and prostitution. In 1919, the local Colored Women's Federation of Clubs helped organize the National Negro Constitution Conservation League of America, with headquarters in Kansas City. Prominent among its resolutions, the league demanded equal protection of the sexual integrity of black women. You were a candidate for membership, the league announced, "if you believe that the chastity of the Negro Woman should be protected the same as any other race of women," and "that the Negro Woman who is good enough to give her son to fight and die for her country is at the same time good enough to be protected by it." Although the league was short-lived, the fact that its organizers included sexual protection among the civil and political rights they demanded indicated how deeply they felt the lack of such protection.[79]

Unfortunately, blacks debased black women's moral value nearly as much as whites did. Lewis Woods railed against vice dens and social clubs because their black patrons defiled "our women and children" and seduced Negro girls into "the vortex of hell's running stream." He excoriated the black males he had heard on a streetcar for describing the black women passengers as "those teasing yellows, those tantalizing browns and worrisome blacks," thus reinforcing whites' tendency to see black women as objects of sexual

78. Historian Evelyn Brooks Higginbotham calls this the "politics of respectability," a bold assertion of will by which African American club women contested white racism and black sexism simultaneously. Higginbotham, *Righteous Discontent: The Women's Movement in the Black Baptist Church, 1880–1920,* chap. 7. Anne Firor Scott and Paula Giddings likewise discovered that black women's organizations aimed to combat the sexual and moral denigration of black women. Scott, "Most Invisible of All: Black Women's Voluntary Associations," 10; Giddings, *When and Where I Enter: The Impact of Black Women on Race and Sex in America,* 5–117.

79. *The Federation of Colored Charities,* 1914 (bound pamphlet) MVR-KCPL; *Kansas City Sun,* January 25, 1919, February 15, 1919. Nor were black Kansas Citians alone in this concern. The African American women's club movement included the protection of black women from rape as an element of its antilynching campaign in the 1890s. Moreover, in 1918 the *Crisis* identified seven problems most needing resolution for the sake of the race. One of them involved "the lack of protection for colored women, girls, and children." *Crisis* (November 1918), 9. Indeed, DuBois and other male activists believed that racial advancement required stable home life and thus the protection of the virtue of black women. Beverly Guy-Sheftall, *Daughters of Sorrow: Attitudes toward Black Women, 1880–1920,* 37–90; Hall, *Revolt against Chivalry.*

curiosity rather than respect. Like Woods, Charles Starks blamed saloons and vice dens and the white authorities who permitted them for "the profane language used by a certain type of Negro." Starks was so incensed by the degrading language he heard on the sidewalks outside his Eighteenth Street office that he placed a placard in his window upbraiding black men who "have no more respect for our women than if they were animals like themselves." Instead of belittling black women, such men argued, the black male must "defend the honor and good name of the women of his race." In so doing, the black man served a double political purpose. For one, he combated the white assumption that all black women were categorically ineligible for the respect accorded white women. Second, the black man who upheld a black woman's rightful claim to respect asserted his own manhood in a society that increasingly denied him the full prerogatives of the male role.[80]

That much became clear in the commotion over Kenneth Oden's arrest in 1915. Oden, a high school student, had kicked and cuffed a white man into submission for insulting Oden's female cousins while the family rode a local streetcar. According to the *Sun,* Oden's act ought to have been the normal response when "a big burly white man ogles and winks and insults a colored girl as many of them have done before in a crowded street car, feeling secure that whatever he does will be endorsed by his fellows and that no punishment will come to him on account of the cowardice . . . of the Negroes present." Unfortunately, Oden's behavior was rare enough to merit front-page treatment and a publicly subscribed defense fund. The *Sun* acknowledged the double standard of justice that discouraged such acts of valor. Had it been a black man ogling a white woman, the *Sun* surmised, "every white man in the car would have felt it his bounden duty to have administered a blow or a kick to this vicious enemy of society." Instead of receiving fines, the white assailants "would have been liberated with words of praise from the court and the culprit would have administered to him the severest penalty upon the statute books."

<hr>

80. *Rising Son,* November 30, 1905, December 22, 1906, September 22, 1905, September 12, 1903; *Kansas City Sun,* September 15, 1917. Other scholars have found the symbolic emasculation of black males to have been a fundamental part of racial subordination. In the antebellum South, Bill Cecil-Fronsman states, yeoman whites "attempted to set themselves apart by insuring that blacks were unable to behave as 'real men,'" i.e. by defending their honor, competing economically, or participating in politics. Cecil-Fronsman, *Common Whites,* 76. In John Dollard's view, whites exercised mastery over black men by denying them the normal role accorded the male in a patriarchal society, namely the defense of "his" female kin from sexual aggression by other males. Dollard, *Caste and Class,* 144.

Moreover, Oden faced a stiff penalty because race hatred perverted enforcement of the law. Only recently, the *Sun* noted, a police commissioner had remarked that he would "'not take the word of any Negro or a number of Negroes against that of a white man.'" Thus, blacks faced a law enforcement system that regarded black men's sexual advances toward white women as social viciousness. Yet, the same system refused either to protect black women from similar outrages or to permit black men the same capacity to defend them that it granted to white men as a conventional part of the male gender role. Precisely for these reasons, the *Sun* maintained, black men must act a man's part in the very way that whites declared out of bounds to them. "It is our duty regardless of consequences whether we are fined, go to prison or die," the *Sun* asserted, "to protect our women, when they are right against the insults of any man white or black."[81]

In other, less specific ways, these men linked racial advancement to affirmations of masculinity, and they defined race prejudice, in part, as the denial of African American manhood. Why did some African Americans oppose segregation when blacks so often chose to live among and socialize with each other? W. E. Griffen asked. They resisted imposed segregation, Griffen replied, because it was foremost an insult, and no real man would lightly brook an insult. Rather than merely separating the two races, segregation required blacks to affirm their own inferiority and accept a status that was "trivial, servile, senseless and unworthy." Those very ascriptions "all men in all climes always will resent."[82] Likewise, editors Nelson Crews and Lewis Woods accused blacks who acquiesced in Jim Crow of being spineless, servile, and generally lacking in masculine qualities. "If you have got to throw up your manhood to hold a position, throw up the position," Woods counseled. "We pray that God Almighty will send us men who will fight for their rights and not be afraid to die."[83]

Repeatedly, black men who claimed the appellation "race man" couched their resistance to racial injustice in the language of masculinity. "Stand up for your rights and manhood," the *Rising Son* exhorted, for "the white man will have more respect for the negro as a race when he has displayed his manhood in every channel." If the authorities failed to protect blacks' homes from arson and murder by legitimate means, Crews advised, then black men were entitled to take whatever measures necessary and, "like every true American, defend their homes and lives regardless of the cost or consequences."

81. *Kansas City Sun,* January 30, 1915.
82. *Ibid.,* December 5, 1914.
83. *Rising Son,* January 22, 1904.

What did the NAACP demand? its chapter president asked in 1914. "Just a man's chance in this work-a-day world is what the Association asks." Only by "presenting our cause manfully," however, would African Americans make "permanent progress along the battle line of real justice and freedom."[84] Of course, American men customarily used a masculinized rhetoric in their political discourse in the nineteenth and early twentieth centuries. But they employed those rhetorical devices precisely because their political culture defined participation in politics and the public sphere as perquisites of the male gender, and American men considered full citizenship to be a prerogative of manhood.[85] Any exclusion from full participation in the public realm classified black men as both less than citizens and less than men. Kansas Citian Charles Starks recognized that nexus in his critique of segregation: "Let us assert now the truth of our manhood and citizenship. Be men and fight for what rightfully belongs to us as men." In the face of segregation, "shall we sit supinely by and allow our sworn enemies to heap this evil upon us without protest or any effort to stop it? Or shall we fight this evil like men and intelligent people who have rights, hopes, aspirations, a love of liberty and a desire for improvement in living conditions? All true men must answer this last with a vigorous affirmative."[86]

■ ■ Conclusion

Ironically, when racial tensions developed in Kansas City between 1900 and 1920, they drew middle-class blacks and whites into conflict with each other over a set of values they held in common. Judging from the city's labor history in that period, and from the persistently integrated quality of the North End, key segments of the white working class managed to work out some accommodation with their black co-workers and neighbors. By contrast, members of the business and civic leadership tried to harness racial questions to serve their own ends. Some sought to sharpen interracial tensions in order to cripple strikes or to gain political advantage; others played the statesman, seeking just that degree of fairness for African Americans that would best preserve their own security. But, where racial tensions were most

84. *Ibid.*, January 22, 1904; *Kansas City Sun*, November 20, 1915, November 21, 1914.

85. E. Anthony Rotundo, *American Manhood: Transformations in Masculinity from the Revolution to the Modern Era*, 217–21; Paula Baker, "The Domestication of Politics: Women and American Political Society, 1780–1920," 620–47.

86. *Kansas City Sun*, November 28, 1914.

acute, particularly over housing, it was largely the middle and upper-middle class of both races who engaged in the conflicts. Race entered the public discussion in those decades, but white and black Kansas Citians linked it to very intimate matters. In the decade to follow, that fusion of the public and the personal would continue to shape race relations in Kansas City as middle-class whites articulated their concerns about status and urban domesticity in an increasingly racial idiom in the 1920s.

4

Racial Geography

Partitioning Kansas City in the 1920s

■ ■ ■

FOR THOSE LUCKY ENOUGH to be "typical," life in Kansas City took on a choreographed, almost ritualized movement in the 1920s. Or so an observer for the *New Republic* noticed. The young man who knew the steps and could perform them, Shaemus O'Sheel explained, began his career in a small bungalow on "the broad eastern fringe of the city." With his next step into a higher income bracket, he would find a larger house on a "street deep in mellow old trees," where a Buick or Hudson would grace the garage. "From this point the road of ambition is as clear as a concrete highway," O'Sheel promised, "and the progress of the successful Kansas Citian will be marked by a trail of homes, each one newer and more pretentious than the last, and each one farther south, to the utmost limit of a high-powered car's ability to whisk him to and from business." Once airplanes became a commuter commonplace, O'Sheel expected to find Kansas City's suburban boundaries a hundred miles from downtown.[1]

Always peripatetic, Kansas Citians were certainly on the move in the 1920s. And, as O'Sheel shrewdly observed, both the movements and the neighborhoods that were their destinations were closely associated with social status. Residence became a badge of social standing, an investment that secured the future, and the means by which a man guaranteed a certain style of living for his family—one safe from the moral and physical hazards to which urbanites are subject. Because a lot was riding on a man's choice of homesite, he keenly felt his anxieties about property values and stable

1. O'Sheel, "Kansas City, the Crossroads of the Continent," *New Republic* (May 16, 1928), 378.

neighborhoods. And not everyone traveled the road of ambition as effort-lessly as O'Sheel proposed or found a neighborhood of lasting prestige. By the close of the 1920s, middle-class white Kansas Citians had found a shortcut to security in racialism. If they could just keep black Kansas City at a distance, they could define what middle-class status meant in a collective sense and stake their own individual claims to that status. But separate could not be equal in this formula. If African Americans enjoyed the same style of living as oneself, one's claim to high status was clearly bogus. As one young white man put it, Negroes were fine people "in their place." He just did not want them "stepping on his face and climbing higher than he."[2] Consequently, race became part of the ritualized elements in the choreography of status.

■ ■ Property Values and White Kansas Citians

Certainly racial conflict deepened in Kansas City in the 1920s. While race relations were improving elsewhere, the Federal Council of Churches reported in 1925, they were deteriorating in northern cities. According to the report, Kansas City, Detroit, and Cleveland experienced the worst tension, largely because of disputes over housing.[3] Obviously, the geographic expansion of the black community contributed to the friction in Kansas City, but that expansion intruded on a white population that was already apprehensive over the quality of their neighborhoods for reasons that had no immediate connection to race.

When middle-class whites began scrutinizing their terrain, what they saw disturbed some of them enough to launch an "Anti-Ugly Movement" in the early twenties. The movement accomplished more publicity than genuine results, but it revealed the sort of concerns such whites had over issues of urban space. In part, the anti-uglies shared the earlier desire of the elite to dress up the city for company. They aimed to replace the approaches to the city, which carried motorists through unsightly industrial districts, with land-scaped trafficways and to provide visitors a more impressive first view of the city by erecting a war memorial opposite Union Station. But the anti-uglies were more troubled by rapid changes in land use in Kansas City. Although they hoped that vigorous policing and reinvestment in the North End were

2. Quoted in press release, "Kansas City Race Relations Tense, Reports Walter White," December 10, 1926, Group G, Box 107, NAACP Papers, LOC.
3. *Kansas City Call,* December 18, 1925.

about to restore that district, the central business district appeared to be headed on another migration southward in the direction of Union Station. Furthermore, downtown Kansas City needed a thorough cleanup to make it safe and accessible for women and children. Searching for a means to anchor the business center, anti-uglies revealed the depth of their anxiety in articles that labeled the North End a "cancerous growth" that instilled "continuous fear" in property owners.[4]

Quick shifts in land use most concerned the anti-uglies because they jeopardized residential real estate values. Kansas City was foremost a city of homes and home owners, its leaders liked to say.[5] Preserving home values deserved the city's best efforts. A vigorous campaign by civic and commercial organizations advocated zoning ordinances as the best guarantee of "conservation and beauty in city building, just as haphazard growth stands for inefficiency, wastefulness, and ugliness." Without these controls, "fine home districts, good for a hundred years ordinarily, have been reduced in twenty years to second and third class properties." With zoning, advocates hoped, "no one per cent of the people shall tear down the loveliness ninety-nine per cent are working to maintain." The city council approved a so-called anti-ugly ordinance in 1922 that restricted the location of stores, cleaning establishments, and service stations, and it enacted its first zoning ordinance in 1923. Proponents hoped that zoning would guide development "in directions that will serve the best interests of all the people" by eliminating the old "haphazard hit and miss proposition, with store buildings and apartments so placed that they depreciate the value of residence property." Still not satisfied, the *Kansas City Star* urged in 1926 that the city establish a permanent "Clean Up and Stay Clean Department" at City Hall. Even so, property owners had to rely chiefly on their own devices to preserve the value of their homes. In 1923, home owners in the vicinity of Seventy-Fifth Street and Holmes Road pooled their funds and bought an adjoining parcel of land where a developer proposed to build small cottages. The investors reported that they had nearly beggared themselves in this way, but they feared that the developer's project would have reduced the value of their properties by $2,000

4. See for example, *Citizens' League Bulletin*, October 3, 1925, October 5, 1921, November 13, 1926, January 20, 1923, December 21, 1929. The *Citizens' League Bulletin* began referring to an "Anti-Ugly Movement" in 1922 and calling its proponents "anti-uglies."

5. See for example, Mayor Albert Beach's statement listing home ownership as Kansas City's primary economic activity, ahead of finance, transportation, industry, and retailing. *Citizens' League Bulletin*, May 21, 1927. In fact, only a third of the city's homes were owned by their occupants in 1920, a lower proportion than in many similar sized cities. *Fourteenth Census: Population*, vol. 2, 1294.

to $2,500. Other householders who found their residential neighborhoods invaded by tiny shops, parking garages, or service stations brought suit to remove the enterprises. So widespread was this concern over property values that Independence Boulevard Church brought legal action in 1924 to remove a nearby property that the congregation claimed depreciated the value of church grounds. In this case, the offending property was a hospital.[6]

■ ■ Housing and Black Kansas City

Clearly, whites' protests about declining property values were not just a smoke screen for racism, for the sudden appearance of a gas station or a billboard could excite nail-biting tension or actual retaliation from home owners. Their worries about the stability and beauty of residential real estate were deep and genuine. When the city's black population pressed against the physical boundaries of the ghetto, however, race became inextricably connected to white householders' existing concerns over the financial and social value of the neighborhoods they occupied. The black eastside experienced irresistible pressures to expand in the 1920s. During that decade, the black population in Kansas City increased by 26 percent, including growing numbers of southern blacks after 1922.[7] Most newcomers and displaced older residents were forced to find what housing they could in the black eastside. The growing number of black businesses, schools, churches, and social organizations radiating from the commercial center at Eighteenth and Vine Streets made the eastside doubly attractive, but construction of each

6. *Citizens' League Bulletin,* December 31, 1921, December 2, 1922, December 8, 1923; *Kansas City Star,* May 1, 1922, May 31, 1926, April 4, 1923, June 13, 1924; Ralph P. Swofford, *Important Facts about Kansas City.* While zoning ordinances in Atlanta, for example, specifically excluded African Americans from "white" areas, zoning ordinances in Kansas City made no reference to race, nor did their supporters. See Ronald H. Baylor, *Race and the Shaping of Twentieth-Century Atlanta,* 54–55.

7. *Citizens' League Bulletin,* January 26, 1924; Joe E. Herriford, "W. W. Yates School," in "Schools-Public," Vertical File, MVR-KCPL; *Reports of the Superintendent of Schools, Kansas City, Missouri.* 1921–1927, 1927–1930. The Citizens' League estimated the number of southern newcomers at 250 per week in 1924, though its figures seem to have been exaggerated. At the rate of 250 in-migrants per week, the black population would have increased by 13,000 per year. Its total increase for the decade was less than 8,000. Indeed, school district records showed that the population of school-aged black children fell sharply between 1923 and 1924, from 12,000 to 8,600 youngsters, before returning to the former figure in 1928. Thus, Kansas City may have been a waystation to the north rather than a permanent destination for many southern migrants. See John Bodnar, Michael Weber, and Roger Simon, "Migration, Kinship, and Urban Adjustment: Blacks and Poles in Pittsburgh, 1900–1930," 548–65.

new store or school subtracted from the available housing stock. Families crowded wherever they could, averaging four and one-half families per residence and compounding the health and sanitation problems in the black sector of the Eighth Ward. Costs for these miserable accommodations ran as high as thirty-six dollars per month—a sum equal to the total monthly income of many black wage earners.[8]

Desperate for a decent place to live, middle-class blacks relied on black realtors to find homes for them outside the boundaries of the ghetto. Fortune J. Weaver had earned the title "The Locator" during his tenure as a realtor in Kansas City in the first decade of the century. A race-conscious businessman, Weaver also operated rooming houses and an employment agency for black job-seekers. But it was his contacts with white-owned realty firms, and his ability to convince white property-owners to rent or sell to African Americans, that made Weaver an influential figure. In 1923 he offered to pay ten dollars for any tip on a house he eventually bought. To induce whites to turn over entire blocks to black purchasers, he announced that he would pay cash for houses in lots of twenty-five. Other real estate agents, black and white, encouraged white flight with the "straw man," a white or light-skinned person who would buy a house in a white residential block. Once the house had been resold to a black buyer, the block was "busted," and the remaining white residents would likely sell out en masse, leaving the wily realtor with several listings to offer to blacks at inflated prices. Black-owned Square Deal Realty and Loan Company preferred to advertise that it had entered "negotiations" with white property-owners to convince them to sell. One very successful parley in 1922 allowed Square Deal to put the entire 2500 block of Tracy Avenue up for sale "only to highly respected Negroes." For down payments of $500 to $3,000, purchasers could move into bungalows priced at $4,000 to $7,500. That year, Square Deal claimed to have made more than one million dollars in real estate sales.[9]

Given these real estate practices, "busted" neighborhoods tended to resegregate rapidly, and the borders of the black eastside expanded along an irregular line by incorporating whole blocks of housing. Anxious to escape overcrowding in the eastside core, black home-buyers apparently cared more about finding decent homes than about the skin color of their neighbors. C. A. Franklin, publisher of the black newspaper the *Kansas City Call* and a watchdog of African American interests, often praised white property-owners

8. *Kansas City Call,* March 2, 1923.

9. Naysmith, "Population in Kansas City, Missouri," folder 5, 214; *Kansas City Call,* November 16, 1923, April 3, 1926, March 5, 1922, August 24, 1923.

who told him that they were willing to "sell up" to blacks rather than live next door to them. Each time whites "released" an entire block to black purchasers, the *Call* announced the event with eye-catching photos and headlines. These instances of white flight did not trouble Franklin greatly, for "it is time wasted to try to prove to whites that they should not refuse to live neighbors to Negroes."[10]

■ ■ Conflicts over Housing

While block-busting and similar real estate practices would be condemned in later decades, in the 1920s they served useful purposes for the black community. After all, the black family who moved into a "busted" block on the eastside's fringe acquired a piece of the American Dream: security and pride of home ownership in a comfortable and healthy neighborhood that still lay within easy reach of the commercial and social center at Eighteenth and Vine. If those neighborhoods quickly resegregated, so much the better, for there was a measure of safety in numbers. The lone black pioneer who penetrated a predominantly white neighborhood, on the other hand, faced daunting risks. Between 1921 and 1928, Kansas City suffered a rash of bombings of black-occupied homes, numbering as many as seven in a single year. By 1923, C. A. Franklin complained, "there was not an unoccupied foot of ground where Negroes could go and live without having to fight to do so." Vigilance committees, and a Negro Protective and Improvement Association organized in 1923, failed to stem the attacks. Protests to the police commissioners by the NAACP received only a bland assurance from the police department that its officers were providing adequate protection. In fact, the NAACP and the *Call* claimed to have evidence that the police left threatened houses unguarded at the "right time" and failed to make arrests, even when a suspect had been tracked down by police dogs. Casting about for a solution, the local NAACP branch considered suing the city for permitting "bombing outrages" to occur with impunity, and it tried to get bombing cases before the grand jury by hiring a private detective to collect evidence.[11]

10. *Kansas City Call,* May 28, 1926.
11. Letter of John L. Love to Walter F. White, May 17, 1923; Letter of Myrtle F. Cook to Robert M. Bagnall, June 19, 1924; Letter of John L. Love to Walter White, May 14, 1925; all letters in Group G, Box 107, NAACP Papers, LOC; *Kansas City Call,* January 19, 1923, May 13, 1922, September 2, 1922, June 20, 1924, October 14, 1927. According to the *Call,* where such matters were most likely to be reported, no perpetrators of bombings or arson were arrested or prosecuted.

Pioneering in a white neighborhood was all the more unsettling a venture because whites' responses were erratic and unpredictable. Although Lucile Bluford grew up at Twenty-Fifth and Montgall, the area raked by bombing attacks in 1911, she recalls playing happily with the children of her white neighbors. Yet, Bluford remembers other nights when her black neighbors sat guard on the homes of friends in other contested neighborhoods, and two houses were bombed across the street from her home when blacks tried to occupy them in 1924. A year earlier, teacher Ida Williams had moved into a neighborhood having several black residents of long standing, only to see her own home damaged by dynamite three times. She vowed to stay on with her aged mother, despite threats of more bombs. By contrast, white residents of a similar neighborhood protected two black women residents when a mob threatened them in 1927.[12]

If the violent outbreaks were unpredictable, the locations where they occurred followed a consistent pattern. Using local city directories, it is possible to reconstitute eight of the areas, shown on Figure 4.1, where bombings and similar acts of intimidation took place.[13] The resulting data reveal some of the characteristics the trouble sites shared and suggest reasons why these areas became so volatile. For one, the areas had distinctive class compositions. Only one incident occurred in a solidly blue-collar neighborhood. It began near the North End when a mob gathered to oust a new black resident from the Garland Apartments in 1925. The Garland was one of several apartment buildings erected in the Queen Anne motif near Independence Avenue in the 1880s. The buildings' architectural style and location went out of fashion soon after they were completed, and the Garland had to be placed in receivership more than once. Apparently, the new owner in 1925 hoped to increase his occupancy rate by letting apartments to blacks, who would pay higher rents for whatever housing space they could find. He renamed the building Lincoln Apartments and assigned a black-owned real estate firm to handle rentals. When residents objected, the Garland's owner told the press that he was determined to rent to black tenants, but the mob of protesters

12. Deposition of Lucile Bluford, 1983, 105–6, Box 102, Benson Papers; *Kansas City Call,* June 13, 1924, February 23, 1923, September 9, 1927.

13. Starting in 1918, *Polk's City Directory of Kansas City* included a "criss-cross" feature, a section listing the name of every business or head of household located at each address on every city street. From these I obtained lists of household heads living at the time of a bombing or antiblack mob action within a nine square block area surrounding the incident's site. I then located each of the household heads in the directory's alphabetical section to determine the individual's occupation. I identified which of the residents were newcomers by comparing lists of residents at the time of the antiblack incident to the lists of residents present in the same area three years prior to the incident.

Selected Sites of Anti-Black Violence

* = Site of bombing or arson.

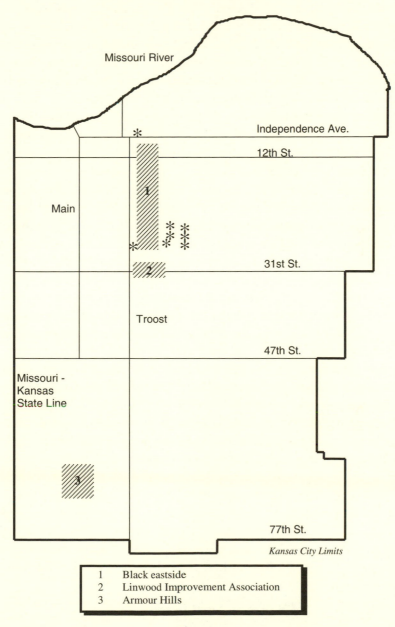

Figure 4.1

forced him to change his plans. No one identified the crowd members by name, but the household heads who occupied the Garland at the time of the incident were almost entirely working class. Of the residents whose occupations were listed in the city directory, 88 percent held blue-collar jobs, half of them in the skilled trades.[14]

The other disturbances occurred along the eastern and western flanks of the black eastside, which formed a peninsula of black residents that penetrated southward into old, white-occupied suburbs. Unlike the incident at the Garland, none of them took place in solidly working-class areas but ignited in neighborhoods that were distinguished by—some residents would say plagued by—heterogeneity. Seven zones, of approximately nine square blocks each, surrounded these sites where one or more bombings or mob actions occurred between 1923 and 1927. Together, these areas encompassed 1,623 households and businesses and 1,308 individual residents whose occupations could be determined from the city directory. The number of businesses in each reconstituted area ranged from three to fourteen, averaging nine businesses per neighborhood. In fact, these seven sites exhibited most of the characteristics that so disturbed the anti-ugly activists. Service stations, repair shops, cafes, and various retail shops were sprinkled among the homes, along with a few machine shops and contracting businesses.

If land use was mixed, so was the population. A significant proportion of families with German, Jewish, and Italian surnames made their homes there. In all but one of these seven neighborhoods where antiblack disturbances took place was a tiny enclave of black residents who had occupied their homes in the neighborhood, apparently without incident, for at least three years before a bomb greeted the arrival of a new black family. Most striking about these reconstituted neighborhoods, as Table 4.1 shows, was the heterogeneous mix of social classes among occupants. Residents were about equally divided between blue- and white-collar workers. Moreover, each trouble spot included residents from the extremes of the class structure—physicians, attorneys, and owners or managers of sizable businesses who lived beside common laborers. But the greatest number made their livings as clerks and salesmen, owners of small businesses, or middle-level managers. In all but one area, the lower-middle-class residents constituted the largest category of occupants. Yet, the lower middle class shared these aged suburbs with

14. *Kansas City Journal,* August 11, 1925; "Structural Kansas City," Native Sons Archives, MVR-KCPL; *Kansas City Star,* August 11, 1925. The man whom the police arrested for instigating the affair was an outsider in terms of class and residence. Listed in the city directory as the president of a cutlery firm, he had his home address on the northeastern edge of the black eastside at a considerable distance from the Garland.

Class Composition of Contested Neighborhoods

Zone	High White Collar	Low White Collar	Skilled Labor	Semiskilled Labor	Unskilled Labor
1 - 21st & Park	4%	36%	9%	36%	14%
2 - 25th & Montgall	6%	39%	32%	18%	4%
3 - 19th & Montgall	5%	34%	25%	25%	11%
4 - 20th & Park	0%	20%	13%	33%	34%
5 - 24th & Brooklyn	10%	47%	9%	25%	10%
6 - 25th & Tracy	9%	45%	10%	21%	14%
7 - 20th & Montgall	0%	51%	20%	24%	5%
Total	6%	39%	18%	25%	12%

Table 4.1

considerable numbers of teamsters, baggage-handlers, streetcar conductors, and others from the ranks of the semiskilled.[15]

Presumably, these neighborhoods became scenes of violence because their white residents were protecting the homes and streets they had occupied for many years against encroachment by blacks. In fact, about 60 percent of the residents who were living in these neighborhoods when an antiblack incident occurred had just moved there within the previous three years. The proportion of newly arrived occupants in each zone ranged from a low of 58 percent to a high of 65 percent. Taking these seven zones together, 988 out of the total of 1,623 households and businesses that were present at the time of a racial incident had only located there within the previous three years. A roughly equal number of residents had moved out in the same period. Consequently, these were fairly transient neighborhoods. Whatever attachments the majority of residents felt for these places, whether loyalty to neighbors and neighborhood or liking for the area's amenities, those attachments had been formed only a short while before the arrival of a black occupant touched off hostilities.

15. The neighborhood with the lowest occupancy by the middle class, identified as Zone 4 in Table 4.1, also had the highest number of black residents, whose lower economic status skewed the head count in favor of the working class. By 1920, city directories no longer identified listees by race. I have designated as black-occupied those blocks on which prominent black individuals (teachers, clergy, attorneys, and other professionals whose names were readily identifiable) were living alongside a cluster of porters, domestics, chauffeurs, and others in occupations typically held by blacks.

It is possible that these neighborhoods developed undesirable character-istics (heterogeneity and transiency) only *because* blacks had moved into them or because they lay in the path of black population movement. To test that hypothesis, two other zones, of four square blocks each, can be studied as control groups. Both resembled the contested neighborhoods in age and type of housing stock. More important, both control group neigh-borhoods suffered similar patterns of rapid turnover and heterogeneity, even though they contained no identifiable black residents and lay outside the routes of black population movement. In other words, heterogeneity and transience occurred independent of and well before black in-migration. One control area lay between Twentieth and Twenty-First Streets east of Benton Boulevard—the unofficial eastern boundary of black expansion. It exhibited a slightly lower (but still considerable) turnover rate of 50 percent between 1922 and 1925 and a heterogeneous mix of class, with a somewhat lower proportion (33 percent) of white-collar occupants. The second lay west of Troost Avenue (the unofficial western boundary to black expansion) and op-posite the southernmost disputed zone. This second control area was more uniformly white collar (80 percent), but it also included blue-collar work-ers and a significant number of residents with Jewish and Italian surnames. Its turnover rate between 1922 and 1925 was appreciable (36 percent) but considerably lower than the rate for contested neighborhoods. Thus, the eastside's old suburbs appeared to be losing their appeal to the native middle class, with or without black residents.

Nor was the simple presence of black residents in a predominantly white neighborhood enough, by itself, to cause violent confrontations over hous-ing. After all, blacks had lived in the troubled areas undisturbed for a number of years before the trouble began. But the continued expansion of the black eastside corridor occurred in an atmosphere of general apprehension over property values and land usage in the 1920s—apprehension that magnified white householders' concern about any threat to stable housing values. In cities like Chicago and Detroit, racial conflict over housing coincided with housing shortages. By contrast, the bombings of black householders began in Kansas City in 1923, near the peak in a period of unprecedented home construction, and the bombings ended in 1927, shortly after homes con-struction began to decline. This evidence suggests that the motive for vio-lence in Kansas City was not competition for a finite group of houses, but contention over the character of specific neighborhoods.[16] The location of

16. Cowherd, "Experiences and Observations," 7–8; William M. Tuttle, Jr., *Race Riot: Chicago in the Red Summer of 1919,* 168–69; David Allan Levine, *Internal Com-bustion: The Races in Detroit, 1915–1926,* 37–48.

the core black community meant that, when the community expanded, it expanded into neighborhoods that had ceased to meet Kansas City's standards for an ideal residential district some time before. Transient and heterogeneous in terms of class and ethnicity, these eastside residential areas added nothing to the prestige of the families who had addresses there. A motley and indiscriminate blend of urbanites assembled in such aging suburbs, where businesses disturbed the peace that was supposed to be the portion of the suburban dweller and altered the original pattern of land use. Families who yearned to sink roots where the character of the neighborhood and the value of their property would endure, where their neighbors would resemble themselves in class, birth, and culture—such families met only frustration here. The admixture of black residents was enough to make those frustrations, quite literally, explosive.

■ ■ Race and Middle-Class Suburbs

Enterprising developers stood ready to administer an antidote in the 1920s. Of course, most white eastsiders could not afford homes in the new subdivisions that sprouted in that decade. But the character of those developments, and the methods by which developers marketed them, illustrated how deeply the middle ranks of white Kansas Citians wished to be isolated from heterogeneity and change. One visionary developer in particular unwittingly suggested the methods by which white eastsiders might repel the "Negro invasion" of their own neighborhoods without using the torch or the bomb. In the 1920s, that visionary, J. C. Nichols, set out to provide middle-class householders with the kind of residential sanctuary he had sold so successfully to the upper class and upper middle class before the war. In 1922, Nichols filed the plat for his Armour Hills subdivision south of his Country Club District. Combining sections of large, two-story houses with sections devoted to smaller bungalows, Nichols designed Armour Hills for the prosperous middle-class home-buyer. Deed restrictions made Armour Hills still more attractive. In fact, Nichols replicated the restrictive covenant he filed with the Armour Hills plat in his other developments in the 1920s.[17]

Those restrictions controlled the size, cost, and placement of each house, the type and location of outbuildings, and the size of free yard space. A further clause banned the sale or rental of an Armour Hills home to blacks.

17. William S. Worley, *J. C. Nichols and the Shaping of Kansas City: Innovation in Planned Residential Communities*, 132.

Contract stipulations also required the Nichols Company's approval for the buyer's architectural plans so that no resident might embarrass his neighbors with a home style that was either eccentric or tawdry. As he had in earlier developments, Nichols vested enforcement of the restrictions in a homes association in which membership was mandatory for all Armour Hills residents, but the Armour Hills project was the first in which the homes association charter was recorded along with the plat and deed restrictions. Numerous other subdivisions in Kansas City and across the country would duplicate the Armour Hills model by combining restrictive deeds with coercive associations of owners.[18] To keep retail businesses from sprouting among the homesites, Nichols's plan set aside specific lots for the location of churches and schools but restricted all other lots to single-family dwellings. Brookside Shopping Center, which Nichols began building in 1919 along the northern edge of Armour Hills, provided space for tradesmen and professionals' offices. The shops were built in uniform style (tastefully Tudor), and, unlike other developers, the Nichols Company retained ownership of the structures and thus could control the kind of tenants who set up for business in its subdivision. More important to Nichols, he hoped that the community spirit he carefully manufactured would guarantee that "very few people in our subdivision would sell to an undesirable purchaser."[19]

Nichols clearly understood the tensions that bedeviled the middle-class householders who were likely to purchase his homesites, for, in Armour Hills, he aimed to accommodate "those who would like to enjoy the advantages of a protected neighborhood in a home of moderate cost." In one of his earliest advertisements for Armour Hills, he promised, "Our model self-perpetuating restrictions are an insurmountable barrier to every damaging and destructive influence. The ridges and slopes of this picturesque tract will be 'home' for families who can have no fear for their surroundings." Fear was warranted, he believed, for "the very home-life of a city is endangered and should be protected" from rapid changes in urban land use. And after all, he reminded the prospective buyer in Armour Hills, "you owe your wife and family a home free from the noise and dirt of the city." If the middle-class family man were not already anxious enough, other advertisers played on his apprehensions, too. "You are thoroughly capable of providing for your loved ones—*so long as you live!*" the Real Estate Board admitted. "But some day— some time—you will cease to be. *Then what?*" Only investment in a home,

18. Helen Monchow, *The Use of Deed Restrictions in Subdivision Development,* 47–49, 60–61; Worley, *J. C. Nichols,* 132–35, 139.
19. Quoted in Worley, *J. C. Nichols,* 267.

the "most valuable and most permanent thing in Kansas City," would ensure a family's place "at the banquet table." Of course, permanence of value depended in particular on the "protective restrictions" that Nichols supplied to stanch the fear.[20] As his biographer William Worley notes, J. C. Nichols built subdivisions for the type of Kansas Citian whose goal was "creating an island of controlled living . . . in an uncontrollable world."[21]

Armour Hills was an immediate success. By 1926, 171 households had located in a six square block area along the subdivision's northern tier. According to city directories, two-thirds of those households were headed by members of the middle class—most of them owners or managers of modestly sized business firms or sellers of real estate and insurance. The remaining third were professionals or midlevel executives, making this neighborhood a bastion of the affluent middle class. Homogeneous in nativity as well as class, this neighborhood had more enduring appeal than the older suburbs, where mixed lots of people moved in and out each year. By contrast, three-quarters of the Armour Hills residents who lived in the reconstituted area in 1926 still lived at the same Armour Hills addresses in 1929. There, life exemplified what Richard Sennett calls the "permanent adolescence" of middle-class America, which faced what it perceived to be an uncertain future in the twentieth-century city by adopting the psychological defenses of the adolescent—the "suppression and avoidance of diversity" along with "the desire for a purified, disorder-transcending identity that emerges in adolescence." The apotheosis of their defenses was the suburb, what Sennett called the "purified community."[22] The suburbs promised these householders the ideal medium for rearing wholesome families, free of the diversity and disorder that blacks, poised on the horizon, embodied.

■ ■ Purification after the Fact—Kansas City's Eastside

In Kansas City in the 1920s, the search for the purified community fueled a boom in residential construction and sales of refurbished older homes that began in 1919 and lasted until sales began to slacken in 1927. Every year between 1921 and 1927 saw more than 2,000 housings starts, with a record-breaking peak of 3,645 new single-family residences built in 1925. But the

20. See for example, advertisements in *Kansas City Star,* May 10, 1925, May 10, 1922, May 31, 1925, June 13, 1926, June 27, 1926, May 3, 1925.
21. Quoted in Worley, *J. C. Nichols,* 256–57, 160.
22. Richard Sennett, *The Uses of Disorder: Personal Identity and City Life,* 66.

mellow, tree-lined old suburbs of the eastside lacked the defensive imple-
ments of Armour Hills or the distinction of an address on the far southside.
Nevertheless, developers like J. C. Nichols had demonstrated to white eastsiders how they might capture some of the exclusivity of the new subdivisions
for their older, formerly suburban neighborhoods. In early 1923, the Southeast Home Protective Association announced its presence in the area south
and east of the black eastside with "dodgers" proclaiming its intention to
secure the value of property between Twentieth and Thirtieth Streets from
Euclid Avenue to Benton Boulevard. The association claimed some of the
virtues of the Armour Hills Homes Association; members pledged, for example, to encourage the planting of trees and flowers and to promote public
improvements in their area. But the organization's prime purpose, according
to its handbill, was to prevent "the encroachment of Negroes" by shunning
property owners, real estate agents, and lenders who enabled African Americans to move into the area.[23]

Not satisfied that these vague threats would cement white solidarity,
the Southeast Home Protective Association shortly began pressuring white
property owners to enter covenants barring black occupancy. Unlike
Nichols's deed restrictions, which accompanied the original deed to the
property, restrictions on older homes had to be attached after the fact to
properties that had not been restricted at the time of their original construction. By March, a notary reported to the *Call* that entire neighborhoods of
whites on the eastside were coming to him to notarize covenant agreements
that were to be in force for fifteen years. The property owners then affixed
these instruments to their deeds at the registrar's office. Neither device was
new; each had been in use in other cities for some time. What was innovative
was the combination of restrictive covenants with homes associations to
back them up. Ironically, the U.S. Supreme Court encouraged the resort
to covenants in 1917 with its decision in *Buchanan v. Warley,* in which the
court overturned a Louisville city ordinance segregating residence in the
city by race. The justices held that the ordinance violated the Fourteenth
Amendment because it was an act of the state, thus implying that covenants,
as agreements among private individuals, would be allowed to stand. As a
Call editorial lamented in 1923, "What the city council and state legislatures
cannot do, that is segregate blacks and whites, a notary with a seal can do,
or at least has made a show of doing in Kansas City."[24]

23. Handbill reproduced in the *Kansas City Call,* January 19, 1923; Cowherd, "Experiences and Observations," 7–8; Worley, *J. C. Nichols,* 221–22.
24. *Kansas City Call,* March 2, 1923. Property owners in St. Louis had been attaching
racial restrictions to deeds on existing homes since at least 1910. Home owners' protective

Despite the apparent approval of the courts, neither protective associations nor covenants could prevent violence or racial turnover. Just four months after the Southeast Home Protective Association began its campaign to improve its district, a bomb damaged every house on a city block within its territory. Nor could these devices make an Armour Hills out of the old southeast suburb. The six square block area surrounding the bomb site in 1923 suffered the same imperfections as other neighborhoods where bombings occurred, including a section where blacks had resided over a long period, a nearly equal mix of white- and blue-collar residents, and a 64 percent turnover in residents since 1920. By 1926, this same area had experienced another turnover of 58 percent in its occupants and a loss of four out of seven business establishments. Its white-collar residents had slipped from 40 percent to 20 percent of the area's population, in part because the block where the bomb was detonated in 1923 now housed black occupants, most of whom were employed at the bottom ranks of the working class.[25]

In fact, restrictive covenants failed to stem "encroachment by Negroes" because whites were unwilling to live up to their sworn agreements. When realtors began using the straw man to bust blocks in Southeast's territory, many white home-owners waived their restrictive agreements by affidavit and put their homes up for sale to blacks in 1926. Likewise, nineteen white home-owners on Tracy Avenue waived their agreements in the same month that two newly arrived black families were bombed on that street in 1927. By November 1927, covenant agreements appeared futile in such districts. Four years earlier, a white woman living in Southeast's most troubled area had filed for an injunction against a white property-owner who had violated his restrictive covenant by selling his home to a black family. The case was unprecedented in Missouri, the *Call* noted, because there had never before been a white who held out long enough for her case to reach the state's supreme court. The Missouri Supreme Court ruled in her case that it was powerless to enforce a covenant in a neighborhood in which the conditions the covenant was meant to preserve no longer existed. Clearly, the restrictive covenant was a frail device if it was not attached to the original deeds in the subdivision. Moreover, deed holders showed as little fidelity to those neighborhoods as they did to their sworn agreements. Even before racial troubles

---

associations emerged in Chicago around 1917, using threats and violent intimidation of black and white property-owners and realtors, but restrictive covenants did not come into use in Chicago until 1927, ten years after the organization of home protective associations in that city. Herman H. Long and Charles S. Johnson, *People vs. Property: Race Restrictive Covenants in Housing,* 12; Tuttle, *Race Riot,* 171–80; Spear, *Black Chicago,* 221.

25. *Kansas City Call,* April 6, 1923.

began, more than half the residents of these contested neighborhoods had seen fit to leave them within a three-year period.[26]

A residential area farther south of the eastside peninsula of black homes appeared to be more promising ground for preserving its all-white character. This district, called Linwood, lay between Twenty-Eighth and Thirty-First Streets from Flora to Brooklyn. In some respects it resembled the racially contested neighborhoods to the north. Its residents were ethnically mixed and fairly transient, 57 percent of residents in 1926 having moved to the area within the previous three years. More than one hundred businesses operated in this thirty-six square block area, but seventy-nine of them were located in the attractive commercial centers on Thirty-First Street or on Brooklyn, rather than being scattered among residences. Moreover, this area boasted a population of somewhat higher status. More than half of its residents ranked in the lower middle class; just a fifth were situated in the bottom two ranks of the working class. This district of detached houses, apartment buildings, and businesses attracted the services of one John Bowman, a realtor whose home and office were located there. As president of the Linwood Improvement Association (LIA), Bowman began mobilizing the district to enter restrictive covenants in 1926. That year, he won public support from a number of churches and apartment owners as well as home owners for his restriction drive, but the experience of neighborhoods to the north already demonstrated how ineffectual those agreements could be. The LIA district, however, enjoyed two geographic advantages. Not only did it lie south of Twenty-Seventh Street (recognized as the southern boundary of the black eastside), but it was bordered on the north by Troost and Spring Valley Parks. Between these two greenspaces was a sparsely populated spit of land occupied partly by black families, who were among the few who lived south of Twenty-Seventh Street.[27]

Developers often used parks and golf courses to buffer their new subdivisions against undesirable land use, and J. C. Nichols had made them an attractive feature of his own developments. Hoping to maximize its advantage by duplicating the park strategy in an existing suburb, LIA decided to ask the Kansas City Board of Commissioners for Parks and Boulevards to condemn the land between the two parks and thus make a solid boundary of greenspace along LIA's northern edge. "Then, for fear Negroes, or some schemers helping Negroes may by hook or crook cross over the park," the

26. *Ibid.*, April 3, 1926, October 7, 1927, November 4, 1927.
27. *Kansas City Journal*, June 8, 1926. This thirty-six block area included 871 households and 109 businesses.

Call reported, LIA managed to restrict more than 60 percent of the area south of the intended park. In mid-May 1926, two LIA officers appeared before the Board of Park Commissioners requesting that, "on account of the encroachment of negroes," the board condemn the property between Troost and Spring Valley Parks and convert it to park space. Board members assured LIA's representatives that "they were in sympathy with their aims, but that they believed the proper settlement was in the hands of property owners, by mutual agreements." According to the *Call*, board members concluded in June that the board could not afford to build a park that would serve as nothing but a "deadline" to black movement. The LIA renewed its request in July, this time bringing a petition signed by thirteen hundred affected property owners and a proposal to pay for the park out of assessments against a benefit district of affected property owners. While the park commissioners considered the petition, some forty white owners of property that was proposed for condemnation came before the board in September to protest LIA's proposal. They reported that they had been unable to refinance their homes because of rumors that their property was due to be condemned. Furthermore, protesters noted, the sixty black families who would lose their homes to the park project had nowhere else to find homes. Unfortunately, the board ignored the white protestors' plea for a clear decision that would end the uncertainty over the future of their homes. Instead, the board refused to take any action at all on the proposal.[28]

Later that month, large delegations of park supporters and opponents met with the park board. This time, the park's proponents stressed the social benefits of their intended greenspace, without mentioning its value as a racial deadline. A parade of witnesses, consisting of owners of businesses and representatives of churches in the Linwood area, argued that their neighborhood badly needed more recreation ground. Residents of the proposed benefit district were ten to one in favor of building such a park at their own expense, proponents claimed. The black speakers present quickly challenged both pretenses. The *Call*'s editor, C. A. Franklin, who lived in the targeted area, protested that the park was intended to establish a "line of division" between black and white, a tactic that was bound to fail given the inadequate supply of housing for black families within the proposed boundary. Rev. D. A. Holmes, pastor of a large congregation of black Baptists, flatly

---

28. Monchow, *Use of Deed Restrictions,* 14; Official Proceedings of the Board of Park Commissioners, Item 12984, May 13, 1926; Items 13229 and 13237, September 2, 1926; *Kansas City Call,* June 4, 1926, June 11, 1926; *Kansas City Journal,* July 30, 1926.

stated, "The only issue here is race." Despite proponents' claims of broad support, Holmes warned the board that many churches and public institutions near Linwood Boulevard, as well as less affluent white property-owners, were opposed to the plan, making the proposal a piece of "class legislation" that would never survive a court challenge. The park commissioners still took no action until November, when the board denied LIA's request on grounds that there was no need for additional park land in the intended area.

Undeterred, LIA submitted yet another petition in 1927, this one proposing to condemn only property owned by whites. Unfortunately for LIA, park commissioners insisted on putting this latest proposal to a vote in a public hearing. Nearly five hundred people appeared at the hearing in October, many of them angry about the petition. In particular, whites who owned property in the southern half of the proposed benefit district complained that they would be assessed for the costs of a park that would only benefit the owners of property lying to the north and therefore closest to the park. They were all the more irate because they claimed they were not informed about the scheme until a week before the hearing. The proposal sank in a wave of "no" votes.[29]

■ ■ Housing and the Tactics of Misdirection

LIA never resurrected the park deadline strategy after this signal failure, but the gambit was significant because it exemplified the tactics of misdirection that certain groups of whites employed in the 1920s. By the end of the decade, the tactic would become standard procedure, even among apparent "race liberals," who approached racial issues with a combination of self-serving benevolence and deception. In LIA's case, a fog of obfuscation clouded many of the association's activities. After its initial meeting before the park board, one of LIA's more active members informed a *Call* reporter "that the association would not state in its petition to the council that its real purpose was to establish a deadline, but that it would contend for the park." Consequently, the *Call* set itself as watchdog on succeeding LIA efforts in order to publicize the organization's antiblack character and tactics. But the *Call*'s editorial policy contrasted sharply with the policies of the white dailies.

29. Official Proceedings of the Board of Park Commissioners, Item 13267, September 30, 1926; Item 13309, November 4, 1926; *Kansas City Call,* July 22, 1927; *Kansas City Times,* October 7, 1927; *Kansas City Journal,* October 7, 1927. The Official Proceedings of the Board of Park Commissioners referred to the hearing after the fact but did not record the hearing itself.

The *Times,* for example, printed a sizable report of a meeting in 1926 in which LIA won broad support for its campaign to restrict its district, but the report neglected to explain that it was blacks who were to be restricted. The front pages of the *Star* seldom failed to note each decision by the city to widen a boulevard or install a stoplight, yet the *Star* carried no reports of LIA's park proposals or of the park board's deliberations. Nor did the *Times* or *Journal* give the matter any appreciable coverage until the acrimony of the final public hearing made it too difficult to ignore.[30]

Those articles that mentioned LIA in any capacity presented the organization as responsible and statesmanlike, despite the facts that mobs of men thought to be LIA members had threatened realtors and black householders, and that the *Call* had received a letter vowing that "we want those sixty-two negro homes for a park and we are going to have them if we are compelled to blow everyone of them up." None of these incidents were reported in the white press. Nor did the white press report the actual assaults on black householders. In the rare instances when a daily newspaper mentioned a bombing or arson attack, the report appeared in a small paragraph that failed to note that the incident was racially motivated or that the likely perpetrators were white. The *Star,* in particular, had a "blind spot for most black news." During his tenure as news editor for the *Call,* Roy Wilkins remembered that the *Star* "fulminated over bombings among racketeers in Chicago, and it ran a tough editorial when a bomb was thrown into a cathedral in Sofia, Bulgaria, but when bombs exploded at black homes on Montgall Avenue and Park Avenue in Kansas City, the *Star* was silent."[31] Where a code of civility had once governed the public debate on race, an apparently deliberate policy of silence now concealed from the public at large the fact that some eastside whites aimed to segregate their neighborhoods.

From LIA's point of view, there turned out to be sound practical reasons for concealment, for news about LIA's plan to establish a racial deadline aroused as much animosity as it did support among the whites who were

30. *Kansas City Call,* May 28, 1926; *Kansas City Times,* June 8, 1926; *Kansas City Journal,* June 13, 1926. For the extent of their coverage, see *Kansas City Times,* October 7, 1927; *Kansas City Journal,* July 30, 1926, October 6, 1927, October 7, 1927. In their survey of neighborhood improvement associations in the 1940s, Long and Johnson found that these organizations typically denied "any special preoccupation and concern with the racial issue." Long and Johnson, *People vs. Property,* 44.

31. *Kansas City Call,* November 19, 1926. Roy Wilkins, with Tom Matthews, *Standing Fast: The Autobiography of Roy Wilkins,* 64. Wilkins moved from his home in St. Paul, Minnesota, to join the *Call*'s staff as managing editor in 1923. He left Kansas City in 1931 to become assistant secretary of the NAACP. He edited the *Crisis* from 1934 to 1949, when he became acting head of the NAACP. Between 1955 and 1977, Wilkins led the NAACP as its executive director.

affected by it. Just as the project's original white opponents objected to losing their homes simply for the sake of a racial barrier, several of the property owners who spoke against the project in the public hearing complained bitterly that LIA had used the race issue to stampede residents into signing its petition. The *Call* perceived some class resentments among the park's white opponents, most of whom were small-property owners who believed that they were going to be burdened with the costs of a scheme that wealthier property holders had devised merely to secure the value of their own holdings. Others doubted that their neighborhoods could be made into an ersatz Armour Hills. At least, they were unwilling to pay for the attempt. According to the *Call*, a woman at the public hearing "declared that the neighborhood was suffering from lowered values because it was old, and people were moving to new homes farther out." Another stated that her tenant property had stood vacant long before blacks had moved near it.[32]

■ ■ Race and Civic Housekeeping in the 1920s

Other factors encouraged whites to be circumspect when dealing with housing. In the previous decade, newspaper editors in particular urged whites to avoid inflammatory words or acts that might spark a race riot. Events in Chicago in 1919 simply demonstrated how easily a minor incident could ignite "the magazine of racial hostility."[33] The Citizens' League was especially worried that Kansas City might suffer similar race violence, and the organization took what it hoped were preventive steps. Organized in March 1917, the Citizens' League aimed to promote honest and efficient government, chiefly through electoral reforms and restructuring of the city's governmental machinery. Its original board of thirty directors consisted almost entirely of men who owned medium-sized businesses, but its guiding hand was its secretary, Nat Spencer, who also served as secretary of the Society for the Suppression of Commercialized Vice for two decades. A number of the original directors left the league's board after its founding, but the board's occupational profile remained unchanged. Of the forty-three men and women listed as board members in either 1923 or 1925, the city directory recorded occupations for thirty-seven of them (or for their husbands). All thirty-seven ranked in the upper level of white-collar occupations. Eighteen were professionals—attorneys, engineers, architects, and school princi-

32. *Kansas City Call,* October 7, 1927.
33. *Kansas City Journal,* July 30, 1919.

pals. The remainder either owned midsized businesses or managed departments in larger firms.[34]

Government reform filled most of the league's agenda, but its publication, the *Citizens' League Bulletin,* also promoted street beautification, zoning laws, improved sanitation, and the rest of the precepts that civic housekeepers and anti-uglies espoused. And the league took a keen interest in race relations and the welfare of the African American community, printing articles by black civic leaders and publicizing health and housing problems in black neighborhoods. The league invariably understood blacks' welfare in terms of its own agenda, however. Consequently, the *Citizens' League Bulletin* paid close attention to the race riots of 1919 and their possible implications for Kansas City.[35] According to the *Bulletin,* violence against blacks was a "hair trigger that may so easily touch off a mine of smothered hatred." And just such a mine could explode close to home. In a "diagnosis" of Kansas City in 1919, the *Bulletin* placed the city in the top ranks of industry, finance, education, and religion but termed it politically "corrupt and contented." On the sixth criterion of race relations, the *Bulletin* warned that the city was "sitting on a volcano." The league's concern lingered well after the fires were doused in riot-torn cities, for an event in 1919 reminded the *Bulletin's* editors that seemingly minor incidents could readily spark racial violence. In October, a prominent black physician in Kansas City reported to the *Bulletin* that he had taken a gun to a postal station intending to pistol-whip a white postal clerk who had been rude to his wife. In the end, the doctor stifled his anger and kept his gun in his pocket, but the *Bulletin* suggested that an interracial committee was needed to build the kind of understanding between the races that would prevent similar incidents before they escalated into racial turmoil.[36]

In 1920, the Citizens' League assembled its own Inter-Racial Committee of twelve in Kansas City. The six black members, named to the committee by the NAACP and the Colored Civic League, included two pastors of large

34. *Citizens' League Bulletin,* December 1918. A random sampling from a roster of new members in 1928 turned up one plumber. The rest of the members in the sample were likewise professionals, department managers, and proprietors of medium-sized firms.

35. Although the daily press in Kansas City printed ample wire service coverage of the Chicago riot in particular, the *Star* and *Times* printed no editorials on the subject; the *Journal* printed a single editorial in which it denounced race riots but claimed to know of no effective remedy; and the *Post* reprinted an editorial from the *New York World* condemning the riots as un-American. *Kansas City Journal,* July 30, 1919; *Kansas City Post,* August 2, 1919.

36. *Citizens' League Bulletin,* September 1919, October 1919, November 1919.

congregations, two educators, and two businessmen. The six white members included three businessmen along with three of the most active men in civic reform in the city, namely Nat Spencer, the league's secretary; L. A. Halbert, a founding officer of the Board of Public Welfare; and Walter Matscheck, head of the Civic Research Institute. The committee's purpose reflected its parent organization's preference for a pacific, well-ordered community. The history of rioting in other cities showed that, "after the violence has broken loose the cooler heads of both races get together and the difficulties are in some way adjusted. The sensible thing seems to be to iron out the troubles before, rather than after, racial disturbances." Naively, perhaps, the committee expected to keep the peace by discussing racial issues so as to get "the other fellow's view point." The work was imperative, the *Bulletin* thought, because in cities that failed to take such preventive measures, "lives have been lost, property has been destroyed and the peace of the community has been sacrificed."[37]

The outbreak of violence over housing gave the Inter-Racial Committee its first real challenge, and its response illustrated what a high priority the parent league placed on communal peace at any price. In 1922, the committee proposed to hold treaty negotiations that would "bring interested parties face to face around a table with a map to try to settle by agreement on a policy as to what territory should be yielded by each race in disputed districts and possibly establish a means of arbitration." An improvement committee would then act "to secure as good moral and physical condition for colored districts so as to make the colored people satisfied with their neighborhoods."[38] Because propinquity inevitably led to confrontation, and confrontation led to riot, municipal reformer Delbert J. Haff hoped that some syndicate of white capitalists would develop "a separate locality where the colored people may establish a complete and separate society."[39] This locality should be, not just separate, but wholesome and tidy, for the better class of black Kansas Citians demanded attractive and sanitary conditions, too. In short, the league aimed to partition the city into racially homogenous segments. While their means differed, the league's civic housekeepers

37. *Citizens' League Bulletin,* March 1920. The black members were Rev. William Alphin, Rev. S. W. Bacote, J. Dallas Bowser, R. T. Coles, John Love, and A. Frank Neal. The other three white members were O. J. Hill, R. M. Maxwell, and B. M. Stigall. The idea of an interracial committee was not an original one. In 1919, Will W. Alexander organized the Commission on Interracial Cooperation to promote better understanding between the races in the south and to ameliorate the treatment southern blacks received. Morton Sosna, *In Search of the Silent South: Southern Liberals and the Race Issue,* 21–22.

38. *Kansas City Call,* April 15, 1922.

39. *Citizens' League Bulletin,* April 8, 1922.

shared that goal with real estate developers like J. C. Nichols and with the members of the Linwood Improvement Association.

At first glance, the league's concern over housing conditions for blacks might appear to be wholly compassionate. But its response to other problems affecting African Americans revealed a good deal of expediency in the way the league approached racial matters, and that presaged a pattern of thinking that characterized liberal white organizations for the next four decades. Ultimately, the Citizens' League viewed poor housing as an evil because it compelled blacks to move into white territory, where they sparked potentially dangerous confrontations. Better housing for blacks meant peace and harmony for whites, in the league's calculations. But substandard housing and crowded ghetto neighborhoods threatened whites in other ways, too, for they bred disease. Addressing the need for better health conditions among black Kansas Citians, Dr. Katherine Berry Richardson, the founder of Children's Mercy Hospital and a frequent collaborator with the Citizens' League, noted, "The nurse who takes care of your baby, the laundress who washes its clothes, the cook who prepares the meals for yourself and guests, may come from a place where the cough of the old-time consumptive beats a tattoo on every partition."[40] And, as the Citizens' League repeatedly warned, there was no way to segregate contagion.

The league's apprehensions over health conditions among blacks mounted in 1926, when Dr. William J. Thompkins, black Democratic leader and now a physician in the city's health department, published a study showing that the incidence of tuberculosis among blacks was four times that of whites in Kansas City. According to Thompkins, the black mortality rate in Kansas City was higher than that in New York City and Chicago. The white dailies joined the league in calling for improved housing for blacks in order to end this menace to whites' health. A cleanup of the ghetto was, in the words of the *Times*, simply a "practical self-defense procedure."[41]

In one of its rare comments on lynching, the *Bulletin* further revealed how much self-interest governed league members' approach to race issues. Lynching must stop, the article contended, because "it lowers the moral standards of communities, breathes contempt of law, utter defiance of authority, and a reckless challenge of established order."[42] Implicit in the arti-

40. *Kansas City Star*, June 29, 1923; *Citizens' League Bulletin*, May 2, 1925.

41. William J. Thompkins, "Report to the Health Commissioner of Child Hygiene and Communicable Diseases, Kansas City, Missouri," Lincoln Collection, MVR-KCPL; *Kansas City Times*, June 10, 1926; *Kansas City Star*, June 10, 1926.

42. *Citizens' League Bulletin*, March 18, 1922. Historically, liberal whites often opposed injustices toward African Americans because whites were harmed by them. Thomas

cle was the suspicion that lower-class whites were unruly bigots, lacking in their respect for civic order and easily aroused by their undisciplined prejudices. Once aroused, the white mob might strike at white-owned property or better-off whites themselves. The writer failed to mention that African Americans might have something to fear from lynchings. In this case, as in the instances of housing and health, blacks' welfare counted merely as the means to achieving a clean, orderly, and harmonious environment for whites. Nor did the league probe too deeply into the causes of the social problems blacks faced. For example, the *Bulletin* lamented that fifty-five blacks were murdered in 1928 and fifty in 1929. Few were arrested for these crimes, the *Bulletin* noted, and fewer still convicted, while the "massacre" received scant attention in the white press. Apparently, the *Bulletin* concluded, the murder of a Negro was not treated as a serious offense. Yet, the journal could go no farther in finding a cause or suggesting a solution; the most it could propose was an effort to induce "higher standards of citizenship" and a respect for law among blacks.[43] In its shortsighted view of race relations, the Citizens' League refused to consider measures that would upset the existing order, such as systemic changes in how the law was enforced.

■ ■ Conclusion

Racial segmentation in Kansas City was an expedient. The Citizens' League helped to establish racial partition because it preserved communal peace. Middle-class whites distanced themselves from blacks because that seemed

---

Jefferson condemned slavery because it brutalized whites, who were "nursed, educated, and daily exercised in tyranny" by their ownership of human chattel. Garrisonian abolitionists condemned slavery as a sin for which white America would pay retribution before God, and Free-Soilers decried it for degrading the value of free white labor. Likewise, southern progressives acted on the belief that injustice to African Americans harmed whites by sparking violence and by "lowering the standards of southern social, economic, and political life." Dewey W. Grantham, *Southern Progressivism: The Reconciliation of Progress and Tradition*, 233–34.

43. *Citizens' League Bulletin*, March 2, 1929; January 11, 1930. The Citizens' League shared several of the limitations of northern progressives of the prewar period who sought merely to improve conditions within black neighborhoods in order to prevent conflict. Likewise, liberal white southerners in the Southern Commission on Interracial Cooperation put racial peace through mutual understanding at the top of their agenda, condemning lynching because "the wrong that it does to the wretched victims is almost as nothing compared to the injury it does to the lynchers themselves, to the community, and to society at large." Maurine Beasley, "The Muckrakers and Lynching: A Case Study in Racism," 86–91. See also, Thomas Philpott, *The Slum and the Ghetto: Neighborhood Deterioration and Middle-Class Reform, Chicago, 1880–1930*, 298–300; Sosna, *Silent South*, 20–41.

the most efficient way to distance themselves from more worrisome, less eradicable bogies—the shortcut to stable property values, well-ordered streetscapes, and staid rectitude. Racialism was no less venomous for being a means to an end rather than an end in itself, however. Spatial apartheid was to became moral apartheid in the 1920s, for middle- and upper-middle-class whites would establish a kind of moral quarantine around their own residential districts that not only excluded blacks from designated geographic areas, but also excluded them from some of the most fundamental benefits of membership in civil society.

5

Under Quarantine

The Social Meaning of Race in the 1920s

■ ■ ■

O<small>NE DAY IN</small> 1927, police officer H. H. Byers arrested the light-skinned Ruth Walton and her dark-skinned husband, Aubrey, on a morals charge because they were sitting beside each other on a curbside bench. When Mrs. Walton protested that she was a black woman and the legal wife of Mr. Walton, Byers replied that she was "the whitest nigger I've ever seen" and took them off to the station house. The Waltons provided proof at their trial that Mrs. Walton was black and that the couple was legally married, whereupon the prosecutor tore up the charges. But police court judge Carlin Smith promptly reached for the charge sheets and wrote out his own complaint against the Waltons for occupying a room for immoral purposes (on the grounds that if they were married they were spending time together somewhere besides public benches). With himself as the sole complaining witness, Smith fined the couple five hundred dollars and sent them to the county detention farm. Judge Smith later admitted that he had erred in imprisoning the Waltons, and he regretted that Ruth Walton would now be branded an immoral woman by her police record, but he justified himself by citing his concern for "purity" and his repugnance for mixed marriages.[1]

Over the decade of the 1920s, lynch mobs would murder an estimated 281 blacks in the nation as a whole.[2] While Kansas City escaped the orgiastic violence of a race riot or a lynching, black Kansas Citians experienced other kinds of racially motivated brutality, of which the Waltons' experience was an example. The perpetrators were anonymous arsonists, uniformed police,

---

1. *Kansas City Call,* July 1, 1927.
2. Walter White, *Rope and Faggot: A Biography of Judge Lynch,* 6.

black-robed judges, and—tragically—African Americans themselves. Meanwhile, African American women encountered a peculiar kind of brutality all its own in the sexual humiliation meted out by white police and judges. At the same time that they physically partitioned their city, middle-class white Kansas Citians also partitioned personhood in the 1920s. By this process, they defined their own racial and class identity, for to be white and middle class now meant to be an ordinary person. Being black came to mean being something less than ordinary. Because this kind of brutality was more diffuse than a riot, it was easier for whites to deny its very existence. But the conspiracy of denial and misdirection failed to cloud the vision of certain watchful African Americans, who scrutinized whites' thoughts and actions in print, thus providing a glimpse into a mentality that whites were often too cagey to confess publicly.

■ ■ Quarantining Crime

Physical separation of the races had all sorts of uses, whites discovered in the 1920s. The so-called garbage crisis provided an early demonstration. The crisis began in 1921, when the Citizens' League complained bitterly about a faulty garbage collection system that left refuse to stew in even the nicest neighborhoods for weeks at a time. Once they collected the trash, garbage-haulers had no way to dispose of it short of feeding it to pigs in stinking swine lots. By 1923, the city had sorted out its collection problems, but it was stymied in its efforts to find a site for a garbage-reduction plant that would extract salable oil and grease from the wastes. No one wanted the dumping station in his backyard. But in 1926, the Citizens' League announced with profound relief that the garbage crisis was over, for the city had found a location for the reduction plant. What the league neglected to mention was that the site the city chose for the garbage plant was Twenty-First and Vine, in the heart of the black eastside. The *Call* thereupon declared war on the "garbage factory" and Mayor Frank Cromwell alike, and the Vine Street Protective Association managed to have the plant location set aside. Several months later, however, the city reneged and placed a garbage yard nearby at Twentieth Street and Woodland Avenue. Trucks dripping swill and drawing clouds of flies rumbled daily through blacks' commercial center to reach the new dump. So thick was the miasma rising from the garbage lot that students had to be evacuated from nearby Western Bible College because they were ill from the stench. Classrooms in Lincoln High and the living rooms of surrounding homes were said to be almost unendurable. "Negro

Neighborhoods Get Oozy Gift" said the *Call* when it announced the city's decision to make the garbage yard a permanent fixture on Woodland—the same decision the Citizens' League had celebrated as an end to the crisis.[3]

Although garbage heaps offended the anti-uglies and literally sickened the black community, this early example of "environmental racism" might seem a trivial matter in light of the city's other racial problems.[4] But the way in which civic housekeepers disposed of the trash problem was significant, in part, because it formed part of an emerging pattern. Segregating neighborhoods by race turned out to be a convenient way to dispose of other unsavory by-products of urban living. Like garbage, crime and vice seemed to collect naturally wherever large numbers of people lived in close proximity. But the garbage crisis demonstrated that a ghetto was a useful dumping ground, a place to warehouse crime and immorality where they would not contaminate the so-called residential districts that the civic housekeepers tended so solicitously.

Nothing smacked of impurity quite like prostitution. Consequently, the Society for the Suppression of Commercialized Vice redoubled its efforts to control the business. After repeated failures, the society won an injunction and abatement law from the state legislature in 1921 that enabled the courts to shut down bawdy houses as public nuisances. Thus armed, the society forced Annie Chambers into retirement and closed several of the most brazen resorts, but many more remained in operation. In 1925, reformers scored what they believed was a victory in their crusade to eradicate the Democratic machine and hence the vice operations that prospered under its protection. Since its founding in 1917, the Citizens' League had sought a revision in the city charter that would establish nonpartisan government under a city manager. By 1924, a charter reform campaign led by the Citizens' League and the Kansas City Civic Research Institute appeared likely to succeed. An astute judge of the prevailing political winds, Tom Pendergast confounded his opponents by coming out in favor of the measure, thus assuring its passage by the voters in 1925. Pendergast reckoned correctly that,

3. *Citizens' League Bulletin,* September 10, 1921, March 29, 1924, November 29, 1924, May 29, 1926; *Kansas City Star,* April 4, 1923; *Kansas City Call,* January 5, 1923, January 26, 1923, November 2, 1923, December 12, 1926.

4. In fact, the nation's mounting problems with toxic and solid wastes have magnified the connections between race and environmental degradation. Robert Bullard's study of environmental hazards and public health shows that, in the last thirty years, a disproportionate number of waste disposal sites and polluting industries have been located in poor, largely minority communities, whose members lack the political clout to exclude these hazards from their midst. Robert D. Bullard, *Dumping in Dixie: Race, Class, and Environment.*

by controlling a majority of members of the new unicameral city council, he would be able to handpick a city manager and thus control every aspect of the city's administration except its police department. Indeed, Pendergast's choice for the position in 1925, former county court judge Henry F. McElroy, served devotedly at the boss's bidding during his thirteen years in the city manager's chair.[5]

Ever a thriving trade in Kansas City, vice now flourished with even greater vigor. "Every club operator, rum runner, pit boss, madame, prostitute, pimp, narcotics peddler, hoodlum, and bartender in Kansas City operated at Pendergast's pleasure and privilege," noted jazz historian Ross Russell.[6] Cabarets, which began to supplant the vaudeville stage as the preferred destination of evening revelers, became illicit trade marts. For the price of a few (bootlegged) beverages, cabaret patrons could hear the hottest jazz west of the Mississippi, visit the gaming tables many clubs provided, or strike their bargains with the pimps and dope dealers who did business in and around the clubs. The town was wide open, but by far the greatest number of its seamy niteries were located in the black ghetto, where it was both cheap and easy to open a jazz joint. The end of prohibition found some fifty cabarets in the six square blocks north of Eighteenth and Vine Streets. Almost none of them served a mixed race clientele; most catered to white "slummers." Edna Mintirn, a white singer and dancer, recalled, "We went down in Nigger Town when we got off [work]. We'd go down and watch 'em jam. Twelfth and Vine, that's where the big shots were, and you could sit in there and get three or four drinks and there was so much marijuana in the air you'd get a buzz. Everybody had smoke comin' up off the ashtrays."[7] For more exotic tastes, some of these cabarets presented female impersonators or catered to white transvestites. Scattered among these nightspots around Eighteenth and Vine were the cabarets, social clubs, gin joints, and policy operations serving a black clientele. Some, like the New Entertainers Cabaret and the Goldenwest Cabaret (which advertised "no drinking, no rowdyism"), were aggressively respectable showcases for jazz musicians.[8] Most were as willing as the white clubs to provide the full range of illicit and illegal entertainment.

5. Lyle W. Dorsett, *The Pendergast Machine*, 76–86; "Prostitution," Vertical File, MVR-KCPL. In 1923, Miss Chambers reopened her establishment as a chaste rooming house for railroad men and took up evangelical religion. In the early 1930s, she began leading tours through her house and treating the curious to accounts of her life. At her death in 1934 at age 92, she bequeathed her property to the City Union Mission. "Annie Chambers," Vertical file, MVR-KCPL; *Social Improvement News* (September 1943), 12.
6. Russell, *Jazz Style in Kansas City and the Southwest*, 8.
7. Quoted in Nathan W. Pearson, Jr., *Goin' to Kansas City*, 102–3.
8. *Kansas City Call*, December 29, 1922, March 25, 1927.

Whether they catered to a black or white clientele, almost none of these niteries were located in the residential districts south of Thirty-Ninth Street. Given the high proportion of native middle-class voters in the city's electorate, Tom Pendergast's political survival required that he expand his base of support to include the residential wards. His tactics included organizing southside political clubs in which bridge parties and ladies' teas replaced the boozers and poker nights favored in the northern ward clubs. To have allowed the vice rackets into those same residential districts would have undone all his careful (and effective) efforts to woo white, middle-class voters. But the quasiofficial restrictions that kept vice operations out of their own neighborhoods failed to satisfy the members of the Society for the Suppression of Commercialized Vice, who trusted that publicity through their own publications and the *Citizens' League Bulletin* would force the mayor and police to shut down the business. Members roamed the streets day and night, publishing the locations where harlots and pimps solicited them and describing the various methods by which brothels and hotels plied the flesh trade. Meanwhile, the Law Enforcement Association, an allied organization, published maps showing that vice (including prostitution, narcotics, and gambling) was clustered in the central business district, the old commercial center in the North End, and the black eastside. In reporting vice dens to the public and to the mayor, however, the Society for the Suppression of Commercialized Vice and the Citizens' League complained only about the resorts that were located *outside* the black enclave.[9]

Despite the society's labors, vice persisted in all three districts, but the pollution of black neighborhoods apparently did not trouble the sworn enemies of the social evil. Like the machine itself, the white reformers partitioned their city by a "moral geography" that declared vice to be unthinkable in their own territory but acceptable in districts where respectable whites seldom ventured. Consequently, vice became a fact of life, not only for the black men and women who engaged in those enterprises, but for every resident of the black eastside, regardless of station or personal values. So thick were the dens around Lincoln High that prostitutes accosted schoolboys on school grounds, and young girls on their way to classes endured rough language and lecherous taunts from the men—white and black—who frequented the bawdy houses, gin mills, and gambling cribs outside Lincoln.[10]

9. Dorsett, *Pendergast Machine,* 81–85; Reports of the Society for the Suppression of Commercialized Vice in "Prostitution," Vertical File, MVR-KCPL; Law Enforcement Association of Kansas City, Missouri, *Crime Survey and Comment,* 1929.
10. *Kansas City Call,* March 20, 1925. The term *moral geography* was coined by historian Perry Duis to describe a compromise by suburbanites, who tolerated vice and saloon

■ ■ Moral Geography and Gender

By encouraging the proliferation of vice in black neighborhoods, moral geography reinforced the dual gender system that pledged the community to protect the virtue of white women only. Any black woman, no matter how she dressed or comported herself, might be propositioned by men of either race while she walked to the shops or to club meetings in the vice-ridden ghetto. If she happened to be light skinned, she was also subject to sexual humiliation by the cop on the beat, for the same police department that permitted vice to flourish in the ghetto also tried its best to prevent white women from being contaminated by it. Repeatedly, white officers stopped light-skinned women when they were seen in company with dark-skinned men. At best, the officers examined a woman's fingernails to determine her race and let her go once they were satisfied that she was indeed African American. More outrageous was the case of a black clergyman who was taken to a police station house along with a light-skinned female member of his congregation when police found them on a public bench, where the minister had been counseling the woman on religious matters. By 1926, the Kansas City Branch of the NAACP ranked police beatings and "stopping of fair colored girls riding in automobiles with darker escorts" as second among the five factors causing severe racial tensions in Kansas City.[11]

Indignation over gratuitous insults of this kind peaked in black Kansas City with the Walton case. According to longtime residents, "not even intense political campaigns have aroused such feeling" as the Waltons' experience excited in the local African American community. More than thirteen hundred black Kansas Citians signed petitions demanding arresting officer Byers's dismissal from the force, and C. A. Franklin joined a delegation of black clergy in cornering Judge Carlin Smith. In response to Smith's claim that he was defending purity, the clergymen retorted that he ought to be equally vigilant in "keeping white men away from colored women as well

---

operations so long as they were confined to selected tenderloins. Thomas Noel also notes that geographic segregation permitted middle-class males to patronize the tenderloins while keeping their own neighborhoods pristine. Duis, *The Saloon: Public Drinking in Chicago and Boston, 1880–1920;* Noel, *The City and the Saloon: Denver, 1858–1916.*

11. Press release, "Kansas City Race Relations Tense, Reports Walter White," December 10, 1926, Group G, Box 107, NAACP Papers, LOC; *Kansas City Call,* September 17, 1926; Wilkins, *Standing Fast,* 66. One wag managed to flummox the white officer who stopped him for driving with a light-skinned woman passenger by telling the officer that the woman was white but that she was not a Caucasian. As expected, the unfamiliar word confused the officer, but the black man reassured him that it was contained in Mendel's Law, which he could look up at the station house. Rather than betray his ignorance of this particular point of law, the officer let the couple go.

as colored men away from white women." Instead, the black delegation pointed out, Smith fined white men as little as ten dollars for associating with black women. Given the sizable number of light-skinned black women in the city, protesters declared, the latitude permitted to police officers created an "intolerable situation" in which "almost any Negro is subject to insult and arrest." Despite African Americans' outrage over the Walton incident, little came of their protests. Officer Byers was transferred to another station in a white neighborhood, but he kept his badge.[12]

Nor was the police crusade for racial purity halted. Despite the fact that mixed race couples were often apprehended and fined on morals charges, nowhere in the city ordinances were interracial associations even mentioned, let alone banned. Yet, police and the courts apparently enjoyed wide latitude in interpreting local morals laws where race was concerned. Police raided houses numerous times where white women were presumed to be consorting with blacks. In 1928, officers carrying riot guns forced their way into a house where two white women had just entered. The officers withdrew when the women turned out to be light-skinned African Americans. Even Roy Wilkins, managing editor of the *Kansas City Call,* and his wife, Minnie, had to answer to the police in 1930 because Mrs. Wilkins, caught in the glare of the headlights of an approaching patrol car, appeared to patrol officers to be white. The incident convinced Wilkins to accept an administrative post in NAACP headquarters in New York and leave the "Hard Heart of America." As Wilkins told a New York acquaintance in 1930, "any policeman in [Kansas City] knows that stopping race mixing is a more sacred duty than stopping any bank robber."[13]

While less brutal than either a rape or a lynching, the social dramas that Kansas City's police and judges performed still had many of the same earmarks, functioning as symbolic rapes to maintain a racial hierarchy. Thus, light-skinned African American women had to endure petty and arbitrary violation as police officers accosted them on public streets, pawed their hands looking for signs of racial descent, or took them into custody. Each such incident made it clear that black men were forbidden even the suggestion of intimacy with white women—a ban which the armed might of the city's

12. *Kansas City Call,* July 1, 1927. The city ordinance governing the renting of rooms for immoral purposes applied specifically to prostitution. Because it was not a court of record, the Municipal Court did not make transcripts of its proceedings, and the white press made no mention of the Walton case. Consequently, the *Call*'s is the only surviving account of the trial.

13. Chapter 7, Article I, *Charter and Revised Ordinances of Kansas City, Missouri,* 1909; Chapter 7, Article I, *Charter and Revised Ordinances of Kansas City, Missouri,* 1928; *Kansas City Call,* March 23, 1928; Wilkins, *Standing Fast,* 84, 98–99.

constabulary and the majesty of its courts were pledged to enforce. And these incidents set limitations on white women's autonomy, for protection came with a price in the form of white women's obedience to and dependence upon their protectors. Presumably, any white woman who might be found accompanying a black man in a public place was there by choice and had not asked to be protected from her companion. In the view of police officers, however, she was not entitled to that choice but must have "protection" imposed upon her. In effect, the police officer's rights were at stake and not the white woman's. On the other hand, white women in Kansas City collaborated in the manufacture of sexualized white supremacy as they neither protested the victimization of blacks that was done for their sake nor complained of the strictures placed on their own movements for the sake of protection.[14]

Editors Franklin and Wilkins clearly understood the dynamics of power implied in these petty rituals. As the *Call* noted, whereas Missouri law prohibited the intermarriage of blacks and whites, "there is no law in this land w[h]ich prevents people of different races from walking, talking, and riding together." Lacking a statutory justification, such incidents of harassment were, in the words of the *Call*, examples of "ignorance made arrogant and sufferable only because a gun swings at the hip of a prejudice-filled bully." Yet, the bullies wore their city's uniform and articulated by their actions a clear message on behalf of the [white] public they served. "Women of unquestioned standing and repute are being followed by Kansas City police and harassed," Franklin warned; "if there is no order from the higher officials of the department to that effect, then at least there is an understanding among the officers which amounts to the same thing." Writing in his own column in the *Call*, Roy Wilkins suggested that white women ought to feel "cheapened and degraded" by such gallantry. "Either white womanhood is not so lily white," he concluded, "or else Judge Smith and his ilk are insufferable cads."[15]

Yet, if these actions impugned the chastity of white females, the black community suffered still greater harm. Not only did black women arbitrarily experience sexual humiliation, but black men figured in the white imagination solely as potential assailants of white virtue. The city avoided the mob executions of suspected black rapists that terrorized African Americans else-

---

14. As John Dollard described, "The race conscious white man has a proprietary interest in every white woman. He also acts as if an attack upon or approach to the white woman were an attack on himself." Dollard, *Caste and Class in a Southern Town*, 381.

15. *Kansas City Call*, July 1, 1927, September 17, 1926. Wilkins's "Talking It Over" column was a regular feature of the *Call*'s op-ed page.

where, but black men reportedly became increasingly cautious around white women. In 1926, several men told the *Call* that they no longer gave their seats to white women on the streetcars because their offers were interpreted as "getting familiar."[16] And the disproportionately harsh sentences given to black men who were convicted of raping white females served to remind black men that white authorities regarded them as sexual menaces. Social dramas like these, played out in the city's streets and courtrooms, contributed to a gendered category of racial inferiority—a lesser class of personhood. That category was further defined when blacks tried to eliminate vice from their own neighborhoods. A Women's Inter-Racial Council was organized in 1925, in part to eradicate the vice dens surrounding Lincoln High. In a display of good faith, the police department assigned extra officers to the Lincoln area and staged a number of raids at the start of the fall school term. But these were Band-Aid solutions—demonstration raids that relieved some pressure on police and left a far greater number of crap games, speakeasies, and brothels to operate undisturbed in the heart of the black community. In any case, assaults on ghetto vice had little chance of succeeding. Officers of the Colored YWCA reported to the *Call* in 1925 that city insiders had told them not to expect much from a few police raids, since most of the dives around Lincoln High had police protection and could not be touched.[17]

Moreover, a significant number of blacks made their livings from illicit enterprises or had political ties to the machine, which relied on vice protection for revenues. African American men like Felix Payne, Piney Brown, and Ellis Burton not only prospered by providing entertainment to whites in the clubs they managed, but also challenged the claims to leadership of "respectable," largely Republican opinion makers in black Kansas City. Capable of "fixing things" with a judge or swinging a job for a party loyalist, such men had important positions as brokers between black Kansas Citians and the seat of power. Less influential blacks found welcome employment as bartenders, shake dancers, or policy runners. Wide-open Kansas City attracted a growing number of black jazz performers, musicians, and singers who came to rely on the club managers for handouts. One recalled that "Piney was like a

16. *Kansas City Call,* December 17, 1926. There were no lynchings in Kansas City proper in this period, but a mob executed a black rape suspect in nearby Excelsior Springs in 1925. The *Call* gave thorough coverage both to the event and to the fact that a Kansas City prosecutor spoke approvingly of it. See, for example, *Kansas City Call,* August 14, 1925. According to the lynch victim's roommate, the killing also convinced a large number of black men to leave Excelsior Springs for Kansas City. See "Deposition of Richard Waller," Box 118, Benson Papers. It therefore seems likely that the lynching had a chilling effect on black men's behavior in Kansas City.

17. *Kansas City Call,* July 3, 1925, September 25, 1925, June 19, 1925.

patron saint to all musicians. . . . Piney was a man, he didn't care how much it cost; . . . if you needed money to pay your rent, he would give it to you and take you out and buy booze. He was a man you could always depend on for something if you needed it." For countless more black Kansas Citians, the club scene provided a release from the frustrations of ghetto life. "Lots of old wash women would go out and work in the service . . . for white people and come back there and chance it on the policy wheel," recalled a Kansas City jazzman.[18] Hope lay in the dream book and the numbers slips, and even a fixed wheel or a pair of dice were more likely to bring good fortune than a life of hard labor at "colored pay." A night spent dancing to some of the best music in the country might be an inadequate compensation for the disappointments and humiliations of the working day, but it was not an insignificant one. Consequently, vice drove a wedge through the black population, making a united effort to eradicate it impossible. While a corrupt city administration and police force actively fostered vice in the black community, and white reformers—the avowed enemies of vice and police laxity—ignored its presence in black neighborhoods, a sizable segment of black Kansas Citians either participated in or profited from it and resisted its eradication.

■ ■ The Moral Geography of Justice

Just as moral geography transposed the terms of the moral equation for African Americans, a roughly similar phenomenon inverted the logic of the justice system. Police brutality and judicial inequity had been a constant plague to the black community in Kansas City, but both reached crisis proportions in the 1920s. Typically blamed on "redneck" or "ethnic" officers who assaulted blacks out of simple bigotry (with the connivance of corrupt, usually Democratic machines), police brutality in Kansas City followed an entirely different pattern. In fact, African Americans learned that they had more to fear from "good government" types whom the middle-class reformers put in police uniforms. When a policing crisis grew out of a conflict between the civic housekeepers and the bosses over the character of law and order, the two white factions combated each other for control of the streets, creating in the process the paradox by which blacks were policed too little and too much.

The contest began in early 1920 after a local salesman committed suicide because of losses he had sustained in a gambling den. This particular gaming

18. Pearson, *Goin' to Kansas City*, 97–98.

room was located in the Sixth Ward Democratic Club and had the protection of Justice of the Peace Casimir J. Welch. Already frustrated with the city's law enforcement, white business interests decided to take matters into their own hands. Within the week, members of the Kansas City Livestock Exchange established a vigilance committee and threatened to wreck every gambling parlor in sight of the stockyards if they were not closed down. The Democratic governor and his appointees to the Kansas City Board of Police Commissioners ignored the threat. Alarmed, the members of a roundtable of civic club presidents, with backing of the Chamber of Commerce, launched the Law Enforcement Association (LEA) that year. With a somewhat more prestigious board of directors than either the Civic League or the Society for the Suppression of Commercialized Vice, the LEA had twenty-three officers and board members serving in 1925, including three presidents or vice-presidents of important banking institutions, the industrialist William Volker, and real estate developer J. C. Nichols. The remaining members were either lawyers or presidents of medium-sized businesses. More important, the LEA cooperated with the Society for Commercialized Vice, and Nat Spencer, secretary of both the antivice society and the Citizens' League, acted as liaison among the three organizations. Sharing outlook and personnel with other civic housekeeping organizations, the LEA would shortly take command of the civic housekeepers' assault on crime. So great was its members' horror of lawbreaking and judicial laxity, in fact, that the LEA would make itself a parallel, quasiofficial institution of law and order.[19]

The Law Enforcement Association assaulted crime on multiple fronts. Its members supplied prosecutors and police with lists of gambling dens and brothels and places of assignation, and it pressured police to suppress streetwalking. Acknowledging Kansas City's reputation as a center for distribution of morphine, opium, and cocaine, the LEA found the drugstores, soft drink parlors, and cigar stores where narcotics were sold, and it hired a detective out of its own treasury to assist the United States Narcotics Bureau in investigating drug rings. But the association did not confine its attentions to so-called victimless crimes. Kansas City's frequent burglaries, armed robberies, and auto thefts not only discouraged trade but devoured a portion of businessmen's profits, so that insurance rates in Kansas City were double

19. *Kansas City Times,* March 5, 1920; *Kansas City Star,* March 9, 1920; *Citizens' League Bulletin,* May 7, 1927. According to Robert Fogelson, similar organizations developed in other cities in the 1920s. The organizations Fogelson describes, however, concentrated their energies either on pressuring officials to get tough with criminals or on restructuring police departments themselves, whereas the LEA also assumed some policing duties directly. Robert M. Fogelson, *Big-City Police,* 41–66.

those in New York City, Los Angeles, and Chicago. Consequently, the LEA demanded swift arrest and conviction of every sort of wrongdoer.

Not content simply to lecture the public or to lobby politicians, the members of the LEA (allegedly one thousand strong) put aside their labors as insurance agents, attorneys, bankers, and merchants and took to the field, where they dogged the steps of police officers on the beat, followed up to see that arrests led to convictions, and participated in raids of vice dens. They attended municipal court sessions and threatened public exposure to judges with lenient sentencing records. Although they hectored uniformed officers, members also subscribed to a reward fund that paid a bounty to policemen or to private investigators who managed to capture a crook. The association even claimed the credit for winning a pay increase for police in 1923. In all, this doughty band of vigilantes assigned itself an astonishing list of public law-enforcement functions, and it invited other "good citizens" to report crimes to the LEA or to the Society for the Suppression of Commercialized Vice instead of the police.[20] LEA had become nearly a shadow government.

For all its many labors, the LEA failed to rid the city of wrongdoers. In fact, the Missouri electorate deserved some of the credit for one of LEA's few victories when the voters put Republican Arthur Hyde in the governor's chair in 1921. Having promised to let "the crooks know the police will shoot," the new governor ousted his Democratic predecessor's appointees from the three-man Kansas City Board of Police Commissioners. In their place, Hyde appointed two men who had the approval of the LEA to serve with the mayor, an ex-officio member. LEA then hired two attorneys to assist the new commissioners in a cleanup of Kansas City. Matthew Foster, Hyde's chief reform appointee to the police commission in 1921 and later president of the park board, took command of the commission and began to implement LEA's agenda. By trade the manager of his father's large real estate holdings in Kansas City, Foster's first venture into public service as Jacob Billikopf's administrator of the municipal welfare bureau put him in the civic housekeepers' camp.[21] And Foster, like Nat Spencer and many of the individuals designated here as civic housekeepers, appeared on the membership lists or boards of directors of several civic housekeeping organizations.

20. *Citizens' League Bulletin*, December 18, 1920, May 23, 1925; Law Enforcement Association, *Crime Survey and Comment*, January 1, 1929; Law Enforcement Association, *Report to Members*, September 1, 1922, May 1, 1924, November 15, 1928, December 1, 1925.

21. LEA, *Report to Members*, May 1, 1924, July 1, 1925; LEA, *Crime Survey and Comment*, January 1, 1929; *Kansas City Star*, December 19, 1921; Dorsett, *Pendergast Machine*, 70; *Kansas City Times*, June 3, 1946.

By obtaining seats on various citizens' oversight bodies, such as the Board of Park and Boulevard Commissioners, the Board of Police Commissioners, or the Board of Pardons and Paroles, this "interlocking directorate" of civic housekeepers made the civic housekeeping program a powerful, though not unrivaled, force for ordering the local polity.

Under the new commission's command, the police began an immediate "clean-up," making scores of arrests daily. Not everyone was impressed with the commission's new show of force, however. The labor newspaper *Missouri Mule* described Foster as a man "born with a silver spoon in his mouth and who has never done an honest day's work in his life," identifying him as the "chief of the bayonet squad" that broke the general strike of 1918. According to the *Mule,* the commission's crackdown amounted to nothing but "a yellow-dog circus of advertising" in which the police arrested dozens of insignificant bootleggers and dope fiends while leaving crime kingpins unmolested. But Foster clearly understood that perceptions mattered to the middle class, particularly its perceptions of safety and sanctuary in the so-called residential districts. One of his proudest achievements as police commissioner was to station motorcycle patrolmen in booths placed throughout the residential districts. His objective was, he said, to induce a "sense of security" in the residents of the favored districts by ensuring them immediate protection from a nearby officer.[22]

Foster was able to put his stamp on police affairs because of the peculiarities of state control, which gave the police commissioners considerable influence over staffing. Consequently, the hiring system was inherently political. Applicants were required to submit character references from people who knew them well, but they generally understood that at least two of these endorsements should come from precinct and ward captains of their chosen parties if their applications were to be taken seriously. When the department needed new personnel, the police commissioners selected candidates from a pool of these application forms, which clearly identified each applicant's party loyalties. The board might ask the chief of police for advice on occasion, but, in practice, the two commissioners whom the state's governor appointed to the task actually recruited and hired the city's police force. And the election of a succession of Republican governors in the 1920s meant that the Republican anticrime element determined the makeup of Kansas City's police force. In 1921, Governor Hyde's reform commissioners made a thor-

22. *Missouri Mule,* February 7, 1920, February 5, 1921; Matthew A. Foster, "Effective Police Protection for Residential Sections."

ough housecleaning by appointing 88 new men to the uniformed force in that year alone. By 1929, out of a uniformed force of 588 men, only 85 had been hired before the Republican takeover in 1921.[23]

In 1928, the Kansas City Chamber of Commerce asked the Civic Research Institute to make a detailed investigation of the city's police department. The resulting study provides a detailed picture of the kind of police force the reformers had created. The Civic Research Institute originated as a civic department within the Chamber of Commerce in 1917. Under its director, Walter Matscheck, the institute became a separate organization promoting "scientific government," efficient administration, and nonpartisanship in civic affairs. Consequently, the Civic Research Institute operated in alliance with other civic reform organizations, like the Citizens' League and the Law Enforcement Association, and its leaders joined the interlocking directorate of civic reformers in Kansas City. Given his penchant for scientific information, Matscheck turned to August Vollmer to carry out the police survey. A police chief himself, Vollmer was one of the leaders of a national movement to reform urban policing by professionalizing police forces.[24]

In Kansas City, Vollmer found ample grounds for each of the reform measures he advocated. According to his detailed study, the local department's organization was lax and clumsy, its record keeping and budgeting primitive, and its equipment outdated. Denied the firm guidance of a well-managed and properly constituted command structure, the hapless police officer also came under countervailing pressures from outside the department, including, according to Vollmer, "the constant interference by ignorant or misguided citizens with their plans for public betterment," along with "grafters" and "unprincipled politicians." Pulled this way and that by outside influences and demoralized by grafters and shirkers among their colleagues, conscientious officers hardly knew where duty lay. The men who served under these conditions lacked most of the qualifications that would have fitted them for policing even under the best of circumstances, Vollmer concluded. Only 6

23. August Vollmer, "Survey of the Metropolitan Police Department of Kansas City, Missouri," 58–59, 65–67.

24. Among the leaders of the Civic Research Institute were Matscheck, Nat Spencer, Henry Beardsley, R. E. McDonnell, Burris Jenkins, and William Volker. Each of those men held at least one directorship in the Citizens' League, the Society for the Suppression of Commercialized Vice, or the Law Enforcement Association. Theodore A. Brown and Lyle W. Dorsett, *K.C.: A History of Kansas City, Missouri*, 146–51; Dorsett, *Pendergast Machine*, 72; Henry C. Haskell, Jr., and Richard B. Fowler, *City of the Future: The Story of Kansas City, 1850–1950*, 124; William M. Reddig, *Tom's Town: Kansas City and the Pendergast Legend*, 115–17; Fogelson, *Big-City Police*, 51.

percent of the uniformed force had prior experience in law enforcement before joining Kansas City's police department. The majority of the force had
taken up policing as a second or third career. Of the 494 uniformed officers
whose prior occupation Vollmer identified, the greatest portion (46 percent)
held semiskilled jobs before receiving their appointments, most of those as
chauffeurs or mechanics. Another 28 percent reported skilled occupations,
and 18 percent held white-collar positions or owned businesses before don-
ning the uniform. Consequently, the force was predominantly, though not
overwhelmingly, working-class in origin. Roughly 70 percent had no education beyond the eighth grade, and more than half had left school after the
sixth grade. But the men who had some high school or college training were
just as likely to be walking the beat as filling the upper echelons. Very little in
these men's backgrounds entitled them to their positions, Vollmer believed,
except their Republican affiliations—a fact that may have accounted for the
woefully high number of officers who quit within a year of joining the force.[25]

Generally ill fitted for the job when they began it, even the best-inten-
tioned officers received very little encouragement to perform their duties
effectively. Just two weeks of cursory training sufficed before officers went
on patrol. Their pay was low and their equipment inadequate, and they
lacked any sort of pension plan. Given the politicized staffing system, they
faced instant dismissal each time the governor's chair changed hands. Little
wonder, Vollmer concluded, that officers provided for themselves by taking
bribes or selling their influence. Summarizing his findings for the Chamber of Commerce, Vollmer wondered that the department functioned at all.
"Hampered by lack of modern equipment, miserably compensated for ar-
duous duties, unprotected by pension provisions, unsupported by the press,
pulpit and public, ridiculed and berated by other law enforcement officials,
kicked around by unscrupulous politicians, it is remarkable, indeed, that the
policemen have been able to maintain any semblance of law and order in this
growing community."[26]

Vollmer's report had nothing to say about the excessive use of force, but
contemporary studies identify several factors that contribute to police brutality in modern cities. Those factors, Vollmer's data showed, were also present
in Kansas City in the 1920s. Among the contributing circumstances contemporary scholars cite is the "declaration of war" on crime by civic leaders
or public officials who have no contact with or knowledge of real conditions
in the streets. Under intense pressure from civilian anticrime crusaders to

25. Vollmer, "Survey," 54–62, 69, and foreword.
26. *Ibid.*, foreword.

crack down on criminals, and convinced that they can not meet crusaders' exaggerated expectations by legitimate means, some police officers become mere time-servers, while others become "hard-nosed" cops, rolling up impressive arrest records and making collars by any means to placate crusaders or the public. The very emphasis on arrest statistics that accompanies a war on crime further encourages cynical overzealousness. When police officers perceive that they are underpaid, underequipped, or otherwise unappreciated by the community, they are likely to develop a siege mentality, by which they see themselves as the lonely and embattled remnant holding off the savage hordes. Under the circumstances, officers believe they are justified in using extralegal measures to control the enemy. If the police operate in a social milieu that identifies a particular group as outcasts or pariahs, officers tend to see all members of that group as potential offenders and to have difficulty distinguishing between law-abiding and lawbreaking members of the pariah group. That is particularly true if the prevailing social ideology holds that criminal propensities account for the group's pariah status in the first place. It matters little whether the offending officer is a bigot or bleeding-heart liberal, a blue-collar working stiff or a college graduate. According to these studies, the institutional environment and the policy makers at the top play a greater role in fostering the excessive use of force than the officer's individual character does.[27]

Certainly such an anticrime crusade enveloped Kansas City's police department in the 1920s in the persons of its Republican police commissioners and the Law Enforcement Association members who dogged policemen's steps. The anticrime element attacked prosecutors and judges for laxity, and the machine-dominated bench likewise discredited itself by its leniency toward protected vice lords and crooks. Whipsawed between pressures to crack down on crime and the temptation to augment their pay by accepting graft from criminal kingpins, whom the courts would treat gently if cops did arrest them, many of Kansas City's police officers may well have seen African Americans as the easiest targets for hard-nosed policing. In any case, the anticrime campaign of the 1920s was accompanied by a marked increase in incidents of police harassment and abuse among black Kansas Citians.

An illustrative case occurred in 1926, when two police officers spotted a young black man named Dorsey Stewart in the act of stealing a ham from

---

27. See, for example, Jerome H. Skolnick and James J. Frye, *Above the Law: Police and the Excessive Use of Force;* Paul Chevigny, *Police Power: Police Abuses in New York City;* and Independent Commission on the Los Angeles Police Department, *Report of the Independent Commission on the Los Angeles Police Department.*

a meat van. Witnesses told the *Call* that, without so much as a warning, an officer who stood forty feet from Stewart opened fire with a riot gun. The wounded youth made his way to his nearby home, where pursuing officers reportedly shot him dead as he lay gasping near his own doorstep. Witnesses heard an officer snarl, "Take that you black _____," as he fired point-blank into the wounded Stewart. On leaving the scene, one of the policemen was overheard to say, "Well, that's one nigger I got anyway." Angry blacks demanded that the officers be charged with murder. The police commission promised an investigation, and a coroner's jury soon convened to determine whether Stewart's killing was justifiable. The coroner made a special effort to summon witnesses, and the *Call* pleaded with witnesses to come forward with their accounts, but just one man appeared to describe the officer's final, point-blank shot. His testimony was mooted when the assistant coroner reported that he could find no pistol slug in Stewart's body. With no other evidence to consider, the coroner's jury ruled that the officers had fired in the line of duty. The jury warned, however, that the police should take more care in the future just to cripple suspects.[28] Five years later, a black man swore in his dying statement that a white police officer had talked him into robbing a gas station. While the white officer stood guard outside, the black man broke into the station and rifled the till—only to be shot by his white accomplice, who reported that he had apprehended an escaping burglar. The same officer was soon after involved with three other policemen in the savage beating of a black man with their blackjacks and gun butts. The officers successfully claimed that they had to subdue the suspect before they could take him to the station house, just three blocks from the scene of the beating. In this case, the victim's offense was to have run a red light after bumping the officers' car with his own.[29]

Incidents like these merely dramatized the routine maltreatment blacks received at police hands. Police squads, acting without warrants, often raided blacks' homes, where they ransacked apartments, wrecked furniture, and ripped up walls and floors in a search for stolen property. Blacks suspected of even minor infractions regularly received beatings in the course of questioning at the station house. Said the *Call*, "If you happen to be Black and one of

28. *Kansas City Call*, March 26, 1926, April 9, 1926. As was typical when blacks were the victims of violence, the white press ignored Stewart's killing and the subsequent inquest. According to the Medical Examiner's Office of Kansas City, no transcripts of coroner's inquests or record of proceedings was made. Autopsy reports from the 1920s were accidentally destroyed in the early 1950s. Consequently, the *Call*'s account of the killing and inquest are the only ones to survive.
29. *Kansas City Call*, August 21, 1930, February 27, 1931.

those Kansas City policemen takes a notion to stop you and take you to the station, the Lord and all his angels can't keep you from the beating of your life." No one—not even a clergyman—was safe, the *Call* predicted in 1928. Soon after, Rev. W. F. Taylor of Metropolitan Spiritual Church answered a late-night sick call. He seldom went out after dark because of his fear of the police, but the case was urgent. On his way to his parishioner, Rev. Taylor spotted a white man in street clothes battering a black man. When Taylor tried to stop the fight, he was savagely beaten himself. Unfortunately for Taylor, the white man was an off-duty officer who was "handling" a suspected thief. In this case, the officer was indicted, but black victims rarely had Taylor's obvious credentials of respectability, and their police tormentors seldom earned more than a verbal reprimand.[30]

Democrats blamed the Republican Board of Police Commissioners in general and Matthew Foster in particular for police abuses in the black community. There were considerable grounds for their claim, for it mattered who sat at the top. Not only was the uniformed force almost entirely Republican, but it was the Republican police commissioners who ultimately decided which officers to investigate and which to punish for excessive use of force. If, as the *Mule* claimed, the Republicans' anticrime crusade was mostly "grandstand antics," then easy collars and rough treatment of black suspects allowed officers to make a show of rigorous policing that might quiet the critics of police laxity. When ill-trained officers or uniformed bullies went too far in "handling" a suspect, the commissioners' refusal to punish them whenever black suspects were involved assured officers that they would suffer no penalties for abusive actions so long as their victims were black.[31] Blacks were fair game.

Still, there was a fair amount of hypocrisy in Democrats' charges. As the Waltons had discovered in 1926 and the Williams case later demonstrated, a Democratically controlled judicial system could behave just as cravenly as the beat cops. In 1927, police arrested nineteen-year-old Cleo Williams and another black teenager for the rape of a white teen. Described by the *Call* as being "in body a man, in brain less than a child," Williams confessed to

30. *Kansas City Call,* July 23, 1926, August 6, 1926, February 3, 1928, April 20, 1928.

31. Studies of modern police departments show that official policies matter. Complaints of police brutality from minority communities are less frequent in departments where the command staff and trainers make it clear that an officer's personal prejudices must not affect the way he or she performs on the job. But police administrators who fail to penalize officers for excessive use of force give it their tacit approval, and its incidence increases in those departments. See for example, William A. Geller, "Police and Deadly Force: A Look at the Empirical Literature," 218–22, and Skolnick and Fyfe, *Above the Law,* 35–36, 137.

the rape, possibly in hopes of leniency. Prosecuting attorney James R. Page promptly announced, however, that he would seek the death penalty for Williams. "Hang them all," an editorial in the *Journal* advised. "Fortunately, Kansas City has been free from crimes of this vicious character," the *Journal* said, "and the best way of maintaining this status is to make an example of brutal young thugs." At Williams's arraignment, his attorney tried to enter a guilty plea, which customarily prevented judges from passing a death sentence. But Circuit Court Judge Allen C. Southern refused to accept the plea and insisted instead on putting the case before a jury. Desperate, Williams's attorney took the unusual step of entering a guilty plea before that jury, whereupon Judge Southern dismissed the jurors and called the rape victim forward to describe her experience. Claiming to be horrified by her account, Judge Southern promptly rendered a guilty verdict and, without a jury having heard a word of evidence, sentenced Williams to die.[32]

In explaining his peremptory handling of the case, Judge Southern claimed that "there has been a series of these crimes in this community and it appears to me that an emergency exists." Prosecutor Page concurred. In fact, the entire affair had the earmarks of a legalized lynching. On its editorial page, the *Journal* suggested that "other magistrates well may follow Judge Southern's example in the future and refuse to bargain with criminality brought to bay." But the paper provided even more sensational commentary in the news pages, where it published a portrait of Judge Southern superimposed over a photo of the gallows on which Williams would hang. The accompanying article gloated that Williams's execution would take place on the sixth anniversary of the last hanging in Jackson County, when the condemned was also a black man who was convicted of attacking a white woman. Meanwhile, the *Post* printed a letter from an ex-Texan declaring that lawful execution was too good for a "dirty skunk" like Williams. "If you haven't enough men in Missouri to take these birds out and string them up and set a match to them, you can get all you need from old Texas," the writer promised.[33]

Needless to say, African Americans in Kansas City were outraged by the way Williams's case was handled and by the atmosphere that surrounded the so-called trial. As the *Call* pointed out, and as the *Journal* had already

---

32. *Kansas City Call,* June 28, 1928; *Kansas City Star,* June 27, 1927; *Kansas City Journal,* June 29, 1927, June 28, 1927. While the other young man charged with Williams also confessed, he could not be given a death sentence because he was still a juvenile.

33. *Kansas City Journal,* June 29, 1927, July 14, 1927; *Kansas City Post,* July 21, 1927.

confirmed, there had been no sexual assaults of white women by black men for some time. If Judge Southern believed an emergency existed, the *Call* reasoned, he must be thinking of a recent rash of attacks on white females by white men, in which case the courts ought to deal just as harshly with the white culprits. Instead, Albert Spaulding, the only one of the white rapists to be tried so far, was allowed to plead guilty to the lesser charge of *attempted* rape because he was unable to fully penetrate his tiny, three-year-old victim. He received a mere five-year prison sentence. Clearly, Williams's punishment was "a special color-rebuke to Negroes."[34]

■ ■ Selective Justice and Black-on-Black Crime

While the amount of bloodshed blacks suffered at police hands was appalling, it scarcely compared to the mayhem blacks inflicted on each other in Kansas City. Starting in the midtwenties, nearly every front page of the weekly *Call* featured a headline announcing, in heavy type and lurid phrases, some murder or assault of a black person by another black. Publisher C. A. Franklin hoped that the shock value of his headlines would provoke in his readers the same horror he felt over black-on-black crime. In March 1924, he reported that black-on-black killings amounted to one per week. In 1927, forty-five African Americans were murdered, nearly all of them by other blacks, compared to fifty-seven homicides in a white population that was ten times the size of the black population. In the first three months of 1928, the murder rate among blacks reached one killing every six days.[35] As the toll mounted, Franklin began printing a cartoon figure of a gallows on his front page, along with the most recent tally of black-on-black homicides.

Initially, Franklin attributed the problem to "liquor, larceny, and love," the fatal combination that caused gamblers' disputes and lovers' quarrels to be settled with a razor. Likewise, the black Ministerial Alliance sent a petition to the police chief in 1924 demanding that officers close down the social clubs operated by and for blacks. The pastors warned the chief that the clubs were "known to everyone to be nothing but the very lowest type of gambling joints with gambling always going on and frequently cutting and shooting

34. *Kansas City Call*, July 15, 1927. Fortunately for Cleo Williams, black Kansas Citians raised a defense fund, and attorney L. Amassa Knox managed to have his execution delayed by filing a motion for a rehearing on the grounds that Williams was denied due process. With a difficult court fight ahead of them, delegations lobbied the governor, and in 1928, Republican governor Sam Baker commuted Williams's sentence to life imprisonment. *Kansas City Call*, July 22, 1927, July 6, 1928.

35. *Kansas City Call*, March 27, 1924, January 6, 1928, March 23, 1928.

scrapes." But Franklin soon began to look deeper for the cause of black-on-black crime. The malady stemmed from the way justice was administered in the black community, he concluded, and he demanded a thorough overhaul of the very structure of the justice system. How could blacks respect law and order, he asked, when the very men who were sworn to enforce the law abused them? Because African Americans in Kansas City feared the police for their brutality and disrespected them for their corruption, many felt justified in concealing criminals and abetting crimes. Eyewitnesses to crimes refused to come forward and innocent bystanders shrank from any contact with the legal system out of a justifiable dread that they might be mistreated themselves. After all, why should they help bring fellow African Americans to justice when justice on their behalf was so often perverted? Franklin wondered.[36]

While the police used excessive force in black Kansas City, Franklin condemned their laxity in other respects. Protected vice dens led youngsters like Cleo Williams into lives of crime, he believed. In fact, Franklin noted that the black residents of Roundtop had tried to close down the Roundtop joint that Williams frequented. If police had not chosen to ignore their pleas, the editor conjectured, then Cleo Williams might never have committed his crimes. Whether or not the social environment of the gin mill had led Williams astray, Franklin was justifiably enraged by a double standard that excused one kind of criminal behavior by blacks and ordered summary execution for another: "If moral cesspools are permitted in districts where Negroes live, we protest against the community exacting a penalty from poor stupid children who go wrong, and then letting conditions run on which make them what they are."[37]

Not only did the crap games and gin mills thrive under the lenient supervision of the force, but Franklin accused the police of allowing blacks to carry concealed weapons in careless disregard of the law. If officers removed those weapons from blacks with the same diligence that Franklin believed they exercised in the white community, jealousy and vengeance would not turn so quickly to murder. So long as concealed weapons were considered acceptable, however, "cutting scrapes" would continue. Such laxity left blacks with little way to protect themselves except vigilantism. "Every Negro murderer should have tried along with him his accomplice, Kansas City with its harsh judgment, its refusal of rights and its half justice," Franklin asserted, for unequal law enforcement "has driven us to individualism which in time

36. *Kansas City Call*, March 7, 1924, January 25, 1924.
37. *Kansas City Call*, May 13, 1927.

of differences between man and man, leads to personal combat, and murder." Recounting the incident of a black woman who was threatened by a black man over a disputed debt, the editor noted that the woman's husband had sought a warrant to protect her. When the authorities refused to issue one, the husband armed himself for a shoot-out to defend his wife. "Settling differences by personal combat is a relic of the days before civilization established law and order, and required of the individual that he submit his claim to courts," Franklin concluded. "But the Negroes' proneness to take the law into their own hands is due to lack of confidence in the law and the courts."[38]

Punishment could be savage for crimes in which the victim was white, as Cleo Williams's case demonstrated, but Franklin claimed that city prosecutors often refused to take an accused murderer of either race to court if the victim were black. When cases involving black victims did reach trial, convicted defendants received light sentences, and judges treated blacks with considerable leniency when they were charged with "victimless" infractions. In 1926, Franklin singled out a Republican and new county prosecutor named Forest Hanna for praise. According to Franklin, Hanna had won convictions and stiff but fair sentences for crimes against blacks. More prosecutors apparently shared city attorney James R. Page's belief that the majority of black voters wanted black criminals to be, as he put it, "helped out" of legal difficulties or protected from prosecution. Page declared publicly that his own leniency would win more black adherents to the Democratic Party. Franklin labeled the statement pernicious and insulting, and he found much more to protest in a lenient judicial system that discounted the value of black lives and black property. "Our recourse to personal combat does not show that we hold our lives cheaply, so much as it expresses utter disdain for the public agencies as a means of justice for Negroes," he warned. "But what good does it do to tell the Negroes not to adjudicate differences in a way costing many times the value involved, when the white people of Kansas City, presumed to be much wiser than we, keep on thinking they can sow injustice and reap peace and prosperity."[39]

With the black homicide rate spiraling upward in 1928, a number of influential African Americans came to agree with Franklin's analysis of black-on-black crime and its causes. In answer to demands by the *Call*, local black leaders gathered in 1928 to discuss the murder crisis and to form a law and

38. *Kansas City Call*, March 7, 1924, October 7, 1927. John Dollard also concluded that selectively lenient law enforcement institutionalized violence and disorder in the black community. Dollard, *Caste and Class*, 279–80.

39. *Kansas City Call*, October 8, 1926, January 7, 1927, October 7, 1927. Hanna served just one term as county prosecutor, from 1926 to 1928.

order committee that would address the problems in the legal system that contributed to black-on-black crime. Summing up the committee's mission, businessman and political leader T. B. Watkins asserted, "Dives and joints are wide open. The forces of evil are in the saddle on every side. The frequency of murders of race men and women without any convictions has become appalling. The taking of human life, although the greatest crime against organized society, is treated with the same leniency as petty larceny and many times with a punishment less severe. The cause and the remedy must be found."[40] Little came of the committee's formation, however. Ultimately, the Democratic black electorate and its white angels in the Pendergast machine would do more to solve the police brutality crisis in the decade to come.

■ ■ Conclusion

Franklin's analysis was astute, nonetheless. By the end of the 1920s, issues of crime and punishment did define black status in Kansas City by relegating blacks to a partial citizenship. At the most fundamental level, organized society accords its members some basic social services, such as protection from the antisocial behavior of others. One needs only to have the status of "ordinary person" to merit those benefits, but the individuals who bore the responsibility for providing protection earned fear and contempt within black Kansas City. Police harassed and abused blacks with the tacit approval of the men who had been given the highest authority for police protection in the city. Meanwhile, a lenient judicial system declared that black crime victims stood outside the shelter of the law—that their welfare was somehow extraneous to the concerns of the courts and the statutes. Consequently, lenient prosecutors and judges only appeared benign; their benevolence institutionalized disorder and irrationality by punishing the innocent and pardoning the guilty. Whites might prey upon blacks—and blacks victimize each other—with impunity. Where the dispensation of justice was concerned, black Kansas Citians qualified as something less than ordinary persons.

In the same way, the protocols of sex and gender that guided civil officers and civic reformers relegated black Kansas Citians to less than ordinary persons' status. To be black and female was to be, by definition, sexually accessible to any male, a status that protected vice helped to institutionalize within the black community. Incidents of harassment and humiliation at the hands of police reinforced that identity. For black men, even the most

40. *Kansas City Call*, February 17, 1928.

innocent action—whether buying a house in a white neighborhood or speaking to a white woman on a public trolley—might draw sharp reprisals because those acts suggested social and potentially sexual intimacy. In a decade in which white middle-class home owners and civic reformers redoubled their efforts to shelter white women and children from immorality, black men and women who tried to exercise the same prerogative met indifference or hostility. The distinction was not a trivial one, for the "city of homes" prized the patriarchal family as the guardian of domestic and civic virtue. To declare African Americans ineligible for those protections was to place them outside the moral equation that society claimed was its foundation. The result was a dual gender system. Black women were to have no place on the pedestal with chaste womanhood; black men were to have no role as patriarchs defending the approaches to the pedestal.

Moral quarantine and the inequitable legal system also contributed to the collective image-making process by which whites defined blacks, and by opposition, themselves. In consigning vice to the ghetto, moral quarantine assumed that it was "all right" for blacks to live in the midst of commercialized sin because they possessed the unrestrained urges on which sin fed. At the same time, whites who lived in the purified residential districts acquired an opposite identity as persons of rectitude and decency. The paradox of police brutality and judicial laxity reinforced whites' perception that blacks were incapable of abiding fully by the law—that African Americans and criminality were synonymous. The fact that an inverted justice system encouraged violence and lawbreaking on ghetto streets further strengthened the criminal stereotype. Both images served to justify blacks' isolation: by holding African Americans at a physical distance, one distanced oneself from moral taint and criminal depravity. The surest way to establish that distance in the 1920s was to select a home in one of the residential districts—the selectively purified communities.

The impulse to live in such a district was powerful because residence was so tightly bound with "social-group position." The household that located in an Armour Hills not only certified its middle-class status, but also laid claim to certain social rewards by virtue of its residence in a favored district. Those rewards included secure property values, shelter from vice, a haven against crime, and respectable neighbors. City officials, civic reformers, and realtors affirmed that these rewards were rightfully due by protecting selected districts from vice, crime, and blight. Race figured in this equation in two ways. First, the collective image-making process, begun in previous decades and institutionalized in the 1920s, declared African Americans to be the personification of immorality, crime, and declining property values. Keeping them out was essential to the purification process. Second, African Americans comprised the oppositional category that backlit white middle-class status. If being a middle-class white meant immunity from vice and crime—if it meant living in a homogeneous and permanently wholesome neighborhood—then the existence of another population that was categorically denied those social rewards gave the rewards a scarcity value. The contention over housing cemented an image of blacks as a kind of antimatter that could dissolve one's middle-class status on contact. The ways in which middle-class whites safeguarded themselves from that contact established conventions that future generations of white Kansas Citians would follow. Together, residential segregation, moral quarantine, and the inverted justice system supplied the mechanisms by which racial perceptions forged in the early century would be transmitted across time to future generations of Kansas Citians.

None of this was inevitable. Some whites in Kansas City could have challenged those perceptions, but they were part of the problem. Civic housekeepers labored to make the city a better place to live, but that coterie of reformers could ill afford to question blacks' status or the character of race relations in Kansas City because they had contributed so heavily to defining both. In their zeal to tidy away the disagreeable, they consigned vice to the ghetto along with the garbage heaps. Their crusade for strict law enforcement helped unleash an abusive police force upon blacks. Their solicitous care to make the residential districts into sanctuaries for middle-class decency and secure investment legitimized middle-class efforts to validate its social prestige by excluding blacks. When the consequences for African Americans were unmistakably pernicious, the civic housekeepers had no solutions to offer except their own shopworn social palliatives: charter reform and a city manager to reverse political and moral corruption, a housing code to improve blacks' health, separate (but pleasant) residences to reward the "better class of Negro."

The public discussion of race was all the more impoverished by the conspiracy of silence that surrounded racial issues in the 1920s, for the segmented, partially purified community required communal peace. So, whites went whistling through the cemetery pretending there were no racial conflicts that could not be solved by interracial amity and good will. Their code of silence made it doubly hard for African Americans to combat racial inequality, for it was too easy for whites to dismiss blacks' protests as social hypochondria, wearisome complaining by the sufferer of an imagined malady. Thus, in the next three decades, black Kansas Citians tested a variety of ways to dramatize that the malady was real—and that the assumptions feeding it were false.

6

Magician's Tricks

Black Activism and White Response, 1920–1940

■ ■ ■

IN THE YEARS between the world wars, African Americans in Kansas City engaged in myriad collective activities. They established new congregations of worshipers and expanded old ones; provided care for the aged, the sick, and the helpless; and nurtured fledgling business enterprises. Some joined together to enjoy painting, music, drama, and dance, and others to compete in amateur athletics or to cheer the Monarchs, the premier team in the Negro National League. While the character of race relations in Kansas City affected those organizations and activities, few of them addressed race questions as their central purpose. African Americans in Kansas City simply acted together in various ways to make their own lives meaningful in terms that they, not whites, defined.

At the same time, however, other African American organizations did make race their central concern by trying to educate whites on race issues. In the long run, their efforts laid the groundwork for a postwar civil rights movement in Kansas City. In the short run, their actions helped shape how whites thought about race and race relations and how they defended their privileges. The tactics whites used to hamstring race-conscious blacks in the 1920s and 1930s would be an enduring legacy too, for they would be used to impede racial justice in coming decades as well. Specifically, whites in decision-making positions refined the tactic of misdirection—the conjuror's art of diverting the eye to conceal the trick. For example, they invented the "myth of the bigoted client" to justify the construction of color lines. And seemingly sympathetic organizations continued to harness black Kansas Citians' interests to serve whites' ends. Thus, blacks' collective actions changed whites' perceptions of race and how race ought to shape civic life, often in ways that ran counter to African Americans' goals.

■ ■ Race Consciousness and White Response in the 1920s

One of the challenges for race-conscious blacks in the interwar years was finding ways to force whites to acknowledge that color lines existed in Kansas City, let alone that they must be erased. In the 1920s, a cadre of middle-class black leaders who styled themselves "race men" and "race women" proposed to forge that awareness by means of protest and political independence. In November 1919, six months after launching the *Kansas City Call*, C. A. Franklin saluted local race men and women, whom he credited for "the growing 'race consciousness' of Negroes" and the "resistance that is taking them upwards with leaps and bounds."[1] Thereafter, the editor both reported and promoted their activities during the 1920s. Little inclined to ideological discussion, race men and women defined themselves by their deeds. They were knowledgeable about black history and culture and identified themselves proudly as Negroes; they brooked neither racial insult nor exclusion; and they strove to advance the race both by example and by using their personal talents or advantages to assist other African Americans, individually and collectively. Any black Kansas Citian who fell short of their standards for race consciousness earned their contempt.

Race men and race women comprised a loose alliance of old-line professionals with newly prominent executives of businesses and civic agencies. Thus, their number included men like L. Amassa Knox and D. A. Holmes, who had figured as community leaders before the First World War and who comprised something of an "old guard" among race men in the 1920s. Knox was a Virginia native and a graduate of Howard University's law department. Shortly after his graduation in 1898, he entered the Missouri bar and, in 1904, opened a practice in Kansas City. By 1907, Knox was counted among a handful of African Americans who were challenging the local Republican Party for wider participation in GOP affairs. Coming from a less privileged background, D. A. Holmes was born in Randolph County, Missouri, in 1877 to former slaves. He supported himself as a laborer and farmhand before receiving the call to preach. In 1901, he was ordained by the First Baptist Church of St. David, Illinois, where he was named assistant superintendent of a countywide Sunday School organization made up almost entirely of white

1. *Kansas City Call*, November 1, 1919.

congregations. Holmes later claimed that the experience taught him both the wisdom of interracial cooperation and the skills for achieving it. In 1914, Holmes took a pulpit in Kansas City, Kansas, and, in 1921, answered a call to pastor the prestigious Vine Street Baptist Church in Kansas City, Missouri. Under Holmes's leadership, the Vine Street congregation completed a new sanctuary in 1927 and renamed itself Paseo Baptist Church to mark its new location.[2]

Among the leaders who emerged following the First World War and allied themselves with older race men were entrepreneurs like Homer Roberts and T. B. Watkins. When Roberts returned to Kansas City from military service overseas in 1919, he found that a number of his friends wanted to buy cars out of their accumulated wartime wages. Roberts decided to parlay his expertise in auto mechanics into a livelihood, initially selling reliable used cars and later offering new models. By 1923, Roberts Company claimed to have the largest black-owned car dealership and the only black-owned auto salesroom in the United States. As an avowed race man, Roberts employed only African Americans on his sales, clerical, and mechanical staffs and took pains to hire only black contractors and construction crews to build his new showroom. Like Holmes and Roberts, Theron B. Watkins was also a self-made man. Born and raised in Carthage, Indiana, Watkins first took an interest in undertaking when, as a boy, he helped out in the funeral home owned by the white family whose son was Watkins's best friend. After attending Indiana University for two years, Watkins worked as a Pullman porter and barber in St. Louis before entering embalming school. Soon after finishing his embalmer's course, Watkins came to Kansas City in 1918 and opened a funeral parlor. Within a few years, his was a flourishing business.[3]

Still, no one exemplified the race men more completely than their chronicler, Chester Arthur Franklin. Franklin was born in Dennison, Texas, in 1880, but his parents, a teacher and a barber, moved to Omaha, Nebraska, in 1887 to ensure their only child an education. When young Chester showed little interest in the barbering trade, the couple established the *Omaha Enterprise* so that their son might have a vocation. It proved a happy choice. Franklin left college after two years to take over the paper from his ailing father and moved the family to Denver in hopes that the change of climate

---

2. "L. Amassa Knox" and "D. A. Holmes," Vertical file of the Ramos Collection, MVR-KCPL.
3. *Kansas City Call,* August 31, 1923, August 22, 1924; "T. B. Watkins," Vertical file of the Ramos Collection, MVR-KCPL.

would repair his father's health. The Franklins purchased a newspaper there, and Chester and his mother, Clara, kept the presses going after the elder Franklin's death in 1901. But Denver's black population remained too small to support the kind of publication Franklin had in mind. In 1913, he moved to Kansas City, Missouri, where he operated a printing shop for six years until he could afford to resume newspaper publication. Starting with just two thousand copies in May 1919, Franklin, his mother, and later his wife, Ada Crogman Franklin, built the *Call* into the largest black newspaper in the southwest, with a staff of twenty-one and sixteen thousand subscribers in 1928.[4]

Frequently in the 1920s, this race-conscious amalgam resisted new impositions of the color bar by urging protests and boycotts. Sometimes protest worked. In 1922, for example, their complaints convinced the mayor's office to cancel a watermelon-eating contest scheduled for black children as part of the mayor's free picnic. That same year, the City Federation of Clubs, a consortium of black women's clubs, organized a successful boycott of a special Jim Crow showing at a local theater, pressured furniture store owners to offer equal credit terms to white and black customers, and convinced a merchant to stop advertising candy as "nigger toe brittle."[5] More often, however, protests failed for lack of a clear target. Repeatedly in the 1920s, those whites who were directly responsible for erecting color bars denied responsibility for their own actions and declared themselves powerless to remove the barriers they had imposed, blaming their white patrons whose prejudices these officials and business directors claimed they must accommodate. White decision-makers of various types adopted the trick of misdirection—a trick that served the city's park board particularly well in the 1920s and 1930s.

In 1924, Kansas City's Board of Parks and Boulevards announced that it was setting aside certain tennis courts, picnic grounds, and ball diamonds for use by African Americans—not to exclude them from other public facilities, the board assured, but to provide them adequate recreation. A protest committee responded that black Kansas City would "rather the board save its money than build this separate picnic ground," and a municipal court judge ruled in 1925 that African Americans were legally entitled to the use of public parks. Henceforth, the board had to work undercover.[6]

---

4. William H. and Nathan B. Young, Jr., *Your Kansas City and Mine*, 12–13, 130–31, 145.

5. *Kansas City Call*, July 15, 1922, February 18, 1922.

6. *Kansas City Call*, August 29, 1924, October 9, 1925, July 22, 1927; *Kansas City Star*, August 15, 1928. Bathhouses in the park system had been segregated for some time, and African Americans were excluded from Swope Park's swimming pool, bathhouse, and

In 1927, a group of black Camp Fire Girls were ordered out of a shelter-house in Swope Park, where they had spread their picnic during a rainstorm. Despite threats from park attendants, the girls' leaders refused to budge until a park superintendent confirmed that the pavilions were now reserved for whites. Mr. A. Coffin, father of one of the Camp Fire Girls, lodged a formal complaint. A protest committee of black residents promptly appeared before the board to remind its members that Swope Park, jewel of the city's park system, had been given to the city by Colonel Thomas Swope in a quit claim deed stipulating its use as a "public pleasure ground." The deed further stipulated that the property would revert to the Swope heirs if the city should violate the terms of the gift. Board members agreed that Kansas City's public included its black citizens, and board president Matthew Foster swore that the board had given no orders to exclude blacks from Swope Park. Nonetheless, park employees informed Mr. Coffin that they had been ordered to oust blacks from Swope's pavilions. The park board had warned its employees, however, that if blacks put up any resistance, board members would deny having given the orders. Park officials claimed to have complied with the terms of the Swope gift even while they violated those terms, but, because the park board officially denied that segregation was its intent, black activists had no grievance for legal action. So, with unofficial-looking "whites only" signs appearing in Swope, black parents avoided the Camp Fire Girls' humiliating experience by confining their outings to the Paradeway, a greenspace along the Paseo where blacks and working-class whites shared some meager recreational facilities.[7]

Because the park board had made no attempt to hide the segregation of Swope Park's golf courses, Homer Roberts and attorneys Carl Johnson and L. Amassa Knox brought suit against that particular violation of the deed's terms. Foster, admitting that he was surprised to learn that blacks even played golf, vowed that they certainly would not be allowed to play it on Swope's courses. Ellis D. Parsons, president of the Swope Park Golf Club, resorted to a more subtle and increasingly common defense of segregation. Separate facilities were necessary, he argued, to preserve community order and protect

---

golf links. However, they had been permitted previously to enjoy Swope's grounds and pavilions.

7. *Kansas City Call*, July 29, 1927. The terms of the deed were reproduced verbatim in the *Kansas City Call*, August 12, 1927. The absence of an actual city ordinance barring blacks continued to pose a problem. For example, a district judge dismissed a discrimination suit against the city in the early 1940s on grounds that, without an ordinance, park employees acted alone, without the city's authority. Consequently, the city could not be held liable. "Memorandum on Several Motions Filed by the Defendants to Dismiss," BA4.FRA22, C. A. Franklin Collection, Black Archives of Mid-America.

black residents from the wrath of the white public. "Any attempt on the part of the Negroes to carry on litigations in this manner," Parsons warned, "just has a tendency to lower the standing of the Negro race by trying to force themselves where they are not wanted and would lead toward race riots in the future."[8] Without any statutory authority for preventing the plaintiffs' use of the public facility, Circuit Court judge Brown Harris had to fall back on a similar argument that segregation was in blacks' best interests. Harris refused to order the city to admit black golfers to Swope's courses on the grounds that blacks had a "right" to their own exclusive golf courses just as, under Missouri law, they had a right to attend schools separate from white persons.[9]

Whites used similar rationalizations to excuse new color lines that emerged elsewhere in Kansas City in the 1920s. When the local chapter of the Veterans of Foreign Wars announced in 1928 that black women would no longer be allowed to sell poppies on Armistice Day, V.F.W. officials denied that they were, themselves, the bigots. Instead, they assumed that white women would be offended by having to attend preliminary sales meetings with black women. Likewise, the managers of downtown clothing stores began forbidding African American customers to try on clothing, hats, or shoes before purchasing them. According to the managers, they wished to avoid "embarrassing the white trade."[10] If white V.F.W. members and store customers truly demanded racial separation in such cases, these functionaries provided no evidence for it except their own presumptions that such a demand existed and that they were helpless to resist it. Both color bans remained in place, for the "myth of the bigoted patron" proved an effective device for justifying discrimination and deflecting blacks' protests.

■ ■ Race and Partisan Politics

When African Americans did mount protests and boycotts, they often failed to surmount what Franklin called blacks' "spinelessness," the refusal to "spend where you work," or to pressure public officials en masse.[11] Nowhere did this supposed spinelessness plague race men more than in the political

8. *Kansas City Star,* August 15, 1928.

9. *Kansas City Star,* August 14, 1928, August 15, 1928; *Kansas City Call,* August 3, 1928, September 7, 1928. According to the *Call,* Judge Harris was not totally benighted, for he showed some annoyance each time he corrected the city attorney for referring to the plaintiffs as "darkies."

10. *Kansas City Call,* July 13, 1923, March 13, 1925, May 25, 1928.

11. *Kansas City Call,* December 10, 1926.

arena, where they surveyed their political choices with some dismay in the early 1920s. The least congenial choice for race men and women, the local Democratic Party garnered a minority of black votes with the usual currency of machine politics: police protection for black-owned gambling and liquor operations, assistance to blacks who fell afoul of the law, and the exchange of liquor, cash, and jobs for votes. Casimir J. Welch, since 1912 the white Democratic boss of the Sixth and Eighth Wards, kept a platoon of black ward heelers who dispensed drinks and pocket money at election time, and, as a municipal court judge, Welch won some personal allegiance from blacks in his ward by leniency toward black defendants. While Welch's tactics failed to attract a majority of African American voters, those black votes he did win were the deciding factor in his control of the Eighth. Outside his ward, Welch negotiated the shifting alliances and antagonisms that fractured Democratic politics. As ward bosses Tom Pendergast and Joseph Shannon competed for party dominance in the early 1920s, the Democratic black vote became an increasingly attractive resource for the ambitious bosses to tap.[12]

Unfortunately, the GOP, dominated by middle-class and upper-middle-class whites, was scarcely more attractive to race-conscious black voters. The so-called boss Republicans, led by Thomas R. Marks, offered African Americans a modicum of patronage, and the faction ran a black candidate, William C. Hueston, for alderman from the Eighth Ward in 1918. But Marks represented the same "padrone system" of vote buying that race activists vilified among Democrats. Moreover, Hueston's unsuccessful candidacy helped fuel antiboss sentiment among white Republicans in the city's southern suburbs. In 1920, reform Republicans ousted Marks from party councils and captured control of the party's city convention two years later. Disgusted with black and white Republicans alike, a group that included Franklin, Knox, Holmes, and a handful of black physicians pinned their hopes on "the dream" of political independence. In 1922, they ran T. B. Watkins as independent candidate for Eighth Ward alderman, only to see Watkins defeated. The would-be independents blamed black Democrats for putting bribery above race loyalty and the large number of blacks who simply failed to register.[13] Franklin began publishing the addresses of unregistered voters in hopes of shaming the black electorate into political independence.

The cadre of race men did see L. Amassa Knox win a seat in Missouri's legislature in 1928, but steadily growing numbers of black voters preferred

12. Dorsett, *Pendergast Machine,* 60–63.
13. Larry Grothaus, "Kansas City Blacks, Harry Truman and the Pendergast Machine," 68–70; *Kansas City Call,* March 4, 1922, April 1, 1922, April 15, 1922, June 15, 1922.

machine politics over political independence. In municipal elections in 1922, Republicans carried the black precincts by margins of two or three to one in every race except the Eighth Ward aldermanic contest. By the fall elections in 1926, the GOP's majority had slipped to a mere 59 percent of the black vote. Even that slender margin disappeared four years later when the local Democratic ticket garnered a majority among black voters in municipal elections in 1930, carrying 60 percent of the black electorate in the Second Ward and 52 percent of black ballots in the residential Fourth Ward. The black Democratic majority continued to swell thereafter. November elections in 1932 gave Democrats a 70 percent majority in black precincts. By 1938, African American voters in three election districts preferred the local Democratic ticket by four to one, compared to a 61 percent Democratic majority among voters citywide.[14]

There are a number of ways to account for the swing of African American voters from Republican to Democratic ranks. Pendergast's most recent biographers claim that fraudulent ballots made up most of that new black Democratic majority, although contemporary observers reported a sizable shift among the certifiably "real" black electorate, which, except for a brief flirtation with the reform faction in the 1940s, remained firmly in Democratic ranks after 1930. According to conventional wisdom among whites at the time, the new black Democrats were mainly crapshooters. Typical was the observation by the *Kansas City Times* in 1930 that "for the first time big G.O.P. Negro precincts went Democratic. This is explained by the Democrats, and most Republicans, to have been due chiefly to the unrelenting activity of the [Republican] police against a certain element of the Negroes . . . whose bail bonds the Democrats supplied after every raid."[15] Other students of Kansas City's political history attribute blacks' machine loyalty to unprecedented benefits in employment, health and social services, and public relief the machine provided to its black constituents.[16] The ques-

14. *Kansas City Call,* April 8, 1922, November 5, 1926, March 28, 1930, November 11, 1932, November 18, 1932, April 1, 1938. Reform of the city's charter in 1925 resulted in redistricting, so that the Second Ward included the North End and the black commercial center along Twelfth and Eighteenth Streets and the Fourth contained more affluent blacks' residences south of the black commercial center. Technically, voting units in municipal elections were called Election Districts rather than wards. Because sources use the term "ward" to discuss municipal vote tallies, I have used that term for the sake of clarity. Note, too, that the local Democrats won a small majority of black votes in 1922, but the margin proved temporary. Dorsett, *Pendergast Machine,* 75.

15. *Kansas City Times,* March 27, 1930.

16. Lawrence H. Larsen and Nancy J. Hulston, *Pendergast!,* 104–5; Brown and Dorsett, *K.C,* 201; Grothaus, "Blacks, Harry Truman and the Pendergast Machine," 65–82.

tion is important for two reasons. First, whites controlled both local parties. Determining the means by which both parties either won or lost black ballots provides some insight into whites' perceptions of African Americans and their place in the local political and social structure. Second, bloc voting was a form of collective action by which black Kansas Citians sought to improve their position in Kansas City and, by extension, to redefine what white Kansas Citians understood their proper status to be. It is important to measure their success by determining how and to what degree the Pendergast regime represented a change in white attitudes or actions regarding race.

Much of the credit for the early shift in black votes belonged to Republican insensitivity, ineptitude, and ill fortune. The party displayed a callous disregard for the interests and feelings of black voters as soon as Republican reformers took over the local GOP in 1922. At the head of the GOP local ticket was Matthew Foster, whom Governor Arthur Hyde had appointed to the Kansas City Board of Police Commissioners in 1921 with instructions to drive out bootleggers, gamblers, and prostitutes. Declaring that a vote for Foster was a vote against vice in the ghetto, the Negro Women's Division of the Republican Central Committee threw its support behind the ticket. The *Call* seconded the choice. The price of reform came high, however. The GOP's antivice campaign, for example, engaged in race-baiting by targeting "crap-shooting Negroes who should either get jobs or get out of town."[17] According to an editorial in the labor newspaper, the *Missouri Mule,* a Republican committeeman had declared in 1920 that "we want no nigger votes for the anti-boss ticket." Perhaps, the *Mule* suggested disapprovingly, Matt Foster "will arrange a 'neck-tie party' out in the Tenth Ward to disfranchise [*sic*] the colored men, too." Instead, the reformers' capture of the Republican City Committee cost blacks representation in the party's city convention in 1922. When the convention refused to nominate a black candidate for alderman, William C. Hueston claimed in a furious speech that Foster had organized the antiboss faction of silk-stocking suburbanites for the sole purpose of keeping blacks off the Republican ballot.[18]

For the rest of the decade, Republican insensitivity continued to alienate African Americans. In 1924, for example, Democrats revealed that their opponents in the GOP had delayed opening the newly built Jackson County Home for Negro Boys because of its "luxury appointments." Charging that nickel-plated faucets and tile floors were too plush for black delinquents,

---

17. Grothaus, "Blacks, Harry Truman and the Pendergast Machine," 69.
18. *Missouri Mule,* March 27, 1920; *Kansas City Call,* March 18, 1922, March 25, 1922, April 1, 1922.

Republican politicians had proposed that the home be used to house the overflow of white inmates of an old-folks home. After segregating the seating at a party rally in 1926, local Republicans compounded their error two years later when Kansas City Republicans hosted their party's 1928 national convention. Black delegates to the convention found that, for the first time in their party's history, they would be barred from the hotels where white delegates stayed. Instead, local Republican leader Conrad Mann arranged to house them in private homes and in a YMCA in the ghetto. Holding Mann responsible for Republican insensitivity, C. A. Franklin wryly noted, "Mr. Mann is the author of the classic statement: 'We wish to accord the visiting Negro delegates the same courteous treatment we always give our own Negro population.'"[19]

Still unenlightened in 1930, Kansas City Republicans staged a rally in which a speaker included the word *nigger* in his address. The party's nominations tended to underscore its disregard for blacks' self-esteem and its inability to recognize the issues that mattered to black Republicans. For example, the Republican mayoral candidate in 1930 was George Kimball, a former president of the hated Linwood Improvement Association. By contrast, Bryce Smith, the Democratic mayoral candidate in 1930, had worked openly to secure funding for black schools while he had served on the school board. Describing the black Republican organization as a skeleton in 1930, C. A. Franklin charged that the fault lay in Republicans' "sublime stupidity" in refusing to campaign seriously for black votes or to provide meaningful benefits to a black constituency.[20]

19. *Kansas City Call*, March 14, 1924, November 7, 1930, February 13, 1923, April 20, 1923, April 13, 1928, April 6, 1928, September 25, 1931. Customary Jim Crow in Kansas City did not, by itself, explain the Republicans' decision. According to an article in the *Call* in 1931, some downtown hotels did allow blacks to attend meetings in the hotel and visit white guests so long as their names were placed on an approved list and the black guests rode the freight elevators. Presumably, given Franklin's outrage over the decision, Kansas City hotel keepers might have been induced to rent rooms to black delegates if pressed by the GOP convention committee.

20. *Kansas City Call*, June 12, 1931, June 17, 1932, January 7, 1927, March 21, 1930, June 13, 1930, November 7, 1930, April 3, 1931. Once in office, the Republicans' presidential nominee at the Kansas City convention further scuttled local Republicans' chances among Kansas City's black electorate. Herbert Hoover tried to appoint a racist, J. J. Parker, to the Supreme Court, and his Secretary of War Patrick Hurley chose to segregate the parties of Gold Star Mothers, whom the federal government sent to Europe to visit the graves of their sons. Some of the black Gold Star Mothers crossed the Atlantic on what were described as cattle boats. Hurley also disbanded the black Ninth and Tenth Cavalry units—objects of pride to African Americans—and dispersed their members to several posts, including nearby Fort Leavenworth. The *Call* reported these outrages assiduously and reminded readers of Hoover's blunders as the 1932 election approached.

Besides the damage Republicans did themselves, the Ku Klux Klan's intrusion into local politics helped brand the GOP as the party of race-baiting and Jim Crow. The Klan first emerged in western Missouri and eastern Kansas in 1922. By 1924, the Kansas and Missouri districts each claimed to have 100,000 members, some 5,000 of them congregated in the vicinity of Kansas City, Missouri, and Kansas City, Kansas. A large but indeterminate proportion of those members were professionals, clergymen, businessmen, newspaper publishers, and lodge brothers—the very ranks for whom Republicans claimed to speak. In both states, the Klan claimed to represent patriotism, Americanism, and morality (including the "protection of our pure womanhood" and the "sanctity of the American home"). Reserving most of its vitriol for Roman Catholics and immigrants, the order declared that it had no quarrel with blacks who kept their place, and neither state saw many incidents of night-riding or intimidation directed against African Americans.[21]

Nonetheless, black voters in Kansas City, Missouri, were understandably uneasy when the Klan entered Missouri politics in 1922. Since the local Democratic factions sheltered most of the immigrant vote and many of the city's Catholic voters, the local Klan endorsed the Republican ticket and targeted Catholics Tom Pendergast and Joseph Shannon for destruction. Another Democrat, James A. Reed, appeared to be the natural ally of the KKK in his bid for re-election to the U.S. Senate. Reed had been an outspoken race-baiter since 1908. As a U.S. Senator, he opposed the Dyer antilynching bill, condemned the League of Nations as a nest of "Hottentots," and proposed to amend immigration law to bar immigration by blacks. Yet, the Klan also tried unsuccessfully to unseat Reed because he was thoroughly "wet" on the liquor issue. Naturally enough, the local Democracy denounced the KKK, though during the election campaign in 1924, Missouri Democrats experienced some embarrassment when their gubernatorial candidate, Arthur Nelson, could not convince the voters that he had never been a Klan member. Republican Sam Baker, who firmly renounced Klan support, carried the governor's race. In Kansas City, however, local Democrats again condemned the KKK and criticized local Republicans for failing to do the same. In fact, the Republican Albert Beach won the mayor's seat with open support from Klansmen.[22]

21. Lila Lee Jones, "The Ku Klux Klan in Eastern Kansas during the 1920s," 10, 21–23, 34–38; David Chalmers, *Hooded Americanism: The History of the Ku Klux Klan*, 36, 135; Kenneth T. Jackson, *The Ku Klux Klan in the City, 1915–1930*, 239; Barbara J. Rush, "The Ku Klux Klan in Kansas City during the Twenties," 71, 81, 88, 103–5.

22. Rush, "Ku Klux Klan in Kansas City," 155–58, 164–70; *Kansas City Call*, April 1, 1922, October 27, 1922.

Political events on the Kansas side linked the Klan more closely to Republicanism. At the first appearance of klaverns in his state, Henry J. Allen, the Kansas Democratic governor, publicly excoriated the hooded realm and directed his attorney general to begin litigation that would oust the order from Kansas. Meanwhile, Harry Burton, Democratic mayor of Kansas City, Kansas, entered public debates with a Klan spokesman from Boston in order to castigate the organization, and he demanded that city employees either quit the Klan or quit their jobs. The Kansas realm figured more prominently in the elections of 1924, when Republican gubernatorial candidate Ben Paulen accepted the Klan's endorsement and stymied an attempt to insert an anti-Klan plank into the party's state platform. The Democratic candidate, Jonathan Davis, renounced the KKK.[23] Paulen won. Although he likely would have carried the state without Klan endorsement, his victory and the Klan-centered campaign that preceded it attracted the attention of the *Call* and deepened the association between the GOP and the Invisible Empire in the minds of Kansas City, Missouri's black voters.

Relations between police and the black community showed even more clearly how cynical Republicans' treatment of African Americans was. As Democrats never tired of pointing out, police violence against blacks had mounted after 1921, when Republican governor Hyde appointed Matthew Foster to head the Kansas City Board of Police Commissioners. Although the Shannon and Pendergast factions promised to eliminate the abusive policing that a GOP-controlled commission fostered, their promises were empty ones.[24] So long as control of the city's police lay in a police commission whose members were appointed by Republican governors, local Democrats could do little to shape police policy or discipline. Already shocking in the 1920s, the incidents of police brutality in the black precincts grew even more savage between 1930 and 1932.

One of the worst cases involved Darius Hendricks, the janitor at the Waldo Theater. Hendricks was arrested in early February 1931 on suspicion of robbing the theater's safe. Although the uniformed patrolmen who arrested Hendricks "talked nice" to him while taking him to Station House #3 for interrogation, the station's chief left him in the keeping of five plainclothes detectives from police headquarters, who spent three hours beating Hendricks with a baseball bat, gardening tools, and wire coat hangers. Still refusing to confess, Hendricks was released with multiple and permanently crippling injuries. Within a week, police arrested the actual thieves and secured their

23. Francis W. Schruben, *Kansas in Turmoil, 1930–1936*, 159, 192–93.
24. *Kansas City Call*, March 28, 1924, April 4, 1924.

confessions, and the Hendricks case went before the Board of Police Commissioners for review. The commission concluded that Hendricks had received his beating, not from police, but from the robbers themselves after he stumbled on them during the robbery. The commissioners further warned black Kansas Citians to "hold themselves quiet on this matter and not have such things printed in the papers." Since the *Call* was the only paper in Kansas City to have mentioned the case, it was clear whom the commission intended to muzzle. Instead, the African American community began raising funds to press the Hendricks case in court.[25]

In March 1931, the Board of Police Commissioners considered the Hendricks incident in a lengthy public hearing.[26] Despite attempts by the commissioners to "bull-doze, bull-rag, and confuse witnesses," Hendricks refused to change his account of his beating. From a milling crowd of twenty-five policemen, Hendricks identified five men who had beaten him. A sergeant at the stationhouse previously had named those same five as the men who interrogated Hendricks. Further support for Hendricks's claims came from the convicted thieves, who provided affidavits swearing that they had not assaulted the janitor. Given the obvious seriousness of Hendricks's injuries, the robbers would have had to spend as much as an hour beating Hendricks before making their escape with the safe's loot. Yet, the five accused detectives denied that they had touched Hendricks, and the captain in charge of the station testified that, in his twenty years of police service, he had never known anyone to be beaten by police.

The police commissioners agreed only to take the thieves' evidence under advisement, and they closed the hearing with a condemnation of C. A. Franklin for trying to start a race riot when he protested police behavior. "It was plain throughout the hearing," the *Call* reported, that the commissioners and their attorney "were attempting to confuse the witnesses, tangle up the whole proceedings and prove that the police never laid a hand on Hendricks, but that Hendricks was beaten by the robbers." Instead of seeking judiciously to find the truth, they "made common cause with the five policemen charged with beating an innocent man." The consequences were grievous, Franklin declared in an editorial. "There are patrolmen and detectives who are above these terrible cruelties which shame the very name of the law in this community. But Negroes know too well that there are also men in

25. *Kansas City Call,* February 13, 1931, March 13, 1931, February 20, 1931, February 27, 1931.

26. No records of police commission proceedings prior to 1949 survive. The *Call* however, reported hearings testimony at length and sometimes verbatim.

the board's employ who need only opportunity to do us harm, and with this the attitude of the commissioners, they practically have permission." Calling the police commission "a travesty," Franklin reported that he had lost all faith in the police board under Republican control. In the fall of 1931, the Hendricks case came before a grand jury, which refused to hand down an indictment. Alarmed by this and other examples of official callousness, the Inter-Racial Commission of the Kansas City Council of Churches informed Governor Henry Caulfield about the most recent cases of police brutality and about the police commissioners' tendency to ignore blacks' complaints of police abuse. The Republican governor promised to investigate, but nothing came of the promise.[27]

Throughout the 1920s, the well-heeled Republicans who had seized control of the party under Matt Foster's guidance made the local GOP the political voice for the same set of racial perceptions that underlay segregated housing, inequitable law enforcement, and the unholy union of race and gender. Republican leaders segregated their political gatherings and excluded African Americans from the rewards of citizenship that accompanied political participation and power. The party's flirtation with the Klan was made possible, in part, by a shared perception that the purity of woman and the sanctity of the home were at risk from dangerous "others"—whether Catholic, Jew, immigrant, or African American. Republicans were responsible for basing official policy upon the belief that African Americans deserved, not the protection, but the scourge of law. Black voters apparently recognized the congruities. Assessing the results of local elections in 1924, Republican C. A. Franklin concluded that blacks were departing GOP ranks because of Republican high-handedness, police brutality, and the Klan.[28]

■ ■ The Pendergast Machine and the Black Electorate

While Republicans did their best to sever blacks' old political allegiances, Tom Pendergast strove to establish new ones. As of 1925, Boss Tom had solidified his control of local Democratic politics by forging alliances with key faction leaders, including Cas Welch. Pendergast thus became the beneficiary and suzerain of Welch's "Little Tammany" organization of black and white Democrats in the Sixth and Eighth Wards. At the same time, Pendergast

27. *Kansas City Call,* February 27, 1931, March 13, 1931, March 20, 1931, November 13, 1931, September 11, 1931, November 13, 1931, January 8, 1932.
28. *Kansas City Call,* April 4, 1924, April 11, 1924.

outflanked municipal reformers by using charter reform and the new city managership to take control of city government. These accretions of power provided Pendergast both the motive and the means to attract black voters to the local Democracy. So long as he lacked control of the Board of Police Commissioners, however, the chief attraction Pendergast had to offer was patronage for black Democrats. Only in March 1932 was Tom Pendergast able to make good his pledge to eliminate police brutality. That month, the Missouri State Supreme Court granted Kansas City home rule of its police department. Municipal reformers like Walter Matscheck of the Civic Research Institute had sought home rule to improve efficiency by eliminating divided responsibility for policing. The Supreme Court concurred in 1932 that it was unconstitutional to require the city to pay for police operations that were under state control. Reformers' victory proved hollow, however, when Tom Pendergast once again turned a reform measure to his own ends. Because the city charter approved in 1925 authorized the city manager to appoint a director of police, the combination of home rule and his own control of the city manager's office gave Pendergast almost unlimited control of the police department.[29]

The results in the black community were dramatic. The Democrats quickly purged the police force of Republican holdovers, including seventeen black patrolmen, and replaced them with politically reliable officers. A few months later, the new Public Safety Director, Eugene Reppert, demonstrated the department's good faith. "Without waiting for complaint, with no delegations of Negroes demanding investigation," Franklin recalled, Reppert fired a police officer for shooting a black suspect without sufficient cause. The *Call* promptly declared, "The reign of police brutality is over!" In fact, reports of police brutality almost disappeared from the pages of the *Call*. Because the *Call* had been dogged in reporting abuses previously and continued to criticize the machine vigorously for other offenses, the lack of such reports likely reflected a real decline in incidents of police abuse. The black electorate rewarded the boss by giving still larger vote tallies to the Democratic ticket. According to the *Call*, "The reason is not far to seek. With the coming of Home Rule, and the police under city control, Negroes for the first time in many years have not been harried by brutal officers. It is this new deal given by the city administration which increased the Negro vote for [Democrat] Bryce B. Smith and his colleagues."[30] If the halt to police terror played the

29. Walter Matscheck, "Kansas City Studies Its Police Department," 453–57; Matscheck, "Kansas City Wins Police Home Rule," 342–43; Brown and Dorsett, *K.C.*, 194.

30. *Kansas City Call*, March 9, 1934, April 22, 1932, April 29, 1932, September 23, 1932, November 25, 1932. In 1938, D. A. Holmes accused the *Call* of concealing

deciding part in adding blacks to Pendergast's coalition though, it likewise proved to be almost the only significant benefit African Americans would obtain from that alliance.

■ ■ The Black Community and the Penalties of Machine Rule

The machine had other rewards to disburse, including recreation centers, swimming pools, and hospitals. In fact, the machine did construct an unprecedented number of social service facilities in the African American community. Judge of the County Court Harry Truman, in particular, saw to it that blacks won a tubercular cottage and girls' home as well as a boys' home. And Truman ousted Dr. D. M. Miller, the Democrat appointed to head the Jackson County Home for Aged Negroes, when it was made clear that Miller had physically abused the home's elderly inmates.[31] More often, however, the facilities the machine built in the African American community fell short of promises given and of the actual needs of the community. Worse, machine rule meant that social services in the black community were hostage to political considerations among whites.

Among the promises the Pendergast organization made to the black community was a pledge to improve health care. The pressure to meet that promise intensified after the city's Democratic administration named Dr. William J. Thompkins an assistant health commissioner in the city's Department of Hygiene and Communicable Diseases in 1927. He remained in that post until 1934, when Roosevelt appointed him Recorder of Deeds for the District of Columbia, thus making Thompkins a member of the president's unofficial Black Cabinet. In almost every respect, Thompkins was the archetypal race man. Born in Jefferson City, Missouri's capital, in 1884, the young Thompkins worked as bellboy in a hotel, where he came to know most of the leading figures in state politics. After receiving his medical degree at Howard University and interning in Washington, D.C., he came to Kansas City to practice medicine in 1906. In 1915, he became the first African American to serve as superintendent of Old City Hospital, the public facility reserved

---

a recent outbreak of police brutality in order to protect the Pendergast organization. The *Call*, however, refuted Holmes's allegations. With a case-by-case analysis, the *Call* argued that the incidents Holmes cited either did not constitute police brutality or did not represent a consistent policy of abuse such as the black community experienced under Republican police administration. *Kansas City Call*, March 25, 1938.

31. Grothaus, "Blacks, Harry Truman and the Pendergast Machine," 77–79; *Kansas City Call*, November 11, 1927, December 2, 1927, December 31, 1926, January 7, 1927; May 4, 1928.

for black patients. Under his administration the hospital rose from a class D to class A rating among several accrediting agencies.[32] A businessman as well as a physician, Thompkins headed Mid-West Life Insurance Company until 1924 and published the *Kansas City American* newspaper between 1928 and 1943.

Yet Thompkins was never counted among the cadre of race men who surrounded C. A. Franklin and whose activism Franklin applauded. Most likely his politics rendered him ineligible for membership in that coterie of Republicans, for Thompkins led the Central Negro Democratic Organization of longtime black Democrats in Kansas City. Thus Thompkins's appointment to the city's hygiene department represented an alliance between Pendergast forces and the old guard of black Democrats. Thompkins further offended race men like Franklin by seeming to subordinate blacks' political interests to the interests of the local Democratic Party. When he stated publicly that "Negroes do not desire and are not ready for Negro leadership," the *Call*'s editor noted that Thompkins's actions "remind us of the old white steer that saved his life for many years by the adeptness with which he led the other cattle out of the pens, through the cattle chute and to their doom on the killing floor."[33] Having claimed "racial uplift" as their own province, race men were ill pleased when Thompkins proved more adept than they at publicizing and ameliorating blacks' living conditions.

After his appointment to the hygiene department, his survey of housing and tuberculosis rates in the ghetto helped build support for a new public hospital for blacks. In December 1925, the Democratically controlled city health board made good the pledge by announcing plans to build a new facility on Hospital Hill near the public hospital for whites. Almost immediately City Manager McElroy allowed the hospital project to bog down in a dispute over the hospital's location.[34] Finally, after tying up hospital construction for almost two years in his attempts to placate whites' objections

32. *Kansas City Times*, April 11, 1934. Thompkins served as recorder until his death in 1944. *Kansas City Call*, April 11, 1944.

33. *Kansas City Call*, October 3, 1924, January 14, 1927; *Kansas City Times*, May 11, 1934; Grothaus, "Blacks, Harry Truman and the Pendergast Machine," 73. Thompkins also supplied Democratic national headquarters with survey data on living conditions among black Americans that were used in campaign speeches, and in 1924, the Democratic Party's national headquarters named him to head its western Negro division.

34. The original site on Michigan Avenue, coincidentally on property owned by Democratic faithful and black nightclub manager Felix Payne, was located conveniently near the black population, but it lay in the area the Linwood Improvement Association hoped would serve as a barrier against black encroachment. After LIA threatened to sue the city to keep the hospital out of its bailiwick, McElroy chose a site on Hospital Hill near the city's other public hospital. Protests from Research Hospital, a private institution

to various sites, City Manager McElroy opened brand-new General Hospital No. 2 on the city's Hospital Hill in February 1930. At its opening, it was the most up-to-date and fully equipped black hospital in the United States. Within six months, however, hospital service began to deteriorate because of a patronage war within the machine. In August 1930, Cas Welch fired Dr. Howard Smith, the hospital's superintendent and a Pendergast appointee. In Smith's place, Welch appointed his own political crony, Dr. D. M. Miller, the same Dr. Miller who had lost his job at the Home for Aged Negroes for abusing the residents. In the months following Miller's appointment, the *Call* received a growing number of complaints from patients about careless diagnoses and faulty treatment, including one from a patient who successfully sued a hospital staff physician for maltreatment. At the same time, a hospital survey by the Kansas City Chamber of Commerce sharply criticized General No. 2 for mismanagement and poor housekeeping.[35]

As Welch replaced more Pendergast appointees with his own staff members, patients reported to the *Call* that employee morale had so broken down that bedpans were left unemptied for up to twenty-four hours, and patients often passed an entire shift without seeing a nurse. Although the hospital was required to provide treatment free of charge, hospital staff pressured patients to sign over their insurance benefits to the hospital to pay for treatment, and they charged fees for filling out and signing insurance claims. In most cases, patients received no more than seven dollars per week in sick benefits—money they needed to feed their families while a breadwinner lay ill. Finally, in late 1932, Pendergast brought Welch to heel, eventually placing competent professionals in staff positions at General No. 2. In the interim, however, his internecine war with Welch cost both the city and its black residents. Investigations showed that hospital payroll had risen by forty thousand dollars each year of Miller's two-year tenure due to padding and expenditure on salaries for nonexistent workers.[36] More important, black patients had received indifferent or faulty care, and the black medical fraternity had suffered considerable embarrassment.

While machine politics threatened to erode the quality of service delivery, the Pendergast organization fell short in supplying civic improvements of the

---

also located on Hospital Hill, further delayed the project. *Kansas City Call*, October 22, 1926, January 7, 1927, July 22, 1927, October 7, 1927, July 6, 1928.

35. *Kansas City Call*, February 28, 1930, August 15, 1930, August 22, 1930, September 9, 1931, January 1, 1932, February 3, 1933, February 20, 1931, July 17, 1931, September 25, 1931, October 9, 1931, October 23, 1931.

36. *Kansas City Call*, November 25, 1932, December 2, 1932, January 6, 1933, April 21, 1933, March 16, 1934.

number and type it had promised the black community. Those promises were beguiling in mid-1930, when the city named ten African Americans to the Committee of 1,000, a citizens' advisory panel to select projects for funding by the Ten Year Plan, an ambitious program of public works construction that slated the black community for better sidewalks and street lighting and a new recreation center on the Paradeway. Yet, five years into the Ten Year Plan, sidewalks in the ghetto still crumbled, street lights were dim, and the much-ballyhooed community center was a "matchbox," with cramped meeting rooms and a tiny pool that leaked the first day it was filled.[37]

In fact, access to recreation facilities remained a problem, one the machine did nothing to relieve. The city's black golfers scored a partial victory when the park board bowed to pressure and allowed them to play Swope Golf Course #2 in 1934 and then reserved that course exclusively for blacks in 1938. While affluent black golfers teed up on Course #2, however, ordinary black residents found it steadily more difficult to enjoy Swope Park. Police and park workers succeeded in ousting more and more African Americans from the park or corralled them in a shelterhouse "reserved for your people." When protests to Democratic mayor and Pendergast toady Bryce Smith produced no results, the local NAACP chapter announced that it would fight segregation in Swope Park. Likewise, the machine refused to use its considerable leverage to raze color barriers in city-owned facilities. Instead, segregation expanded its reach into city facilities under Pendergast, so that African Americans were barred from a café in Kansas City's Municipal Airport for the first time in 1937, and city officials refused to compel the operators who leased the brand-new Municipal Auditorium to eradicate Jim Crow. Apparently, city administrators believed as heartily in the myth of the bigoted patron as private officials did.[38]

There was one area of city administration, however, where the Pendergast forces had both the authority to erase racial exclusion and a commitment to the black electorate to do so, for Democrats had promised repeatedly to provide jobs for black constituents. Certainly, the machine possessed the means to expand employment opportunities for its black constituents in the Ten Year Plan, the enormous bond issue of fifty million dollars to underwrite

---

37. *Kansas City Call*, June 13, 1930, August 1, 1930, August 22, 1930, April 24, 1931, May 29, 1931, February 14, 1936, April 29, 1938, July 1, 1938, June 2, 1939, June 23, 1939; June 30, 1939.

38. *Kansas City Call*, March 22, 1935, August 5, 1932, March 4, 1932, June 4, 1937, February 12, 1937, February 26, 1937; May 15, 1931, June 12, 1931, January 19, 1934, August 31, 1934, October 7, 1938, January 27, 1939, May 6, 1938, June 2, 1939, August 4, 1939.

public works construction. By 1933, the Ten Year Plan had paid out nearly two million dollars in wages to some twenty-two thousand men. And there was more money to spend. Because Tom Pendergast had given early support to Franklin Roosevelt's bid for the presidential nomination, FDR rewarded him with control over virtually all federal relief expenditures in Missouri. Not surprisingly, an extravagant portion of that federal relief money made its way to Kansas City, so that the effects of the Great Depression fell more lightly on Kansas City than other cities.[39]

In fact, the number of African Americans on the city's payroll rose under the Pendergast regime from 89 in 1924 to 438 in 1938. Yet, these benefits represented fairly meager rewards for blacks' continued loyalty to the machine. Aside from increasing city employment for African Americans, the machine did surprisingly little to lower color barriers to black job-seekers. In the private sector, for example, blacks in the building trades found it particularly difficult to retain their positions during the depression. Much of the fault lay with a city administration that Pendergast controlled, for the city's building inspection department denied the necessary permits that would have enabled black plumbers, electricians, masons, carpenters, plasterers, and tile setters to work on buildings that required city inspections. The fact that the machine honored union rules and color lines further worked against its black constituency. Consequently, the number of blacks employed in the building trades shrank in the 1930s in a period in which publicly funded construction jobs kept thousands of white families from abject want.[40] A timely word from Tom Pendergast could have righted matters, but as long as African Americans continued to give him their votes, the boss had scant reason to challenge the prejudices of his white constituents on their behalf.

■ ■ The Moral Geography of Jazz

In Pendergast's day, most white observers echoed the *Kansas City Times*'s belief that blacks voted for the machine to protect vice. The *Call* replied angrily that vice attracted few black voters to Democratic ranks. Gambling and

39. Brown and Dorsett, *K.C.*, 196–200.
40. "Minutes, July 7, 1932," in *Minutes of the Monthly Meetings of the Board of Directors of the Urban League of Kansas City,* Archives of the Urban League of Kansas City; "Monthly Report of the Executive Secretary," November, 1935, *Minutes of Urban League;* "Executive Secretary's Report," November 6, 1935, *Minutes of Urban League; Kansas City Call,* September 8, 1933, September 29, 1933, June 8, 1934, September 29, 1931, December 14, 1934, August 4, 1939, August 12, 1938, August 19, 1938.

bootlegging dives might be proliferating in the city, but "their operators and their customers are too few to affect the thousands of Negro voters." Most of those thousands who voted Democratic were churchgoers and housewives, the *Call* noted. "Even the fertile imagination of the reporter who wrote that twaddle would hardly charge the women who handle family finances and the host of church members with voting 'to protect crap games.'"[41] The increase in black Democrats in largely residential precincts lying well to the south of the vice operations further convinced the *Call* that honest citizens made up the bulk of the machine's black supporters.

Nonetheless, the Pendergast regime fostered a "wide-open" entertainment industry that gave employment to many African Americans and nurtured a golden era of jazz in Kansas City. Pendergast's seizure of the police department ensured that gamblers, club owners, brothel keepers, and vendors of liquor and narcotics, who once secured protection from individual police officers or machine judges, now enjoyed the tacit approval of an entire police organization. Moreover, the machine's lavish expenditures on public works meant that working-class and middle-class whites had money to spend on leisure. A host of new nightspots and resorts opened to accommodate them—many of the enterprises located in the ghetto north of Twentieth Street, nearly all of them supplying jazz performers to entertain the crowds. While theaters and clubs shut their doors all over the depression-plagued southwestern states, jazz musicians migrated to Kansas City, where the gigs were plentiful. Mary Lou Williams, the pianist for Andy Kirk's Clouds of Joy, recalled the period: "Kansas City was under Tom Pendergast's control. Most of the nightspots were run by politicians and hoodlums, and the town was wide open for drinking, gambling, and pretty much every form of vice. Work was plentiful for musicians, though some of the employers were tough people. . . . I found Kansas City to be a heavenly city—music everywhere in the Negro section of town, and fifty or more cabarets rocking on Twelfth and Eighteenth Streets."[42]

Club dates were still abundant when another black pianist came to Kansas City in 1937. "All the cats were working you know, and they used to have plenty of bands around," Jay McShann remembered. "Plenty of clubs, plenty of places to play and everybody's makin' it." Some African American women also found work dancing in clubs. According to John Tumino, "The clubs all had shake dancers, . . . strippers, really, only they were professional dancers, . . . shake their butts and their bodies and their boobs; . . . they

41. *Kansas City Times,* March 27, 1930; *Kansas City Call,* March 28, 1930.
42. Russell, *Jazz Style,* 8–10.

were black." Still other men and women served as numbers runners for the policy wheels or worked in the kitchens of supper clubs. The most influential blacks in Kansas City's entertainment industry, however, were club managers Felix Payne, Piney Brown, and Ellis Burton, whom Sam Price remembered as "godfathers actually for most musicians." Besides the jobs, the free food, and the rent money these managers handed out to musicians, they exercised their political connections to the machine on behalf of black musicians, gamblers, and others in the netherworld of entertainment. While he worked in Burton's club, The Yellow Front, Booker Washington recalled that the police "would raid us occasionally. But no sooner do they take the people down, there was always a bond waiting for them to get out. . . . Burton had connections. . . . He had a strong hold politically to even operate that place." Fortunately for the jazz world, the same men who brokered money and power, whether black club managers or white "gangsters," also loved music with a generous and fatherly ardor. Numerous jazz performers recalled in oral histories that so-called gangsters who ran clubs or simply worked the liquor and gambling trades sponsored and protected them. Sometimes they "bought out" a club for a night of private performances. As Eddie Durham remembered, "Those guys paid you double for anything you ever done in Kansas City. . . . The gangster always protected. . . . Those gangsters would always treat everybody right. If you touched a musician, or one of the girls, you'd go out on your head."[43]

That rich and magnetic mixture drew many of the finest jazz performers to Kansas City in the 1930s. Homegrown talents in Andy Kirk's Clouds of Joy or Bennie Moten's orchestra honed their abilities in local clubs and in "Battles of the Bands" against visiting orchestras led by Cab Calloway, Duke Ellington, and other luminaries. Young players like Count Basie, Hershel Evans, Ben Webster, and Charlie Parker practiced in "KC" jam sessions. Out of the musical ferment came a distinctive Kansas City style with an aggressive "eight to the bar" rhythm driving complex arrangements and improvised riffs. Gradually, that style infiltrated the jazz world outside KC as local bands headed out on tour or won play dates in Chicago's Grand Terrace or New York's Roseland. When Bennie Moten took his orchestra on a forty-five week tour in 1931, band member Buck Clayton recalled being on the forward edge. "We played more swing music than all the bands in New York. . . . So the people liked us. . . . They were just crazy about this music. They never heard this kind of music coming from the west before."[44]

43. Pearson, *Goin' to Kansas City,* 91, 94–95, 97, 99, 101.
44. Howard Litwack and Nathan Pearson, eds., "Goin' to Kansas City," 44–45.

If "Pendergast prosperity" fueled jazz, the machine era also grafted an essentially African American art form onto a lifestyle that many African Americans in Kansas City despised. Gambling remained a regular feature of club life, in the cabarets or in the rooms above the clubs. The money that Felix Payne and Piney Brown lavished on musicians and black folks in trouble came largely from their earnings in the numbers racket. The end of prohibition removed some of the illicit taint from alcohol, but drugs, particularly marijuana, proliferated in the jazz quarter. And, whatever its physiological effects, marijuana use stood outside the law. Jazz critic and producer John Hammond found, when he visited Kansas City, that "weed" was readily available to local musicians. At the Reno Club, where Hammond heard the Basie band, "there was a window in the back of the bandstand," he discovered. "People used to just shovel up pot through the back window and it didn't seem to affect the guys at all."[45] A few musicians, like the tragic Charlie Parker, came to depend on the heroin that was so plentiful in Kansas City.

For black women on the periphery of the jazz scene, a very thin membrane separated the entertainment and prostitution industries. Waitresses and dancers in the clubs were allowed, even encouraged, to "turn tricks." In some clubs, explicit sexual performances, costuming, and contortions by waitresses were part of the regular entertainment. The Chesterfield Club, for example, catered to downtown businessmen who were served by black and white waitresses costumed in nothing but artfully shaved pubic hair. Other cabarets, particularly the so-called black clubs, offered drag acts and explicit performances with animals. While the wide-open town defied conventional norms in most respects, in one regard it preserved convention. Except for the Reno Club, which served black and white patrons on opposite sides of a divider, nearly all Kansas City's nightspots catered to one race or the other. Ironically, mixed-race, so-called black and tan socializing, took place almost exclusively in supper clubs in what was considered the "red-neck" precincts of rural Jackson County.[46]

Consequently, white patrons of Kansas City's niteries observed blacks in a single role—as consorts of gambling, narcotics, prostitution, and deviancy. As Burton Peretti notes of jazz clubs throughout the North, "most white

45. Pearson, *Goin' to Kansas City*, 104–6.

46. Russell, *Jazz Style*, 23; Pearson, *Goin' to Kansas City*, 112–3. According to Burton Peretti, jazz was a patriarchal fraternity that restricted black women to the illicit fringes of the music world. The association of jazz with prostitution encouraged even black jazzmen to perceive black women in jazz circles as "commercialized sex objects." Burton W. Peretti, *The Creation of Jazz: Music, Race, and Culture in Urban America*, 35–36, 100–103, 124.

customers gained little appreciation of black culture, since they came to nightclubs to reinforce their preconceptions about 'primitivistic' art and people. . . . In some respects, the 1920s nightclub scene perpetuated the minstrelsy tradition of onstage humiliation and stereotyping."[47] In particular, black performers and servers appeared to act out the same stereotypes that associated African Americans with crime, sexual disorder, and moral laxity. By welding jazz and the rackets together, the Pendergast machine helped equate the practitioners of jazz with the illicit practices that accompanied its performance. In so doing, the machine nearly co-opted an art form that engaged almost all the African American community in Kansas City and energized its cultural life. Few whites could know that another jazz scene existed outside the seamy niteries—that black Kansas Citians sought venues where they might enjoy the music apart from the same vices that whites believed were endemic to them. These venues sacrificed nothing in quality. If anything, black musicians tried harder to perform well for discriminating, all-black audiences. And many of the same artists who headlined the best whites-only clubs also played for black audiences in "respectable" entertainment centers.

Many of the nightclubs that catered to black patrons, like the Hawaiian Garden and Harlem Nite Club, provided the same raunchy atmosphere and criminal connections as the white clubs. Others, however, advertised more decorous surroundings to attract black patrons. The Castle informed readers of the *Call* that it offered "hot music, a great floor show and good eats" in an atmosphere free of "rowdiness, embarrassment or humiliation." The Cherry Blossom, the first venue for Count Basie and his Cherry Blossom Orchestra, often rented its lavishly decorated space to African American social clubs, whose members staged comparatively sedate dance parties to raise funds. During normal business operations, the Cherry Blossom employed a black policeman to keep order, and the Street Hotel Lounge, a high-tone cabaret, operated in that premier hostelry for blacks in Kansas City. Dance halls accommodated still larger crowds of dancers and music lovers. Numerous dance halls were, in fact, taxi-dance emporia in which the management supplied female dance partners at a dime a dance, and the atmosphere was fairly sordid. But the *Call* assured readers that the Silver Slipper wished to attract a more respectable black clientele with its policy. At the Silver Slipper, the house charged a flat entrance fee and did not supply dancing partners.[48] The premier dance hall for black patrons, however, remained the Paseo Dance Hall at Fifteenth and the Paseo. The most prominent social

47. Peretti, *Creation of Jazz,* 196–97.
48. *Kansas City Call,* April 3, 1931, July 29, 1932, February 9, 1934.

clubs, such as the Cheerio Boys, frequently rented the hall for formal club dances, and the hall hosted its own elegant soirees, including the Crystal Ball and the Musicians' Ball. Paseo Dance Hall, capable of hosting three thousand dancers at a time, was also a favorite arena for "battle of the bands" that pitted out-of-town headliners in competition with local organizations under Kirk, Moten, or Harlan Leonard. The dancing couples at the Paseo were so proficient that passersby crowded the windows to watch and learn the latest steps. Hot though the dance pace was, however, the Paseo Dance Hall maintained a respectable atmosphere by employing a floor manager to call the dance set and keep order on the floor.

Outdoor recreation spots that entertained African Americans also provided jazz music for listening and dancing in respectable environments. Except for Liberty Park, which served only blacks, the city's amusement parks normally excluded African American patrons, even though African American jazz performers monopolized local amusement park bandstands. Occasionally, however, such parks rented their facilities to black organizations like the Wayne Minor American Legion Post for daylong family galas that included hot music and dance. The *Idlewild* excursion steamer, which began taking black passengers on Missouri River cruises in 1928, continued to offer the best jazz performers to black excursionists in the 1930s. Promising that passengers would enjoy wholesome, decorous entertainment, the Idlewild's owner reported to the *Call*, "I am going to have policemen on board to keep an eye on things and they will allow no liquor at all." The decision simply made good business sense, owner George Golden contended. "In my previous experience in using this boat, colored excursions were the most orderly of any on the river. I am going to see that that reputation is maintained." After all, he said, "we want this to be a family affair. Perfect order will be maintained so that men can bring along their whole families to enjoy the outing and get away from the hot city weather."[49]

For African American jazz lovers who found even these entertainment spots too unseemly or too expensive, the Vine Street Varieties provided a wholesome milieu for enjoying hot music. During the 1930s, movie theaters like the Lincoln, the Castle, and the New Centre regularly offered musical performances and live stage revues in addition to screening films made for black audiences. In 1938, the Lincoln Theater expanded this audience for jazz by inaugurating the Vine Street Varieties, with singers, dancers, comedians, and bands performing every Saturday night from its stage. Given its policy of open auditions, the Varieties provided a showcase for new local

49. *Kansas City Call*, July 29, 1932.

talent, including teen-aged performers from Lincoln High, as well as seasoned veterans like Count Basie and singer Julia Lee. The Varieties became an entertainment staple within the black community. Its environment suited families and courting couples alike, while weekly broadcasts from the stage by radio station WHB reached even stay-at-home jazz fans.[50]

The popularity of entertainment outlets like the Vine Street Varieties demonstrated great demand in the African American community for safe and decent surroundings in which to enjoy its own music. And jazz was "its own." A passion for swing cut across class lines, engaging even the *Kansas City Call,* that staid bastion of middle-class rectitude. The *Call* reported in great detail on the engagements, the triumphs, and the disappointments of Kansas City's favorite black musicians, and it trumpeted their appearances, not only in the clubs that advertised in the *Call,* but also in the clubs and dance halls whose managers did not buy the *Call*'s advertising space and whose tables did not seat the *Call*'s black readership. Likewise, the most select of the city's black social clubs made jazz the focal attraction of their gala affairs. The proprietors who catered to this audience understood both their clientele and the racialized social structure that made it difficult for that clientele to find suitable places to enjoy jazz. In fact, the inducements those proprietors advertised were exact counterpoints to the stereotypes that underlay white racism in Kansas City. Because black women were deemed sexually accessible, proprietors advertised a "no whites allowed" policy to insure black women customers against the insults and indignities of amorous white revelers, who might treat them as fair game for sexual advances. If an inverted justice system failed to protect blacks from physical assault, if vice racketeering and police laxity encouraged knifing and shooting scrapes among blacks, other proprietors hired their own police to protect their black customers from black and white assailants. If moral quarantine allowed gambling, narcotics, and prostitution to proliferate at the center of the black community, the Lincoln Theater provided maximum safety from the mean streets by broadcasting jazz into the secure environs of the home. This jazz scene—decent, peaceable, and continent—embodied what Roy Rosenzwieg calls an "alternative culture."[51] Here, African Americans acted out and acted upon a set of values opposite to those expected and demanded of them by the dominant culture. Unfortunately, by capturing jazz for its own ends, the Pendergast regime made it more difficult both for African Americans to

---

50. *Kansas City Call,* May 1, 1931, April 29, 1938, August 19, 1938, March 3, 1939.
51. Roy Rosenzweig, *Eight Hours for What We Will: Workers and Leisure in an Industrial City, 1870–1920,* 64.

maintain an alternative jazz milieu and for whites to recognize that such an alternative culture existed.

■ ■ Pendergast's Eclipse

In the end, events outside the black community gave the victory to the "purity" faction when Tom Pendergast's fiefdom collapsed, providing openings for race men to reassert their claims to speak for black Kansas City. After Tom Pendergast and several of his key personnel received federal sentences for income tax evasion in 1939, investigations of city administration unfolded enough evidence of graft and mismanagement of city affairs to sweep a Citizen's Reform ticket into office in 1940. Seeing a chance to capitalize, race men organized the Non-Partisan Citizens Movement in June 1939. The movement's platform was a preview of the political agenda activist black leaders would pursue in the 1940s. It called for equitable employment based on merit in city and county positions, proposed public housing projects for blacks, demanded an end to racial discrimination in tax-supported facilities, and urged the election of blacks to the city council.[52]

Looking back on the Pendergast years in 1950, attorney and NAACP chairman Carl Johnson recalled that "we were crippled politically" by the Pendergast machine. In Johnson's view, the machine stifled political independence among blacks and raised up "mere stand-ins" instead of real black leaders.[53] And Johnson might have laid other indictments upon the Pendergast organization, for the mass of black voters who cast their lot with the machine were no more successful than the race men and race women in transforming the ways in which whites perceived blacks or acted upon those perceptions to shape the social context in which both races resided. In the end, the machine reinforced more racial constructs than it eroded.

■ ■ Experiments in Activism

African Americans took other collective actions besides ballot casting and boycotting in the years between the wars. During the 1930s, various small

52. *Kansas City Call*, March 17, 1939, March 31, 1939; William M. Reddig, *Tom's Town: Kansas City and the Pendergast Legend*, 311–22; Haskell and Fowler, *City of the Future*, 132–34; Dorsett, *Pendergast Machine*, 129–37. "Citizens Movement Platform," reproduced in *Kansas City Call*, June 9, 1939.
53. Young and Young, *Your Kansas City and Mine*, 27.

groups of black Kansas Citians engaged in alternative forms of activism that helped generate a more militant approach to race issues. The alternatives to machine partisanship that emerged during the Pendergast years helped energize a confrontational impulse that burgeoned in the war and postwar years, when black Kansas City would adopt the tactics of direct action both to challenge segregation and to forge a new understanding of race among some whites. For example, the Kansas City Division 308 of the Universal Negro Improvement Association (UNIA), founded by Winston Holmes in 1922, received frequent visits from Marcus Garvey during the 1920s. Despite Garvey's exile, a faithful remnant of Garveyites apparently persevered in Kansas City through the 1930s. A smaller group, called the "Red Fez" or "red cap" cult by the *Call,* followed their prophet and leader Mohammed Bey in Kansas City, Missouri, and Kansas City, Kansas, practicing a vaguely Islamic and race-conscious religion. While neither the Red Fez nor UNIA attracted large followings (Bey was estimated to have just fifty followers in 1936), they introduced at least some of the black underclass to nationalist or radical ways of thinking about themselves and their place in a white-dominated society. Other black Kansas Citians had their exposure to radicalism from the American Communist Party. Unemployed blacks made up a disproportionate number of the marchers in a communist demonstration against unemployment in Kansas City in 1931, and party organizers and members of the Young Communist League continued to speak in the black community, including black party member Abner Berry and nationally known black communist organizer Angelo Herndon.[54] If the Communist Party did not win many committed party members, its protests may at least have encouraged working-class blacks to think about radical changes that the system of partisan politics dared not address.

The black labor movement mobilized a larger number of ordinary men and women. Among the most stalwart were the local members of the Brotherhood of Sleeping Car Porters. In fact, Kansas City's was one of the first divisions to be organized following the Brotherhood's founding in 1925. By early 1927, the Brotherhood's local division had enrolled 301 out of the 386 porters in greater Kansas City. Throughout the late 1920s and the 1930s, A. Philip Randolph visited Kansas City to speak and to organize, including an appearance before the first Labor Conference in Kansas City in 1928. Local Brotherhood members needed every scrap of encouragement

54. *Kansas City Call,* March 11, 1922, July 15, 1922, October 12, 1923, April 7, 1939, March 14, 1941, October 16, 1936, March 6, 1931, February 10, 1933, September 28, 1934.

Randolph could provide, for Kansas City was an important railroad nexus, and the Pullman Company, owner of the sleeping cars and thus the porters' employer, aimed to crush the local Brotherhood. In 1926, Randolph sent his assistant general organizer, Ashley L. Totten, to head the Kansas City division. Tensions mounted after the Pullman Company withdrew from negotiations before a federal mediation board in 1928. Randolph secured a strike vote to force resumption of mediation, and Totten stashed a small armory of weapons in his Kansas City offices to repel strikebreakers. Randolph called off the strike, but Brotherhood members agreed that Kansas City was one of only three divisions where the strike might have succeeded. Consequently, the intimidation continued. In 1929, Totten was clubbed and seriously injured on a street near his headquarters in the Lincoln Building. Earlier, porters had warned the union leader about Pullman Company officials' statement that "Totten must be gotten out of the way." Testimony in the trials of Totten's two assailants failed to prove that they had acted on company orders, but one witness swore that the assailants were promised police protection if they carried out the assault.[55]

Many of the Brotherhood's locals shut down when the union failed to win tangible gains in the middle of a depression, but the Kansas City division remained in operation. Meanwhile, the Pullman Company used subtler means to break the Brotherhood in Kansas City, including browbeating, threats, and dismissals for porters and maids who refused to forsake the Brotherhood to join a company union. The company also shifted Pullman cars off the rail lines into Kansas City and routed them through other rail centers where the Brotherhood had a weaker hold. When the Brotherhood sought a federal injunction against the company union in 1931, accounts of the extreme intimidation porters had experienced in Kansas City formed a significant part of its case. Finally, in 1934, Congress included sleeping-car workers among the beneficiaries of an amendment to the Railway Labor Act that banned company unions. A year later, the *Call* triumphantly announced the end to a ten-year battle in Kansas City as Pullman porters voted by an overwhelming margin for the Brotherhood of Sleeping Car Porters to represent them.[56]

Other unions also stirred aggressive action by black workers. In September 1938, the CIO's United Packing House Workers of America staged a sit-

55. Jervis Anderson, *A. Philip Randolph: A Biographical Portrait*, 168–69, 153, 182, 196–206; *Kansas City Call*, November 5, 1926, April 19, 1929, July 19, 1929. Totten's injuries were so severe that Randolph recalled him from Kansas City to headquarters in New York, where he made Totten national secretary-treasurer of the Brotherhood.

56. Anderson, *Randolph*, 205, 218; *Kansas City Call*, June 6, 1930, July 3, 1931, November 14, 1930, July 5, 1935.

down strike at the local Armour plant because six members were docked pay for the time they had spent in stating a grievance before the plant's grievance committee. Half the eighteen hundred members participating in the strike were black, as were five of the six workers who had been docked for using the grievance procedure. Equally significant were the wildcat actions that black workers undertook with little or no organizational support, like the walkout of black busboys and dishwashers that left a Fred Harvey restaurant heaped with unwashed plates and cutlery until management rehired a busboy it had unjustly fired.[57] For several years after, this incident was recounted in the *Call* as an example of assertive racial solidarity.

Nor did Kansas City's race men and race women entirely abandon their own tactics of race activism in the Pendergast years. In particular, they sought legislative and judicial remedies for segregation. The most important of these efforts enlisted black Kansas Citians' support for the Lloyd Gaines suit. After Gaines, a young St. Louis resident, was denied admission to the University of Missouri law school on the basis of his race, the U.S. Supreme Court ruled in 1938 that the University of Missouri must admit Gaines to its existing law school or provide equal facilities to black law students. University curators and state legislators chose the latter option, though with a distorted notion of what constituted "equal" facilities. The state legislature voted in 1939 to provide a law school for black students in an abandoned beauty college, with an appropriation totaling $200,000. Unfortunately, Lloyd Gaines never enrolled in that or any school. In March 1939, Gaines spoke to an audience of some one thousand African Americans in Kansas City to thank them for their support of his suit and to assure them that he would enter the law school in the fall. Soon after, Gaines disappeared. By October, a nationwide search involving the NAACP and local black newspapers still had not located the young man, and the *Call* voiced what many had concluded: that Lloyd Gaines had been the victim of foul play. Indeed, Gaines's fate was never determined.[58]

Gaines's probable murder only emboldened certain African Americans in Kansas City. A month prior to Gaines's Kansas City speech, Lucile Bluford

57. *Kansas City Call,* September 6, 1938, June 18, 1937. The strike was soon ended when Armour agreed to arbitration.

58. Daniel T. Kelleher, "The Case of Lloyd Lionel Gaines: The Demise of the Separate but Equal Doctrine," 262–71; Lucile Bluford, "The Lloyd Gaines Story," 242–46. See also, *Kansas City Call,* January 31, 1936, April 13, 1936, December 10, 1937, December 16, 1938, March 10, 1939, April 21, 1939, May 5, 1939, August 18, 1939, March 3, 1939, October 13, 1939, October 20, 1939, October 27, 1939.

was prevented from enrolling in the University of Missouri's graduate school of journalism. Bluford, an honors graduate of the journalism school of the University of Kansas, had been a reporter for the *Call* since her graduation in 1932, and in 1937, she became that paper's news editor. On the basis of her transcript alone, the University of Missouri had accepted her application for admission to the graduate school. When Bluford tried to enroll, however, the registrar discovered that she was an African American and refused to enroll her on the grounds that the Gaines case had not been completely settled. Regardless of Gaines's disappearance and the perils it implied, Bluford renewed her application and was denied admittance. In October, the NAACP's chief counsel, Charles Houston, who had argued the Gaines case before the Supreme Court, came to Kansas City to announce that he would file suit on Bluford's behalf.[59] For more than a decade, Bluford and her supporters would battle to make segregated schooling prohibitively expensive for the state of Missouri by demanding truly equal facilities for higher education.

In the course of reporting these events, C. A. Franklin, the spokesman for race men and women in Kansas City, began to question some fundamental assumptions about how American society worked and to entertain new ideas about how to change that society. Unlike many black publishers, Franklin always showed a degree of respect for militant movements that, like UNIA and the Brotherhood of Sleeping Car Porters, involved largely working-class blacks. Nothing if not eclectic, the *Call*'s editor also examined "the Ghandi [*sic*] program of non-violence and non-cooperation." After all, he asked his readers, "Are not Negroes in much the same position in America as the Indians are in their own country under Britain?" Even a protest of Ten Year Plan expenditures seemed a potent demonstration of Gandhian tactics, for "the quiet dignity of the Negro delegation partook of the Ghandi spirit. . . . It is not the threat which impresses, but the good cause. Nothing can do more to show that a cause is good than the earnestness and dignity of its supporters." The Rev. Joseph Gomez, pastor of prestigious Allen Chapel A.M.E., apparently shared Franklin's admiration for Gandhi, for he gave a series of lectures to inform black audiences about Gandhi's basic tenets. Understanding those principles was vital, Gomez believed, because "the acceptance of the Western Civilization of Gandhi's teachings will mean the elimination of all class

59. "Deposition of Lucile Bluford," 112–15, Box 102, Benson Papers; Diane E. Loupe, "Storming and Defending the Color Barrier at the University of Missouri School of Journalism: The Lucile Bluford Case," BA4.FRA12, C. A. Franklin Collection, Black Archives of Mid-America; *Kansas City Call*, February 3, 1939, October 13, 1939.

and color prejudice." Meanwhile, Franklin declared, "there is a lesson to be learned from India if we have eyes to see."[60]

■ ■ Conclusion

Franklin's optimism seemed badly misplaced. Black Kansas Citians had found a variety of ways to challenge racism in the 1920s and 1930s. So far, the most tangible result of all that activism was that whites simply invented more illusionist's tricks to conceal racialism. Even the Pendergast machine retarded the development of an autonomous black leadership and cemented racial stereotypes—demonstrating that friends can be more dangerous than enemies. Still, new ways of thinking about and acting on race issues simmered in the African American community during the 1920s and 1930s. Two years after Pendergast's fall, black Kansas City would begin to combine these tentative ideas, devising strategies of direct action peculiarly suited to the character of race relations in Kansas City—tactics that provided a growth medium for the emergence of new conceptions about race among a critical minority of white Kansas Citians.

60. *Kansas City Call*, February 13, 1931, January 22, 1932, March 20, 1931. Franklin used various spellings of Gandhi's name, which I have reproduced as Franklin spelled them in each quotation.

7

"Truth Is Fatal"

The Civil Rights Activists, Black and White

■ ■ ■

EARLY IN THE WAR YEARS, when Alvin Brooks was ten or eleven years old, he and his buddies were looking forward to a treat. His playmates, the sons of the white families who were the Brookses' nearest neighbors, had told Alvin about the special pleasures of sitting at a soda fountain sipping a cherry Coke. The real satisfaction, the boys promised, came in the preliminaries—scrunching the paper wrapper down to the end of a drinking straw and blowing the wrapper like a bazooka shell across the drugstore. The boys agreed that, as soon as each had a nickel to spend, they would head for their local pharmacy. Alvin knew the drugstore in question and its druggist. Like his family's home, the store was located among the white-occupied residences that fringed a black enclave in Leeds-Dunbar, a residential and industrial district on Kansas City's eastern boundary. Alvin's adoptive father, Cluster Brooks, hauled the store's trash when his work day as a railroad employee ended, and Alvin often helped his father sort the store's discards and scour out its refuse containers. On the day the boys finally took their seats at the store's soda counter, the pharmacist's son joked with Alvin and his buddies while he served them their Cokes and laughed as they fired off their paper missiles. But before Alvin could put his straw in his Coke, the pharmacist bowled up to the counter, poured Alvin's drink from its glass into a paper cup, and ordered the boy to stand by the door while he drank it. The youngster was horrified. Assuming that he had done something to anger the druggist, he and his friends pleaded with the man not to tell Alvin's father. The druggist simply growled that he would throw Alvin out if he did not stop fussing. Confused, the boys left.

Alvin swore his friends not to tell his mother that he was in trouble with the pharmacist, but the story tumbled out as soon as the youngsters reached the Brooks home. Mrs. Brooks sat the boys down and explained to them that race was the reason for the druggist's behavior and that Alvin had experienced something called race discrimination. While the boys stumbled over the pronunciation of the unfamiliar phrase, Mrs. Brooks made them promise to say nothing of the incident to Alvin's father. That promise lasted no longer than the first. After hearing the boys' story, Mr. Brooks picked up his gun, put Alvin in the trash truck, and drove to the drugstore. Parking the truck so that it blocked the store's entry, Cluster Brooks confronted the pharmacist, gun in hand. He was through hauling the store's rubbish, Brooks told the druggist, and, if the store owner showed any future disrespect to a member of the Brooks family, the elder Brooks promised to return with his gun. Alvin's father then refused to leave the store until the pharmacist addressed him as Mr. Cluster Brooks.[1]

A searing experience for its young participants, this social drama exemplified race relations in Kansas City at midcentury. Numerous such experiences, and his study of sociology, would make of Alvin Brooks a police officer, civil rights activist, and dogged combatant of inner-city crime. But at age ten, Alvin resembled many of his older black contemporaries in having yet to articulate the ways in which race structured his community or determined his place in the social structure. Youthful naïveté explained his buddies' ignorance, yet many of the boys' white elders enjoyed a similar state of fabricated innocence. Racialism wore such effective disguises that whites could deny its existence even while they enjoyed its supposed benefits. The druggist's behavior helped to induce this state of artificial innocence. In the very act of drawing the color line, he refused to identify his actions as race discrimination or to take any personal responsibility for them or for their consequences. Countless other proprietors, public servants, and community leaders practiced the same deceits. It often fell to individuals like Cluster Brooks to decide how much insult they would accept and what steps they would take on their own to redress an offense that appeared more personal than collective.

During and after the Second World War, however, more African Americans were inclined to take collective, direct action to combat racial exclusion.

1. Alvin Brooks, interview with author, October 25, 1993. Alvin Brooks served as a Kansas City police officer between 1954 and 1964. In 1964, he joined CORE and became the local chapter's chairman. Later, he founded the Ad Hoc Group Against Crime, a nationally recognized coalition that marshals grassroots efforts to reform the justice system, combat drug use and street crime, and provide alternative role models for inner-city youth. In 1999, he was elected to the city council of Kansas City, Missouri, and was appointed Mayor Pro-Tem.

Repeatedly, they aimed their protests, demonstrations, and court battles at the bulwark of misdirection and mythology that protected racialism. In the process, black activism helped energize a new breed of white race liberals in the interwar years—by challenging them to act out their principles and by providing a context in which they could act. From the interracial partnerships thus forged emerged a new conceptualization of race and of race relations among a minority of white Kansas Citians. Guided by an integrationist ethos, these liberals reversed the standard formulation among white Kansas Citians, which held that racial separation was a critical ingredient for making the community a peaceable, secure, and wholesome place. Instead, white integrationists proposed that racial separation jeopardized communal peace and safety by corrupting individual character. Through integration, they sought to uplift community and transform human personality. Black activism and black and white integrationists managed to erase color lines in some public accommodations in the postwar period and laid the groundwork for further desegregation of public accommodations after 1958. More important, they forged a new way of thinking about race and identity

■ ■ The War on Two Fronts

In the 1920s and 1930s, fragments of the black community experimented with confrontational tactics or contemplated Gandhian noncooperation to racialism. But the outbreak of war in Europe, and the ensuing scramble among American manufacturers to supply democracy's arsenals, provided the first real test of mass demonstration tactics by large numbers of black Kansas Citians. By late 1940, manufacturers and public officials, in Kansas City as elsewhere, were gearing up to produce the weaponry, munitions, and war matériel their president had promised to help supply the Allied war effort in Europe. Initially, it appeared that African Americans were to be excluded from most of the economic benefits of defense production in Kansas City. The Kansas City, Missouri, School District, which launched an emergency program of manual arts instruction to train defense workers, refused to admit black trainees until persuaded by pressure from the African American community. According to the *Call*, state employment bureaus in Kansas and Missouri tacitly refused to send blacks to fill requisitions by defense contractors, and it took a mass protest rally to force the hiring of twenty-five black carpenters from Kansas City for construction work at Fort Riley, Kansas.[2]

2. *Kansas City Call*, January 1, 1941, February 28, 1941, March 7, 1941.

But for underemployed workers, black or white, the aircraft industry held the most promise for good-paying jobs on the factory line. In March 1941, contractors began constructing an enormous bomber plant in Fairfax, a riverside industrial district in Kansas City, Kansas. Built at federal expense, the plant was to be operated by North American Aviation, a California-based subsidiary of General Motors, for production of medium-range Mitchell bombers. The plant projected that it would eventually employ as many as ten thousand at the Kansas City site. Anxious to secure this rich trove of defense jobs, Mayor Don McCombs of Kansas City, Kansas, assured black voters— who made up 20 percent of his electorate—that North American intended to hire blacks on the line. Consequently, the city's voters approved a bond issue allowing the city to purchase Fairfax airport for North American's use in testing its bombers.[3]

McCombs came to regret his easy assurances. Under a banner headline announcing "NAZISM IN KANSAS CITY," the *Call* informed readers in March that North American planned to hire blacks only as janitors. In answer to a query from the *Kansas City Star*, North American's president, James H. Kindelberger, had stated by telephone that his firm would refuse to employ blacks on the factory line, regardless of their skills or training. Within hours of the *Star*'s publication of his remarks, black Kansas Citians fired off telegrams and letters of protest to Washington. Among those whose comments accompanied the *Call*'s article, mail carrier Maurice Howard summed up the tenor of the protest with the suggestion that "such a statement could be expected from a man so similar to Mr. Hitler and his subordinates."[4]

Because African Americans were being turned away from defense plant gates throughout the country, a Senate subcommittee was preparing hearings on Senate Resolution 75, a resolution providing for thorough investigation of racial discrimination in defense, which Senator Arthur Capper of Kansas had helped sponsor and which the NAACP was pushing. But Kindelberger's bald candor and the firestorm of protest it ignited among Kansas Citians provided NAACP secretary Walter White a means to dramatize the need for an investigation. White condemned North American's president for accepting profits and a salary that black taxpayers helped to underwrite, and he demanded that Kindelberger be subpoenaed to testify before the Senate subcommittee. Meanwhile, Kansas Congressman U. S. Guyer took to the House floor citing North American's "gross discrimination" as reason enough to pass House Resolution 3394 making it unlawful for recipients of

3. *Ibid.*, March 21, 1941.
4. *Ibid.*; *Kansas City Star*, March 17, 1941.

federal funds to discriminate in hiring or dispensation of benefits on the basis of race. In Topeka, the Kansas House passed its own resolution condemning North American's hiring policy and sent the resolution to the White House.[5]

Unwilling to rely wholly on others to speak for them, African Americans in Kansas City looked for some way in which to express their indignation over Kindelberger's decision. A. Philip Randolph's March On Washington Movement (MOWM) suggested a forum. In January 1941, Randolph had registered his dissatisfaction with the Roosevelt administration's attempts to sidestep an outright ban on race discrimination in defense. That month, he announced a pilgrimage to the capital by African Americans demanding their right to "work and fight." Randolph wrote, "Our demand would be simple, single, and central. Namely: jobs in National Defense and placement as soldiers and officers of all ranks we are qualified for in the armed forces."[6] If that central demand were not met in reasonable time, Randolph promised, ten thousand blacks would fill the streets of the nation's capital on July 1, 1941. Still, President Roosevelt refused to meet with a national conference on Negro Participation in National Defense in March 1941. On March 15, two days before Kindelberger's statement, the president included in a fireside chat a somewhat mild admonition that, if black Americans were to have no stake in their country's defense, "then the effort is not one which can command their full loyalty and unstinted support."[7] Thus far, Roosevelt refused to use his executive powers to guarantee that African Americans would have such a stake or to ground their full inclusion in defense on any but self-serving appeals to national interests in wartime.

Randolph had warm ties to the black communities in the two Kansas Cities and could expect a receptive hearing of his proposal there. In a Kansas City speech in 1943, Randolph would credit the *Call* as one of the few black newspapers to have covered his union organizing efforts fairly and would acknowledge Rev. D. A. Holmes as the only pastor in the midwest to have permitted him the use of a pulpit. Moreover, the *Call* joined the vast majority of black presses in 1941 in supporting his call for a March On Washington. Thus, a mass local protest paralleling MOWM appeared an effective way by which to make Kansas City's black voices heard. On March 28, the *Call* urged readers to assemble in unprecedented numbers at a protest rally

5. Letter of Arthur Capper to Walter White, December 21, 1940, and Letter of Walter White to Arthur Capper, January 2, 1941, Group II:A334, NAACP Papers, LOC; *Kansas City Call*, March 28, 1941.

6. *Kansas City Call*, January 31, 1941.

7. Quoted in the *Kansas City Call*, April 4, 1941. Neil A. Wynn, *The Afro-American and the Second World War*, 43.

planned by NAACP chapters of the two Kansas Cities for the coming Sunday afternoon. "Any ordinary attendance at that meeting," the *Call* warned, "will be taken to mean that Negroes don't care."[8]

In fact, an audience estimated between thirty-five hundred and five thousand black men and women from Greater Kansas City turned out for the rally at Memorial Hall in Kansas City, Kansas, on March 30, 1941. As participant Lucile Bluford recalled, "On that Sunday you could see people walking down there, going in cars, trucks, streetcars, every kind of way there, and when the time came the arena was full of people." Dorothy Davis Johnson believed "that's probably the largest gathering of people protesting something that has occurred in my lifetime." By voice vote, the assemblage passed a resolution demanding cancellation of North American's defense contract, and it called for delegates to go to Washington to meet with the White House and with Congressional panels. Among the several speakers at the rally were Dr. A. Porter Davis, who thundered at the gathering to "rise up and fight now or hold your peace forever." Catcalls for Mayor McCombs turned to cheers after the mayor read an angry letter he had sent to Kindelberger, chastising him for misleading the mayor and black voters about his hiring policies and appealing to the executive to change those policies.[9]

Reaction to the meeting was swift on the Kansas side, where city commissioners in Kansas City, Kansas, approved a resolution banning discrimination against black workers at the Fairfax bomber plant, and the packinghouse local of the CIO sent a delegation to Washington to register its own protest. Both houses of the Kansas state legislature passed unanimously a bill making it unlawful for labor unions in Kansas to exclude blacks from membership. And a wire service article published in the *Call* reported that the Office of Production Management, the federal agency responsible for mobilizing

8. *Kansas City Call*, March 28, 1941, February 26, 1943.

9. A. Porter Davis, "Mass Meeting," Group II:C99, Branch File, NAAP Papers, LOC; "Deposition of Lucile Bluford," 117, Box 102, Benson Papers; Dorothy Davis Johnson, interview with author, October 7, 1991; *Kansas City Call*, April 4, 1941. In several accounts, participants have recalled the rally as taking place in 1942 at Municipal Auditorium in Kansas City, Missouri. The rally calling for employment of black carpenters at Fort Riley took place there in 1940, and a mass meeting of black defense workers gathered in 1942 to discuss how to maintain wartime gains in employment. Participants' recollections may have combined the three events. Of the three, the gathering in Kansas City, Kansas, in 1941 was by far the most significant for its far-reaching effects, however. Despite the unprecedented size of this protest gathering, the white press gave it little attention. The *Star* made no mention of it, the *Times* noted it in a small article on the inside pages, and the *Journal* covered it in a small regular column written by Leona Pouncey called "Negro News." None of the white dailies took notice of the protest or its origins on their op-ed pages.

defense production, had been "bombarded" with letters, telegrams, and telephone calls from Kansas Citians demanding action against North American. Accordingly, the House Committee on Military Affairs called William S. Knudson, chief of the Office of Production Management (OPM), to report to the committee on what action he planned in response to Kindelberger's statement to the *Star*. As former head of General Motors, North American's parent company, Knudsen's interests were somewhat suspect, but he assured the committee that neither he nor General Motors stood to gain by denying work to blacks. On the basis of a private meeting with Kindelberger, Knudsen told committee members, he was certain that blacks would receive equal consideration for training at the Fairfax plant.[10]

Sidney Hillman, OPM's co-director, took a slightly bolder step in reaction to complaints from Greater Kansas City and elsewhere. On April 11, he issued what became known as the "Hillman letter" to the country's defense contractors. In it, OPM cited reports that some contractors failed to hire "qualified and available Negro workers." "Such practices," the letter lamented, "are extremely wasteful of our human resources and prevent a total effort for national defense." Consequently, "all holders of defense contracts are urged to examine their employment and training policies at once to determine whether or not those policies make ample provision for the full utilization of Negro workers." This was hardly a stirring call for racial justice on its own merits, and OPM's admonition contained no enforcement provisions, but the Hillman letter represented the first break in the administration's previously obdurate refusal to intervene at all in racial hiring practices.[11]

In mid-May, the Kansas City delegation of protestors reached Washington to find Senate Resolution 75 bottled up in committee. The delegation left the capital with nothing more than vague assurances from committee members and OPM officials that everything practicable was being done to open defense employment to blacks. Worse, the *Call* reported, Hillman had received commitments from aircraft manufacturers to hire and train some twelve hundred black workers but thus far had received no answer whatsoever to his letter from J. H. Kindelberger. That same month, Randolph condemned the "runaround" with a summons to stage "an 'all-out' thundering march on Washington, ending in a monster and huge demonstration

---

10. *Kansas City Call*, April 11, 1941, April 18, 1941.
11. Wynn, *Second World War*, 43; Richard Polenberg, *War and Society: The United States, 1941–1945*, 103. Apparently, public officials from Missouri reserved comment, as no reaction from them was reported in the *Call*.

at Lincoln's monument [that] will shake up white America."[12] By mobilizing "mass power," Randolph hoped to secure Roosevelt's executive order abolishing discrimination in all federal departments, including the armed forces and defense industries.

Still, Roosevelt temporized, arguing that a march that Randolph now promised to be fifty thousand strong would "stir up race hatred and slow up progress." Other close advisors to the president repeated the timeworn caution that the march might spark a race riot. Only in mid-June, thanks in part to Eleanor Roosevelt's intercession, did the president unbend enough to issue his first public statement supporting the principles of the Hillman letter. FDR now joined Hillman in decrying discrimination—but only as a waste of manpower rather than as a civil inequity. MOWM supporters were far from satisfied, and Randolph refused to call off the July 1 march. When the president finally met with Randolph and other delegates on June 18, his chief concern was determining whether the threatened demonstration was a bluff—a suspicion Walter White scotched with an unequivocal promise of 100,000 marchers. Convinced, Roosevelt joined Randolph in hammering out an agreement that omitted desegregation of the military. On June 25, 1941, the president issued Executive Order 8802 banning racial discrimination in employment by defense contractors.[13]

Histories of the March On Washington Movement omit to mention the mass rally by the two Kansas Cities. That mass action, and the protests surrounding it, were nonetheless significant, for the Hillman letter to Kindelberger represented the first breach in the administration's policy of studied indifference to discrimination. Because the tempest of protest that the statement engendered in Greater Kansas City helped considerably to publicize Kindelberger's remarks, Hillman's letter was, in large measure, a product of black Kansas Citians' outrage and the pressure it exerted on the White House and Capitol Hill. More important, the final stumbling block to an executive order was Roosevelt's doubt that MOWM really could muster a massive turnout of demonstrators. What convinced the president and his advisors that 100,000 marchers were a real possibility was not Walter White's unflinching gaze as he issued the promise, but eventual recognition by the White House that a deep disaffection pervaded the African American com-

12. Quoted from Randolph's "Call to Negro America," printed in the *Kansas City Call*, May 9, 1941.

13. Herbert Garfinkel, *When Negroes March: The March on Washington Movement in the Organizational Politics for FEPC*, 54; Polenberg, *War and Society*, 105; Wynn, *Second World War*, 45; Polenberg, *War and Society*, 104; *Kansas City Call*, June 20, 1941, May 2, 1941, May 23, 1941.

munity, which MOWM had galvanized into an enthusiastic and broad-based expression of "mass power." The incidence of local March On Washington demonstrations helped immeasurably to convince White House staff that both the anger and MOWM's threat were genuine. Given that the Greater Kansas City protest meeting was significantly larger than others that MOWM historians cite, and that it sparked action from Kansas officialdom, local participants are justified in recalling their demonstration as a progenitor of the historic presidential order. "We were hoping to make it so big that 'protest' would mean something—which it did," Dorothy Davis Johnson concludes. "We later realized that it probably had more effect on people than we thought."[14]

Locally, MOWM and the Kansas City demonstration had other far-reaching effects. After their initial success with mass demonstration, middle-class leaders who had called the rally began to retreat from Randolph's militant tactics. C. A. Franklin, for example, cautioned against further direct actions to extort concessions from whites. African Americans were better advised to earn respect by waging a Double V campaign—fighting to defeat racist totalitarianism abroad so as to discredit racism at home. Yet, segments of the black working class in Kansas City displayed a continuing commitment to Randolph's methods. Throughout the war, they staged a sequence of ad hoc, direct-action protests entirely independent of middle-class leadership. In May 1943, for example, forty black employees of a local garment company stopped work for one day to protest the firing of black machine operators. A month later, eight black employees of an Army mess hall in Kansas City walked off the job after two black soldiers were denied service there. In March 1945, the African American women who operated elevators in the Jackson County Courthouse struck to protest the beating of a black woman by county deputies.[15] The most significant of the wildcat direct actions, however, occurred at the Pratt-Whitney aircraft engine plant in July 1944.

Circumstances at Pratt-Whitney reflected a pattern common among Kansas City employers. Based on a survey of employers and unions done in 1940, the Urban League of Kansas City found that a cluster of "stock objections" underlay blacks' exclusion from many occupations and workplaces.

14. Dorothy Davis Johnson, interview. The largest local demonstration Garfinkel cites attracted one thousand demonstrators for a parade in Chicago. Garfinkel, *When Negroes March*, 54–57; Paula F. Pfeffer, *A. Philip Randolph, Pioneer of the Civil Rights Movement*, 47;
15. *Kansas City Call*, May 14, 1943, June 4, 1943, March 16, 1945, October 17, 1941, January 23, 1942, May 22, 1942. For the reaction of bourgeois blacks to MOWM, see Lee Finkle, *Forum for Protest: The Black Press during World War II*, 89–90, 123. Wynn, *Second World War*, 47; Polenberg, *War and Society*, 102.

Employers claimed that they would hire blacks if they had only their own preferences to consider, but they expected that union labor would object or that the "Southern consciousness" of many of their white employees would lead to friction on the factory floor. Should they hire blacks, employers worried, they would have the expense of installing separate toilets and drinking fountains because they assumed that white workers would not agree to share facilities. Personnel managers denied being prejudiced themselves but feared that higher officials of their companies would object to hiring blacks. Union officials believed there was no point in recruiting black members because employers would not hire them, and the union rank and file would be unlikely to admit them to membership. In fact, the Urban League pointed out, these presumptions about the bigotry of others flourished in workplaces where they had never been put to the test. In workplaces where racially mixed crews had been tried, black and white workers managed to share the shop floor and the toilet facilities without friction.[16]

Confirming the Urban League's findings, thirteen hundred African Americans employed at Pratt-Whitney discovered in 1944 that their antagonists came from the upper echelons, not from the factory line. While the plant had separate toilets for blacks and whites, no other facilities in the plant were segregated, and relations between the races were described by black workers as "harmonious." Consequently, black employees were shocked to find on coming to work one morning that "whites only" and "colored only" signs had been posted at the plants' six cafeterias. Within an hour, most blacks on the first shift had left their work, and the majority on the second and third shifts walked off the job as soon as they learned of the Jim Crow cafeterias. A conference with management revealed that the signs had been posted at the request of local officials of the International Association of Machinists, which had won the right to bargain for Pratt-Whitney's workers in a recent election. The striking black workers were mystified, since neither they nor the union officials were aware of any specific objections to shared cafeterias from the white workers.[17]

Once the spontaneous job action was under way, however, Pratt-Whitney's black employees registered other complaints against management. Many had been turned down for promotion, while whites with less training and seniority were promoted steadily. Others, including graduates of Pratt-Whitney's own training school, reported that foremen still assigned them to the lowest level, least desirable jobs and failed to replace their worn or

16. Urban League of Kansas City, "The Negro Worker of Kansas City," July 1940.
17. *Kansas City Call*, June 30, 1944.

outmoded machines. The verbal conflicts black workers reported almost always involved foremen instead of line workers. But the Jim Crow cafeterias drew the most fire. Said a teenaged machinist from Tupelo, Mississippi, "When I was down in Mississippi, I ran into the same thing and that is why I left the rotten place. . . . Eighteen years of Jim-Crow is enough for me." A returned veteran asserted, "I served 18 months in the U.S. Army to uphold the high ideals of democracy. But I returned to civilian life to find that we colored people have still a greater fight on this side to gain equal rights and all that goes with them. . . . If we allow ourselves to eat in these jim-crow cafeterias, we show the managers that we approve of jim-crow. And then, further attempts will be made to exclude and deprive us of rights and opportunities that are justly ours." Two young women objected to segregation because "it is implied that there is a great difference between the races—a difference in the quality of the individual" that could be used to justify still other distinctions in opportunities and wages. Nearly in tears, the mother of two sons in uniform pointed out that there was "no segregation of bullets being shelled on our boys overseas."[18] The black workers soon called off their strike so as not to delay war production, but while Pratt-Whitney's cafeterias remained segregated, only about two hundred black workers would use them. More important, segments of the African American working class had indicated a willingness to engage in direct action wherever their treatment contrasted most flagrantly with the principles their country supposedly fought to uphold.

■ ■ Experiments in Direct Action and Interracialism

By the time of the Pratt-Whitney strike, even some of Franklin's middle-class readers were ready to adopt direct action tactics and adapt them to suit the contours of racialism in Kansas City. The catalyst was a performance by Paul Robeson at Kansas City's Municipal Auditorium in February 1942. Robeson had sworn that he would never perform before a segregated audience, and he had been promised that his audience in Kansas City would be integrated. During intermission, Lucile Bluford visited Robeson backstage and asked him why he had broken his pledge by singing in a Jim Crow hall that night. Shocked, Robeson replied that he did not know his audience was segregated. Robeson, it seemed, had been deceived by an example of misdirection that Municipal Auditorium personnel often employed, for the

18. *Kansas City Call*, July 7, 1944.

auditorium was segregated. But the blocs of seats reserved for blacks were scattered throughout the hall in such a way that, from the stage, the audience appeared to be integrated. Robeson returned after intermission to announce that, at the urging of local black friends, he would continue his concert but only under protest. He then abandoned his prepared program to sing the most rousing freedom songs he knew. Whites began leaving the auditorium. "I was proud," Harold Holliday recalled of that moment. "[Robeson] was a big, black, beautiful black son-of-a-bitch. I loved him for that too."[19]

Robeson's performance galvanized the middle-class black leadership, and the local NAACP prepared to lobby for desegregation of city-owned facilities, particularly Municipal Auditorium, the auditorium's Music Hall, and Swope Park. The first step, a *Call* editorial recommended, was an informal conference with the proper authorities. After all, black Republicans were staunch supporters of the Citizens' Association, the nonpartisan organization of reformers who had swept the Pendergast machine from office and now governed the use of public facilities. But traditional strategies failed. Negotiations with the reform administration went nowhere, as Mayor John B. Gage and the city council ducked responsibility, this time by claiming that the private promoters who rented the Municipal Auditorium and not city officials determined whether to segregate seating at their events. Refusing to eliminate Jim Crow at the auditorium, the reform administration actually tightened the racial boundaries in public-owned facilities by sending mounted park attendants and officers in squad cars to herd black picnickers into a "colored" area of Swope Park. The *Call* reported that most black Kansas Citians were self-respecting enough not to obey the orders.

Performances by the Kansas City Philharmonic were barred to blacks altogether. Ruth Seufert, chairwoman of the Philharmonic, explained that she was not color prejudiced herself. "I have a colored maid," she offered as proof. "And I think the world and all of this maid. And this is the truth, sometimes she eats at my own table with my family. So you see I do not feel any discrimination because of color." Unfortunately, Seufert told a *Call* reporter, she had to comply with the wishes of contributing patrons, many of whom did not wish to share a concert hall with black audience members. However, neither the Philharmonic musicians nor their conductor, Efrem Kurtz, approved of the Jim Crow policies. After the Philharmonic's Board of Trustees agreed to sell tickets to African Americans in 1943, the orchestra scheduled a performance by African American singer Carol Brice, over the

19. Harold Holliday, interview by Horace Peterson, Black Archives of Mid-America, September 27, 1976. See also, *Kansas City Call,* February 20, 1942.

trustee's objections, and registered a firm protest against a seating policy that sold tickets to black concertgoers, yet confined them to the upper balcony.[20]

Thus far, conventional tactics of negotiation and lobbying, and a seemingly advantageous alliance between white reformers and black Republicans, had netted little more than polite dismissals and a few crumbs. Midway through the war, however, a cadre of white Kansas Citians emerged who were genuinely distressed by African Americans' grievances and alarmed at the possible consequences if those grievances were ignored. As had happened in 1919, a race riot in Detroit in 1943 convinced a number of Kansas Citians of both colors that some manner of interracial cooperation was needed to quell incendiary rumors and to prevent a similar outbreak in their own city. Among the rumors were reports that riots had already broken out in various spots in the city; that a "bump club" of blacks deliberately jostled white passengers on buses and streetcars; that "Eleanor Clubs" of black domestics were inspired by Mrs. Roosevelt to abandon their employers' kitchens on Sundays and holidays; and that blacks planned to leap en masse into Swope Park's swimming pool on Independence Day. Thus, in August 1943, the Kansas City Council of Social Agencies named a forty-nine member Citizens' Inter-racial Committee to scotch the rumors and to ease racial tensions over housing.[21]

The committee suffered several key limitations, however. For one, influential citizens of both races asked Mayor Gage to call an interracial conference, but the mayor refused. Instead, he shouldered the task of creating an interracial committee onto a nongovernmental organization. By failing to give the committee official standing, the *Call* lamented, Gage provided employers, union officials, and realtors an excuse for ignoring the committee's recommendations. The mayor did send a letter of encouragement to the committee, but its contents demonstrated how narrowly the mayor, and probably many of the committee members, defined their mission. Besides discounting "rumor and false propaganda," the letter directed committee members to "bring home to the people of every race the necessity of stamping out any activities of radical elements."[22] In other words, the interracial committee's

20. *Kansas City Call,* February 27, 1942, July 25, 1941, July 16, 1943, July 7, 1944, December 4, 1942, December 22, 1944.

21. *Ibid.,* August 13, 1943. Thomas Webster, "Community Planning to Improve the Housing Conditions of the Negro Population of Kansas City, Missouri, 1940–1947," Appendix.

22. Quoted in *Kansas City Call,* August 13, 1943. According to Thomas Webster, then secretary of the Kansas City Urban League, Gage's refusal to lend the committee his official support, despite endorsements from the Kansas City Chamber of Commerce and several labor and civic organizations, severely handicapped the committee's work. Webster, "Housing Conditions," 118.

purpose was pacification, not social change. For black and white Kansas Citians who wanted to challenge the status quo, direct action promised more satisfying results than either reform politics or flaccid interracialism had produced thus far.

The nucleus of interracial direct action grew from a tiny cadre of pacifists who organized a branch of the Fellowship of Reconciliation (FOR) in Kansas City in the 1930s. Modeled on a British organization of the same name, the American FOR originated in 1915 among forty Christian activists who sought to reconcile warring peoples by establishing a "world order based on Love." FOR members saw pacifism as an instrument for achieving broad social change and, conversely, regarded social change as a necessary ingredient of world peace. By 1942, its leadership, including executive secretary John Swomley and the country's best-known pacifist, A. J. Muste, were steering FOR toward "dynamic, disciplined, pacifist action" against war and racial oppression, twin evils issuing from the same antisocial and unchristian impulses. That year, FOR established a Department of Race Relations staffed by black Christian activists James Farmer, Bayard Rustin, and George Houser to develop tactics of "relentless non-cooperation." Farmer, for one, demanded a tougher approach than the typical interracial committees had dared so far. "It must strive, for example, not to make housing in ghettoes more tolerable, but to destroy residential segregation."[23] Among the "peace cells" Farmer and Houser established was the Chicago Committee of Racial Equality at the University of Chicago, which served as the original nucleus of the Congress of Racial Equality. For nearly a decade, Farmer and Houser served on FOR's staff while developing CORE's national network of interracial, nonviolent affiliates, relying heavily on FOR's financial contributions.

Early in the Second World War, FOR's little Kansas City band underwent significant changes. Feeling the need for a spiritual foundation to sustain their pacifism in the midst of wholesale carnage, the local FOR members asked the assistance of the Wider Quaker Fellowship, which sent its chairwoman, Emma Cadbury, to help them organize a local Society of Friends.

23. Letter of James Farmer to A. J. Muste, July 8, 1943, Series A-3, Box 2, and "Draft Report—Commission on Inter-Racial and Minorities," c. 1943, Series A-2, Box 4, Committee-Racial-Industrial, Records of the Fellowship of Reconciliation, Swarthmore College Peace Collection (hereafter Records of FOR-Swarthmore). See also, Joann Ooiman Robinson, *Abraham Went Out: A Biography of A. J. Muste,* 20, 111; Charles DeBenedetti, *The Peace Reform in American History,* 95; August Meier and Elliott Rudwick, *CORE: A Study in the Civil Rights Movement, 1942–1968,* 3–20.

Out of that collaboration came the Penn Valley Meeting for the Religious Society of Friends, which held its first meeting in January 1942.[24] In coming years, Penn Valley Friends would provide religious and ethical footings for several white civil rights activists.

At the same time, local pacifists shifted their objectives. Virginia Oldham, a charter member of Kansas City FOR and Penn Valley Friends, recalled that, after Pearl Harbor, FOR's national office advised local branches that "there wasn't anything we could do to stop the war because that was going on and we were in it. But peace began at home and we should interest ourselves in the things that caused dissension and difficulties and one of them was race. We should then begin to work on this problem of race." In 1942, local FOR members invited acquaintances of both races who might be interested in forming a civil rights organization to a meeting. The gathering considered itself loosely affiliated with the Congress of Racial Equality but decided that, in Kansas City, "if we go around talking about racial equality we'll really be in trouble."[25] Consequently, the group decided to call themselves the Committee on the Practice of Democracy (COPOD), a less inflammatory title that encapsulated the group's conviction that integration simply amounted to the application of democratic principles.

According to Girard T. Bryant, one of the few African Americans present at the first COPOD meeting, most of the blacks invited "were afraid to come." Gradually, however, COPOD attracted black members, most of them professionals. Bryant, for example, came to Kansas City in 1926 to teach at Western Baptist Bible College. In 1930, he joined the faculty of the Kansas City, Missouri, School District, serving as a high school principal at the time COPOD was founded and later serving as a college president. He would chair both COPOD and its offspring Fellowship House. COPOD's white members also came chiefly from the teaching, social service, and health professions. For example, Ruth Gordon, one of the few Penn Valley Friends who had been raised a Quaker, was a dietitian and professor of dietetics and

24. Reva Griffith, "Going Forth," typed manuscript history of Penn Valley Meeting, Private Papers of Reva Griffith, 1. See also, Reva Griffith, "Going Forth: Quaker Women and Resistance."

25. Virginia Oldham, interview by Reva Griffith, 1978, Private Papers of Reva Griffith. See also, "Memo on Proposed Institutes on Non-Violent Action as Applied to Race Relationships in the United States," April 30, 1943, General Race Relations Work, 1942–44, Records of FOR-Swarthmore. Meier and Rudwick characterize COPOD as an early affiliate of CORE. At least one other CORE affiliate, in Bartlesville, Oklahoma, took the name Committee on the Practice of Democracy for similar reasons. Meier and Rudwick, *CORE*, 25–26.

nutrition at the University of Kansas Medical Center in Kansas City, Kansas. There she initiated desegregation of the teaching hospital by hiring its first black staff person near the beginning of the war.[26]

Virginia Oldham, who became one of the city's leading antiwar activists and prison reformers as well as a civil rights worker, came to social activism by a less direct route. As a student at Wellesley College, Oldham was distressed by the social isolation her black classmates experienced, in spite of their obvious talent and brilliance. But her own father and elder brother were race prejudiced, and an interracial meeting that Oldham attended in Chicago in the 1920s left her feeling "strange" and "self-conscious" about this brief social contact with blacks. Upon her return to her native Kansas City, Oldham became an English teacher at Central High School because there were few other careers open to women in the 1920s, and she lacked the "brass" to be a journalist, her real heart's desire. Sometime in the 1930s, she accompanied a friend to a pacifist rally because the friend was infatuated with A. J. Muste, the main speaker. Oldham herself was so persuaded by Muste that she joined the movement. "I remember signing this card that I was going to be a pacifist and after I got home I wondered, 'My goodness, what have I done?'"[27] Thus, by a series of seeming accidents, Oldham became one of the founders of the local FOR branch and Penn Valley Meeting and a force behind the establishment of COPOD.

For nearly two years after its organization, COPOD continued to meet informally in members' homes. In April 1944, however, the organization mobilized for a more aggressive assault on segregation. That spring, several hundred blacks and whites gathered at the Grand Avenue Temple in downtown Kansas City for a Race Relations Institute, one of several held in northern cities by the Fellowship of Reconciliation. The institutes employed a similar pattern: on Fridays, a scientist spoke on the absence of scientific evidence for racial inferiority, and a clergyman, preferably local, spoke on racism as a moral issue. On Saturdays, teams led by FOR's "subsistence student secretaries" engaged in direct action projects in local public accommodations. Over the course of three days, participants in the Kansas City institute also studied the philosophy and techniques of nonviolent, "good will" direct action with speakers John Nevin Sayre, FOR's international chairman, and FOR's race relations secretary, James Farmer.

26. Memorandum from Girard T. Bryant to Reva Griffith, February, 1978, Private Papers of Reva Griffith; "In Memory of Dr. Girard T. Bryant, 1905–1993," privately printed obituary provided by Betty Feazel; Griffith, "Going Forth," 4–5.

27. Virginia Oldham, interview, 11.

Out of that gathering came a battery of stratagems aimed specifically at unmasking the tactics of misdirection. As part of the institute's direct action projects, interracial teams visited downtown theaters, restaurants, hotels, and drugstores to determine the exact boundaries of segregation in public accommodations. Those boundaries, they discovered, were somewhat irregular. In one theater, mixed groups might be ushered out before they had taken their seats; in another, the test group would sit through an entire movie before being asked to leave. Certain restaurants and lunch counters seated test groups in out-of-the-way corners and overcharged them or failed to take their orders, while other eateries barred them altogether. Project participants reported that they encountered no apparent hostility from the general public and found managers courteous if sometimes confused by their sudden appearance. Repeatedly, managers admitted that it was wrong to discriminate or claimed, as one theater manager did, that "it's not me personally." But they were afraid to "be the first to break the ice" of long-standing tradition. Asked how he knew his patrons would object to sharing his theater with blacks when none had ever been admitted, a theater owner replied, "Once in the summer some people objected to a sun-burned man, saying he was a Negro."[28]

According to a *Call* editorial, the experiments proved what the *Call* and the Urban League had long recognized, and Pratt-Whitney's black workers learned by hard experience. Namely, "it is the officials, the management of private business and a few 'race' fanatics who split this social order up into warring clans, instead of fostering respect for each other and enjoying mutual assistance." As C. A. Franklin had noted in 1942, "all the petty limitations put on us are the work of officials, not the wish of the white public." Indeed, the editor then claimed, "the white public is faced toward democracy." Without legal sanctions for discrimination in public accommodations, "the insults and injuries we suffer in them are all imposed without authority, and against the trend of white opinion." The institute's survey only confirmed that, so far as public accommodations, the "bigoted white patron" was largely a chimera.[29]

To test that hypothesis, COPOD launched a campaign based on a twofold, and quite literal, definition of the word *demonstration*. In one sense, COPOD aimed to "demonstrate" that whites were ready to tolerate integra-

28. "Test Public Places in Kansas City," 2, Series A-5, Box 7, FOR Literature, Records of FOR-Swarthmore; *Kansas City Call*, April 21, 1944; John Swomley, interview with author, October 29, 1993. See also, John Swomley, "FOR History," unfinished manuscript, Series A-1, Box 2, History-Addenda, Records of FOR-Swarthmore.
29. *Kansas City Call*, August 7, 1942, April 21, 1944.

tion, as when a mixed party of seven young women asked for and received service at a local cafeteria in 1945. Although the cashier abandoned her post rather than wait on them, and one white customer stormed out in protest, "nothing else was out of the ordinary—only glances and a few whispers." In smaller groups of two and three, the test participants shared tables with other diners, who told the interracial pairings "that it was all right—they were glad to have them."[30] In another sense, COPOD members intended to "demonstrate" to whites that segregation was real and widespread, no matter the tricks worked by misdirection. For this, the group targeted Municipal Auditorium and the Music Hall, where the scattering of "colored sections" camouflaged Jim Crow. Although the Philharmonic had begun admitting blacks to its concerts in 1943, seating remained segregated. Consequently, interracial teams of COPOD members attended the concerts demanding to be seated together. Meanwhile, in November 1945, the NAACP began picketing the Music Hall and Municipal Auditorium to force both blacks and whites to acknowledge that auditorium seating was, indeed, segregated, and to "flush out" possible white supporters.[31]

The following winter, the campaign expanded to include several black social clubs and veterans' organizations, whose members chose to picket stage performances like *Carmen Jones* and *Anna Lucasta,* which had black themes and were therefore likely to attract large audiences of African Americans. Meanwhile, the *Call* refused to advertise the performances and urged readers to boycott them. The strategy worked. At the opening night for *Carmen Jones,* only thirteen blacks crossed the picket line out of the eight hundred to nine hundred whom the *Call* estimated would have attended ordinarily. The *Call* printed the names of the thirteen turncoats. So many white ticket holders refused to enter the auditorium that more than a third of its seats were empty, and several of the whites who encountered pickets at the auditorium and music hall reported that they were astonished to learn that the facilities were segregated.[32]

One of those was Betty Feazel, a newcomer to Kansas City along with her husband, Ernie, an airline pilot. The young couple's tight budget required that they choose their entertainment expenditures carefully; they could just manage tickets to two symphony concerts at the Music Hall. When the couple arrived for a performance they found well-dressed young black men walking a picket line. Betty Feazel asked them what they were protesting and

30. "K.C. Restaurant Serves All," 2, Series A-5, Box 7, FOR-Literature, Records of FOR-Swarthmore.
31. *Kansas City Call,* October 20, 1944, November 16, 1945.
32. *Ibid.,* December 13, 1946, December 27, 1946, January 3, 1947.

was told that blacks had to sit in just the last two rows of the Music Hall even though, as taxpayers, they helped fund the facility. Feazel was furious— though not enough to give up the rare pleasure of the concert. The next day, she called NAACP president Carl Johnson to ask what she could do to contest the injustice. Johnson advised her to call Virginia Oldham of CO-POD rather than try to work with the NAACP, and Feazel joined Oldham's interracial group. In Feazel's case, her initial encounter with a black picket line proved the catalyst for a lifelong involvement in social activism, first in civil rights and later as an environmentalist.[33]

The pickets had a less electrifying effect on white officialdom, however. Following the first appearance of COPOD's pickets, city officials retorted that they only rented the public halls. Renters determined whether to seg-regate seating at the events they staged, and the city had no control over renters' policies. With city elections approaching in March 1946, the Citizens' Association unbent only enough to promise that city-sponsored events at the auditorium would not be segregated—but city officials would still leave private promoters to set seating policy for their own events. Even this half-measure was welcome, the *Call* declared, since promoters who had wanted to forgo segregation in the past had reported that city personnel pressured them to impose Jim Crow. As a recent performance before a mixed audience at the arena proved, "it is not the average citizen who insists upon artificial barriers based upon race and color, but those in authority."[34] Now, at least, city officials agreed not to interfere if a promoter wished to mix his audience.

Unfortunately, the city administration waffled on its promise by "advis-ing" event sponsors to "follow the custom in the seating of Negroes." Weary of the "buck-passing," a black delegation confronted the city council in early 1947 demanding that the council set seating policy at Municipal Auditorium. Still, City Manager L. P. Cookingham argued that the city had no legal au-thority over the actions of private events promoters. When the delegation pointed out that a recent Golden Gloves event at the auditorium had been segregated against the stated wishes of the sponsor, the *Kansas City Star*, Cookingham claimed that the *Star* had actually ordered segregated seating. The *Call* labeled the claim a lie, and the picketing continued. The delegation was convinced that Kansas City was "ready for democracy." Only its overly cautious city government stood in the way of progress.[35]

33. Betty Feazel, interview with author, September 21, 1993; Griffith, "Going Forth," 5–6.

34. *Kansas City Call*, June 14, 1946, February 1, 1946, March 22, 1946.

35. *Ibid.*, November 29, 1946, February 14, 1947, February 28, 1947.

A month later came an opportunity to illustrate the point when two events took place without Jim Crow seating at Municipal Auditorium. Predicting fistfights in the aisles and angry brawls by resentful whites, city officials upped their security measures. Instead, according to the *Call,* whites applauded when Carl Johnson took the microphone to say, "This crowd here tonight demonstrates that Negro and white people can enjoy an event sitting side by side in the same auditorium without any trouble." Encouraged by these events, the NAACP drew up an ordinance banning racial discrimination in public facilities, but then withdrew it because of Citizens' Association mayor William Kemp's objections that the measure would include Swope Park's swimming pool. The city council refused even to introduce and debate a second proposal that would ban discrimination in Municipal Auditorium alone. Only after the *Call*'s business manager, Dowdal Davis, made the ordinance a campaign issue in his run for a council seat did the city council relent. According to his widow, Davis agreed to run for city council as a Citizens' Association candidate if the association would support the amendment after the election. Although Davis failed to unseat Thomas Gavin, most popular of the Pendergast holdovers, he drew enough black votes from Gavin to force the association to make good its promise. In May 1951, the council approved an ordinance prohibiting discrimination at Municipal Auditorium, the air terminal restaurant, and new Starlight Theater in Swope Park.[36]

■ ■ Thinking about Segregation

After 1945, the NAACP took over more and more of the leadership of picketing actions at public facilities. For its part, COPOD undertook a new kind of organization with a new purpose. In 1945, Rev. Lawrence Scott, a COPOD member and Baptist minister, suggested that COPOD establish a Fellowship House modeled on an organization located in Philadelphia. In July 1946, members of COPOD, FOR, and Penn Valley Meeting purchased a large Victorian home at 1462 Independence Avenue, and Rev. Scott and his wife moved into the building to serve as directors. Fellowship House planned a variety of activities, including conferences on peace and international relations, a bureau of "liberal" speakers, weekend camps for area stu-

36. *Ibid.,* March 7, 1947, March 21, 1947, May 25, 1951, June 1, 1951. Dorothy Davis Johnson, interview. The NAACP withdrew an ordinance banning discrimination in private as well as public amusements in 1946 because no member of the city council would agree to introduce it.

dents to study labor and race relations problems, and workshops on direct action projects in race relations.[37]

But Fellowship House served an immediate, more fundamental purpose in providing a safe haven where racially mixed groups could meet socially. According to Betty Feazel, COPOD members had been meeting "practically on street corners" because public gathering places barred interracial socializing on their premises. At Fellowship House, African American, Hispanic, Asian, and white men and women shared potluck suppers, discussed the great books, and debated issues of the day in an atmosphere that was both relaxed and liberated from the stifling racial conventions of their community. Sometimes a gathering included a speaker, but Fellowship's meager budget meant that most get-togethers offered nothing more than warm conviviality and an equal opportunity to do the cooking and the washing-up. "It was tremendous fun," Betty Feazel recalled, "because the group was so mixed and you met and heard the views of such different people." Rhea Kalhorn joined after her first visit in 1953 because Fellowship House freed her from the "sterile atmosphere" of a segregated community, which "does not allow you to know another race, culture, or religion." The interracial gatherings served a political purpose, but "members were not just wearing the halo," recalled Kalhorn. They came because the conversation was "better than talking about the cost of butter and diapers." As house member Lucile Bluford summed up the organization, "It was just a cross section of people who got together just to be friends across racial and religious lines, trying to eliminate segregation and discrimination by letting people know each other as individuals and persons. It was just a drop in the bucket, I mean, it couldn't affect the whole town, but it was a beginning."[38]

37. Fellowship Houses existed in a variety of forms. FOR pacifists and wealthy benefactors established one in Boston during the First World War as a sanctuary in which to live the principles of nonviolence and work for peace and economic and racial justice. A Fellowship House established by an interracial committee of Quakers in Philadelphia in 1931 provided the model for a laboratory for racial and religious understanding that was used in Kansas City. The University of Chicago students who comprised CORE's first cell established a Fellowship House during the Second World War and modeled it on the Gandhian ashram as a men's cooperative community. "Fellowship House, Fellowship Farm," 1, CDGA Collective Box, Fellowship House File, Swarthmore College Peace Collection; Robinson, *Abraham*, 25; Meier and Rudwick, *CORE*, 6. During his tenure in Kansas City's Fellowship House, Scott was recognized as one of three FOR members at the forefront of race relations nationally. "Forty Years for Peace: A History of the Fellowship of Reconciliation, 1914–1954," Series A-1, Box 2, FOR-History Addenda, Records of FOR-Swarthmore; Virginia Oldham, interview. See also, *Kansas City Call*, August 9, 1946.

38. Betty Feazel, interview; Rhea Kalhorn, interview with author, October 12, 1993; Deposition of Lucile Bluford, 106.

Still, Fellowship House had a political agenda. The informal get-togethers were intended to promote what Kalhorn called "brotherhood through exposure." Members of different races interacted socially to demonstrate to observers that those interactions were even possible. In the public arena, Fellowship House tried to educate the community about the possibilities of brotherhood with its Wednesday luncheons. All other days of the week, Bretton's popular downtown restaurant refused service to blacks. But owner Max Bretton, who was active in Jewish community relations work, set aside a special table each Wednesday for Fellowship members in hopes that the Restaurant Owners Association would find the courage to jettison Jim Crow. Because Bretton's white customers were unaware that Fellowship House had Bretton's permission to dine, members hoped their interracial socializing appeared to happen naturally. "We wanted to demonstrate to the public and the restaurant owners that this could be a peaceable kingdom," Feazel explained, "that the public would accept integration if only the restaurant owners would allow it."[39]

Other days of the week, Fellowship House conducted "surveys" of public accommodations. Ostensibly to determine what racial policies proprietors maintained, the surveys actually served an educational purpose. At the Forum Cafeteria, for example, Lucile Bluford and Virginia Oldham waited in line until Bluford was refused service. Then Oldham filled a tray at the food line and sat down with Bluford to share the meal. The purpose was "so the people could see that black didn't rub off and black people and white people could enjoy things together," Oldham explained. "Now, the theory of it was to get people accustomed to seeing black people and white people together and to show that nothing was going to happen if a black person sat at this table and a white person sat there, nothing is going to happen," Bluford recalled. "People would have you think that a wall was going to cave in or something if that happened but nothing actually happened."[40]

Despite its atmosphere of racial comity, Fellowship House actually signaled the presence of three remarkably different perceptions of segregation and its consequences among Kansas Citians. For obvious reasons, African Americans who combated Jim Crow in the postwar decade defined the consequences of segregation in personal and pragmatic terms. Margaret Holliday battled segregation in the postwar years because "it limits the individual so very much. It's like two different worlds. . . . Every thing that is wrong is black; right is white. When you do that to one group of people,

39. Betty Feazel, interview; Dorothy Davis Johnson, interview.
40. Virginia Oldham, interview, 12; Deposition of Lucile Bluford, 108.

they begin to think that, and they will be less than what they should be or what they can be." An Urban League staff member and graduate student in those years, Dorothy Davis Johnson, felt that "what segregation did to us, we have not recovered from. . . . It is an injustice to people to imply that there is something so different about them that they must be separated." Just as important, Johnson recalled, segregation placed her and other African Americans under constant threat of violence or humiliation if they overstepped boundaries. "Segregation causes incidents. You see, if you have a whole bunch of blacks . . . and they're told they can't go here, they can't go there, then the tiniest infraction can cause a scene. If those people weren't forcibly held apart, that wouldn't occur." Her sense of danger was magnified by the fact that segregation boundaries varied and were not always clearly defined. "The variation is what is important. You never know what to expect. That's important to the black side of it. You're constantly on the *qui-vive* in a strange situation—a discomfort that I don't think many white people had to experience."[41]

For C. A. Franklin, segregation represented the polar opposite of democracy. It is not surprising that the word appeared in most of his condemnations of race prejudice during the war and Cold War period. In Franklin's calculations, democracy was measured in concrete terms, for in a democracy, a man had a right "to make a living and to enjoy the fruits of his labor equally with his neighbors." Segregation cost African Americans that right by consigning them to decrepit schools and unsafe housing, by depriving them of labor commensurate with their skills, and by barring them from public places of enjoyment. Putting it bluntly, "A man should not have to remain hungry or accept a poor quality of food when he has money in his pocket simply because of the color of his skin." Moreover, segregation was self-reinforcing since it deprived whites of the personal contacts with African Americans that would upset their racial stereotypes—the same stereotypes that justified exclusion of blacks from jobs, neighborhoods, and schools. Racial separation prevented whites from putting their assumptions to the test. "We can't understand how anyone can be so certain of the failure of intelligent, democratic, moral progress which he hasn't yet tried," Franklin declared in 1954. "We can't understand how anyone can tell whether he likes french fried potatoes if he hasn't tasted any." But the worst consequences of segregation were the measures taken to justify and maintain the system, the editor reasoned, for those whites whose interests were served by segregating

41. Margaret Holliday, interview with author, January 31, 1992; Dorothy Davis Johnson, interview.

the races must constantly vindicate the system by "selling to white America the idea that a Negro who works beside a white man, or lives beside him has sinister designs." In order to "prove Negroes bad," segregationists railroaded them into prison, lynched them by the score, and denied them work and homes, "a policy of slow extermination entirely at variance with Christianity and real Americanism."[42] In short, segregation must go because it did direct and measurable harm to black people.

By contrast, many of the liberal whites who engaged in interracial and civil rights activities in the same period condemned segregation because it was bad for *white* people. Asked why she combated segregation in the 1940s and 1950s, Betty Feazel replied that the very people who demeaned others by segregating them were themselves degraded by it. "It lowers their character; it brings out the worst in people," she contended. "You can't keep a man in the gutter without getting down there with him." The catalyst that propelled Robert Farnsworth into civil rights activism was the realization that his own value system had been corroded by contact with segregation. Farnsworth grew up in the north, "having felt that I was very liberal on race issues . . . seeing myself as someone who was challenging the racial assumptions of my students." After spending several years in the south teaching and completing his doctorate, however, Farnsworth returned in 1957 to Wayne State University in Detroit, where he found he had absorbed some of the expectations and assumptions of the segregated south. Black students were numerous at Wayne State and freely used all its facilities, including its cafeteria. "I was shocked at my own response . . . when I went to the university cafeteria—at the emotional response I had in the presence of sixty to seventy per cent blacks—the people in the cafeteria." He concluded, "I had been conditioned to segregation even while I didn't believe in it." His repulsion "made me question my racial attitudes and what I thought I believed. My conscious beliefs were consistent, but it made me examine what I felt." Soon after, Farnsworth and his wife moved to Kansas City. As a result of his self-examination, "we were primed when we got here to get involved in civil rights."[43]

For Rhea Kalhorn, segregation weakened the social values that undergirded civility and decency in her own community: "It was directly contrary to the basis of this country." Segregation "was very undemocratic—made

---

42. *Kansas City Call,* February 23, 1940, February 20, 1942, July 30, 1948, August 29, 1952, January 8, 1954.
43. Betty Feazel, interview; Robert Farnsworth, interview with author, September 27, 1993.

it impossible to look at people as human beings." By promoting inequality, segregation "took dignity away from men." Beth Smith opposed segregation in Kansas City because "when you demean someone in a society, it's an unhealthy society. . . . You miss the potential and the creativity of all those people who are kept apart. Their talents are not brought to the table." According to his wife, Anne, Sidney Lawrence believed that if race discrimination persisted unchallenged, "there'd be a lot of chaos," for where there is discrimination, "there's a lot of hate; there's a lot of ignorance."[44] In sum, segregation created an uncivil society, one populated by citizens of weakened character who, in debasing democratic values, threatened the capacity of all individuals to enjoy autonomy, dignity, and security. The white Kansas Citians who contested segregation did so, in part, because they did not want to live in such a society.

Fortunately, these integrationists believed, bigotry was not caused by character flaws but by something easier to eradicate. At the heart of segregation, and the prejudice on which it fed, lay ignorance—not stupidity or malevolence. Anne Lawrence blamed the fact that whites "just didn't know what the circumstances were." Segregation had "not just harmful effects on blacks but harmful effects on whites because they had no contact with people they feared and despised," John Swomley concluded. Overcoming ignorance by providing that contact, directly or vicariously, formed an important part of white integrationists' agenda. Thus, Sidney Lawrence "went about making people know each other." Formerly an art historian at New York University and USO director in Junction City, Kansas, Lawrence came to Kansas City in 1945 to serve as first executive director of the Jewish Community Relations Bureau (JCRB). "If you asked Sidney what his job was," Anne Lawrence recalled, "he would say it was to make people love one another" by educating audiences and readers about "what anti-Semitism was, anti-black [prejudice], the importance of accepting each other's differences."[45]

Beth Smith joined the Panel of American Women because she was convinced that "people are teachable," that race discrimination "is learned in the culture." The panel originated when Ann Jacobson needed an interesting program for B'nai Jehudah Temple Sisterhood. She thought of assembling a group of adult women based on the example of the National Panel of Americans, which featured students of various races, ethnic groups, and religions

44. Rhea Kalhorn, interview; Beth Smith, interview with author, January 17, 1995; Anne Lawrence, interview with author, January 14, 1995.
45. John Swomley, interview; Anne Lawrence, interview. Sidney Lawrence headed the JCRB from 1945 to 1973.

speaking to other students on college campuses about their experiences as "outsiders." As the panel's historian remembered, the task seemed simple. "But how do you persuade sensitive adult women accustomed to concealing hurts (for the sake of 'social acceptability' or in the name of 'ladylike behavior') to expose in public the wounds of prejudice so the sources can be discussed *with* the public?" Ultimately, these were the facets that made the panel powerful. "Racism was a personal experience," LaDonna Harris recalled of the panel's first years.[46] Simply by telling their stories and their hurts as highly personal narratives, they transformed discrimination from an abstraction to something vivid and tangible.

The panel was meant to be a one-time-only event, but the sisterhood received repeated requests to bring the panel to other audiences. As demand for the panel rose, Esther Brown of B'nai Jehudah turned it into a movable forum for minority women to "tell their stories" about what it was like for them being "outside the mainstream." Speaking most often to groups of other women, panel members sought venues where their audiences were at ease in familiar surroundings. They counted on highly personal, face-to-face accounts of their experiences and feelings to build empathy among their audiences and to establish a sense of intimate involvement between panel and audience. Smith believed that whites often dismissed blacks' demands for social change by asking, "What do they want?" or by protesting that racial change was happening too fast. Once an audience experienced vicariously what it was like to be excluded, demeaned, or stereotyped, panel members assumed that their audience was more likely to understand what "they" wanted and to accept the imperative for change.[47]

According to Smith, the panel most often spoke before women's groups in part because it was a daytime activity and women were available for day-

46. Ann Jacobson, interview with author, June 30, 1999; "History," in *Panel of American Women,* Box 3, Folder 33, in Panel of American Women Collection, 885kc Box 3, Western Historical Manuscript Collection (hereafter PAW-WHMC).

47. Beth Smith, interview. Once launched in Kansas City, the Panel for American Women was developed by Brown into a national network of forty-seven panels in twenty-seven states, including the south, in 1968. Better known for her school desegregation efforts, Brown was a resident of Merriam, Kansas, a suburb of Kansas City, in 1948 when she realized that black children living in South Park, a low-income subdivision of Merriam, were forced by gerrymandered attendance zones to attend school in a two-room shack. When the county school board built a new building for whites that barred black students, Brown launched a "school strike" by establishing temporary classrooms in the homes of South Park's black families. She helped the NAACP instigate a suit that resulted in a state Supreme Court decision desegregating Merriam schools, and she assisted in bringing the *Brown* suit in Topeka. Frank J. Adler, *Roots in a Moving Stream: The Centennial History of Congregation B'nai Jehudah of Kansas City, 1870–1970,* 255–57.

time meetings. But she also thought that women audiences were comfortable talking about personal experiences and feelings and were better equipped than men to participate in the style of dialogue the panel employed. But men also reported that hearing personal narratives made a difference. Asked what propelled some whites into the civil rights movement, Howard Sachs, for example, argued that it often depended on hearing face-to-face about mistreatment: "Experiences of that sort—[happening to] people that we knew that seemed extremely unfair and inappropriate—that caused people to take some action." But the women's panels, with their white-gloved respectability and coffee klatch air, were particularly effective in getting an audience to lower its guard. "There we appeared, looking like your neighbor. . . . We got people to think about how *they* spoke, how *they* treated their neighbor," panel founder Jacobson recalled.[48] A further asset of the Panel of American Women was that the actions it advocated were both prosaic and personal: smiling and sitting next to a black passenger on a bus, asking not to be told an ethnic joke. Seemingly simplistic, these meant taking action, not just a philosophical position, and even traditional, apolitical women could do these things comfortably. Intimacy was disarming and potentially radical.

■ ■ The Transforming Power of Integration

Believing that segregation established the defective community and that interracial contact overcame antipathies, white civil rights proponents expected integration to create what Betty Feazel called "the peaceable kingdom." Integration possessed a transforming power, they believed, that would uplift human character as well as human society. So certain was Rhea Kalhorn of that transforming power that she joined Fellowship House to expose her children to people of diverse races and cultures. She believed that many other parents likewise joined the house in hopes of enriching themselves and their children. It was a "contrived opportunity," she admitted, but an effective one. "My children are tolerant people—wonderful human beings who practice democratic, Christian principles. I am not sure, given the area

48. Howard F. Sachs, interview with author, June 9, 1999; Ann Jacobson, interview. See also, Doris Quin, "Panel of Americans," Box 3, File 1, PAW-WHMC. The panel may also have sought an audience of women because they believed that racism was a learned response that mothers were best situated to eradicate in future generations. Ruth Feldstein, *Motherhood in Black and White: Race and Sex in American Liberalism, 1930–1965*, 40–50.

where they grew up, that they would have been tolerant without a contrived situation."[49]

"I was starry-eyed," Robert Farnsworth recalled of his early years in the local civil rights movement. As a scholar, he was attracted to romantic literature of the nineteenth century and to its creators' belief that human beings were essentially godlike and hence perfectible. "I tend to believe in a progressive human realization that is rooted in those nineteenth century romantics. I believe that truth is fatal." Not only would integration advance the rehabilitation of human spirit, but the very act of seeking racial justice called out the best in others, for "the dramatic confrontation of civil disobedience appealed to people's better nature," he contended. "What civil disobedience is is a willingness to submit oneself to violence without responding in kind. It makes the dramatic connection; it forces a person to react to you in a human sense that goes very deep. . . . If you can get to that core, it's the way in which people address what is right rather than what other people expect of them. Much of the racial prejudice, to my mind, is not really innate in anybody. It's something taught. It's something learned. And what I had found in the South is that I had learned it." If fundamental civil rights could not be established for African Americans, "I would have to abandon all my notions about the essential goodness of human nature."[50]

Where nineteenth-century romanticism provided the theological underpinnings for Farnsworth's civil rights activism, the conjunction of civil religion with their own inclinations toward a Social Gospel shaped the political culture of other white activists.[51] Both COPOD and Fellowship House were intentionally ecumenical, but the Quakers of Penn Valley Friends Meeting formed an essential core of both organizations. Unlike "birthright Friend" Ruth Gordon, however, most of those Quakers were led into the Society of Friends in the first place because its tenets accorded with their own practical idealism. Asked to account for her passion for justice, Virginia Oldham sug-

49. Rhea Kalhorn, interview.
50. Robert Farnsworth, interview.
51. Theologically, these activists reflect the tenets of what Will Herberg describes as the civil religion of the United States, which he characterizes as a belief in the supreme value of the individual and in the brotherhood of all Americans, disquiet over social inequalities, a profound faith in the power of education, and the "religionizing" of democracy. He identifies American civil religion as a system of values, ideas, and beliefs that constitute a faith common to all Americans, however. That these activists possessed an *uncommon* commitment to those same values apparently stems from their adherence to a Social Gospel. That is, they believe that sin is caused by social conditions rather than inherent human evil, and that people of faith can therefore bring about the Kingdom of God by means of social reform. Will Herberg, "America's Civil Religion: What It Is and Whence It Comes," 78–88.

gested that she had grown up with an inner conviction that "you weren't out for yourself, you were out to help others live happily or improve their situation." Her association with Quakers and with Gandhi's teachings provided a religious foundation for her inclinations. Like many of her generation, she claimed, Oldham grew up envisioning God as "somebody off in heaven who ought to do better for the world than he does, and I'm kind of 'agin' Him most of the time. But when you call him Truth and Love then I can grasp that and I think Gandhi's idea [is] that it's a goal that we are struggling toward, it's not anything you achieve. . . . I think I can say that I believe that there is an inner light in everybody." Yet, Oldham claimed that she never had religious meditation during meeting. "All I think of [during meditation] is people and the things people do and the people who need help or the causes that need help or something like that. I'm just not religious." She joined the Quakers because "the main thing was that they were people who did something about their religion."[52]

Both by his actions and his explorations of Christian ethics, John Swomley helped articulate the theological foundation on which many white Christians based their civil rights activism in Kansas City. Swomley's involvement in civil rights came out of his commitment to Christian pacifism, which led him to liberal positions on a broad range of social issues. Partly as a result of his discussions with pacifists, "I was radicalized. I went all the way." Going to work for the Fellowship of Reconciliation in 1939 and becoming first its executive secretary and later its director, Swomley hired James Farmer, whom he had met in the Methodist youth movement, as FOR's race relations secretary. Later he also hired Bayard Rustin. Together, the three honed the Gandhian tactics that Farmer and Rustin incorporated as the strategic and philosophical base for the Congress of Racial Equality.[53] After completing his doctorate on sabbatical from FOR, Swomley came to Kansas City to join the faculty of St. Paul's Theological Seminary. In Kansas City, Swomley became an advocate for peace and civil liberties as well as civil rights.

52. Virginia Oldham, interview, 16–17, 23. Betty Feazel joined Penn Valley Meeting as a result of her membership in Fellowship House and her friendship with Oldham. Rhea Kalhorn, on the other hand, made her first visit to Fellowship House at the urging of her Unitarian minister and found there many other whites who had been influenced by "liberal pastors." Because the Protestant establishment, as exemplified by the National Council of Churches, failed to act forthrightly to condemn racial discrimination, mobilized Protestants were left to find a spiritual community of action with nonmainline denominations or the liberal pastors who acted without institutional backing. James F. Findlay, Jr., *Church People in the Struggle: The National Council of Churches and the Black Freedom Movement, 1950–1970,* 11–47.

53. John Swomley, interview; Taylor Branch, *Parting the Waters: America in the King Years, 1954–1963,* 16, 20, 69.

Shortly before coming to Kansas City, Swomley published *The Word of God in the Nuclear Age,* in which he defined the connection between Christian ethics and social change that activated many of his white colleagues in the civil rights movement.[54] Ultimately, Swomley wrote, "justice has become a major aim of Christian ethics. While the Christian's primary object is a relationship with God, he admitted, "he should seek in his relationship with his fellow men the kind of relationship he wants with God." To be genuine, that relationship required the kind of "respect for personality" that lay in "recognizing the intrinsic value of each person so that he is not a tool to be used, exploited, or humiliated." Consequently, Christians were obligated to seek social change, for in society as it then existed, human relationships grounded upon the inviolable integrity of personhood were impossible. In particular, Christians' responsibilities for social change must draw them across racial boundaries, for "in spite of division and difference we are biologically and psychologically one race in need of functioning as an interdependent whole." Social change would not come easily or quickly, Swomley warned his readers, for Christians must seek to transform their society by accepting suffering rather than inflicting it on others—by an exercise of love, the effects of which were slow to emerge and difficult to discern. Indeed, it was the *process* of seeking social transformation, and not its product, that Swomley found to be the core of Christian living. "In confronting the fact of evil, including injustice, inequality, the power some men use to dominate other men, the prejudices arising from difference, the vested political and economic interests, the Christian is constrained to act as fully as he can in the spirit of love, for the greatest good." Who, then, were the real beneficiaries of social activism on behalf of racial justice? Swomley's analysis implied that white Christians gained at least as much, if not more, than African Americans from their engagement with race prejudice, for they entered communion with God— the ultimate destination of Christianity—by engaging in the struggle. Thus they brought into being the peaceable kingdom wherein authentic Christian living would be less impeded.

A similar coupling of faith and justice drew Jews into the early civil rights movement in Kansas City. "I am a Jew," Beth Smith replied when asked why she began her work in race relations. "Justice is the cornerstone of Judaism. . . . Justice is a central word, a central concept. Every year at the high holidays, it is not your relationship with God that you reexamine but your relationship with your fellow man." In his columns in the *Kansas City*

---

54. Swomley's analysis of Christian social ethics is reprinted in John Swomley, "Christian Dynamic for Social Change," 75–76.

Jewish Chronicle, Sidney Lawrence reminded Jews that the call to "strike at prejudice and encourage democratic human relations" came from ancient Hebrew literature. "'Man was created alone for the sake of harmony among the different people,'" Lawrence quoted from the Mishnah Sanhedrin. "One should not be able to say to the other: 'My ancestor was better than yours.'"[55]

Just as their understanding of Jewish tradition led Smith and Lawrence into civil rights activities, so did their experiences as Jews. "I had a deep sense of 'otherness' myself," Beth Smith explained. Having felt the pain of exclusion—of "being outside the mainstream"—she understood the personal costs of prejudice and the necessity to eradicate it for her own sake as well as others'. Sidney Lawrence had witnessed at close range the extremes of anti-Semitism. Lawrence took a sabbatical in Germany in the late 1930s, where he wrote his wife, Anne, long, anguished letters analyzing Nazism and the plight of German Jews. By the time he arrived in Kansas City in 1945, he understood what horrors intolerance could wreak if left unchallenged. "The Holocaust had a tremendous effect on us," Anne Lawrence remembered. It galvanized Sidney Lawrence's impulse to bridge the racial and religious fissures that separated people into mutually suspicious and antagonistic groups. For Lawrence, a society that cultivated antiblack or anti-Catholic prejudice was one in which anti-Semitism equally flourished.[56]

Consequently, Lawrence was avowedly ecumenical, joining COPOD and Fellowship House and seeking contact with religious groups of every kind. And he was an ideal choice for executive director of the Jewish Community Relations Bureau.

The JCRB interested itself in social issues that affected relations between Jews and non-Jews. As Lawrence explained the bureau's mission in the *Jewish Chronicle*, "We are learning that the fight against anti-Semitism is related to the fight against reactionary totalitarian tendencies in modern society; that the fight for equality for the Jew in all fields is related to the expansion of democratic rights for everyone." Ironically, jurist and historian Howard Sachs recalls, the Jewish community benefited from the mere fact that racial integration was even an issue in Kansas City. Once people began to think

---

55. Beth Smith, interview; Sidney Lawrence, "United We Stand."

56. Anne Lawrence, interview. Smith and Sidney Lawrence evince several of the tenets of "civil Judaism," which historian Joseph Schultz calls the consensus of Kansas City Jewry. As Schultz defines it, civil Judaism includes commitment to good citizenship in the larger community, commitment to social justice, anxiety about Jewish survival and the Holocaust, and "the need for a more intense experience of community." Joseph P. Schultz, "The Consensus of 'Civil Judaism': The Religious Life of Kansas City Jewry," 2.

about lowering the barriers based on skin color, it became "kind of ridicu-
lous" to discriminate based on less obvious distinctions like ethnicity or religion. With this in mind, Sachs notes, Lawrence made it a policy of the JCRB
that "the civil rights movement was vitally significant to the removal of social
barriers affecting Jews."[57]

The JCRB did not reach that position without a struggle, however, for
there were hazards. And Sidney Lawrence worried over every one of them.
How, for example, could he claim on the one hand that Jews were individuals, as different from each other as any other group of Kansas Citians, then
propose that they shared a view of race relations based on their common experiences as Jews? Were individual Jews entitled to their "minor prejudices,"
or must they think alike on this one issue? Would "forthright action" on civil
rights for blacks make Jews appear pushy and aggressive to Christians, and
so reinforce the stereotypes that excited anti-Semitism? Questions of tactics
plagued the JCRB as well. In 1945, the bureau learned that a new subdivision in Leawood, Kansas, was to include covenants restricting Jews. The
bureau's board considered a legal challenge that would focus on religious
discrimination alone because a challenge to race discrimination was unlikely
to succeed in the courts. Consultation with local African American activists
convinced the board not to separate the issues but to forge stronger ties to
Fellowship House as a way of coordinating attacks. As an unnamed board
member concluded, "If we are fighting just for the Jew, whatever gain is
achieved will be only temporary, for as long as there is any minority group
mistreated, the Jew is in that position."[58] As Lawrence ultimately concluded
in his internal debate, Jews would have to redefine what the term *Jewish community* meant—no longer to imply a separate and isolated population but a
population dedicated to constructing communities of relationship. He had
found his way to the beloved community that Christian race liberals sought.

■ ■ Conclusion

Of course, the white Kansas Citians who contested racial discrimination were
a minority. Still, a significant cadre of white activists had emerged along with

57. Lawrence, "United We Stand"; Howard F. Sachs, interview; Howard F. Sachs,
"Seeking the Welfare of the City: A Survey of Public Relations, Economics, and Social and
Civic Activity," 173. Among the other social issues that concerned the JCRB were religion
in the schools, poverty, the public image of the state of Israel, and political extremism.

58. Sidney Lawrence, "Report: On some of the recent work of the Community Relations Bureau," June 29, 1951, Minutes of the Community Relations Bureau, October
16, 1945, Jewish Community Relations Bureau Archives.

a new way of thinking about race. And the rest of the city's white population, they believed, were simply apathetic about civil rights and the segregation of public accommodations. As a *Call* editorial reckoned in 1951, "It isn't the customer at the lunch counter who objects to the serving of a Negro. It is the restaurant owner. It isn't the theater patron who keeps Negroes from enjoying first-run movies. It is the theater manager or the owner."[59] Even the *Kansas City Star* admitted, "There seems almost always to be a lag between the enlightenment of the majority and the timidity of a few backed by an out-moded tradition."[60]

In the same period, black activists devised potent tactics of direct action to demonstrate a paradox: namely, that segregation in public accommodations existed while whites' demand for it barely did. Consequently, as Girard Bryant was fond of putting it, the two races sat down together in public places to prove that "the sky would not fall." The difficulty lay in forcing business owners and city officials to act forthrightly. As activists, black and white, would discover, their chief opposition came not so much from avowed segregationists as from well-intentioned civic housekeepers, from officials and "friends" who aimed for an orderly community, not a beloved one, and who were willing to bargain away justice merely to avoid conflict.

59. *Kansas City Call*, March 9, 1951.
60. Quoted in *ibid.*, November 3, 1950.

8

Expedient Fears

Leadership and the Politics of Denial, 1950–1958

■ ■ ■

S PEAKING THROUGH ITS legal counsel in 1951, the municipal
government of Kansas City, Missouri, assured the populace that its government was exercising its "duty and responsibility under the police power to
preserve peace and order in the community for the protection and welfare of
both races and in the interest of public safety to prevent racial conflicts, riots,
and violence."[1] Reassuring and welcome words no doubt, for Americans had
seen much racial violence in their past. But against what danger was the city
of Kansas City defending its citizens? In this case, it was the peril of mixed
bathing—of swimming by both races in the same public pool. And this was
neither the first nor the last time that officials exaggerated the potential for
racial violence. Fear was useful—an excuse to do nothing to alter the system
of race privilege and penalty. Timidity passed as wise policy.

Officials' reluctance to tamper with long-standing racial custom seemed
to have little to do with the personal biases of business managers or public
functionaries. They simply defined good race relations as the absence of
conflict between the races, and they presumed that changes in racial custom
would provoke resentful whites to retaliate. The anticipated backlash would
be bad for business and for civic order. Accordingly, the shrewd businessman
preserved the color line in public accommodations and "passed it back to his
customers" when challenged. The responsible public official aimed to maintain civic harmony and "good race relations" by a combination of denial and
pacification. And, as was true in the 1920s, many of the supposed "friends of

---

1. *City of Kansas City, et al. v. Esther Williams, et al.,* U.S. Court of Appeals, Eighth
Circuit, 2, Box 8, File 1, Kansas City Commission of Human Relations Collection, Missouri State Archives (hereafter KCHRC Collection-MSA).

the Negro" defined justice for blacks in terms of what was good for whites; they understood racial harmony as peace at any price. All of them underestimated the capacity of ordinary Kansas Citians to coexist in public places.

Unfortunately, official timidity came at grievous cost, for Kansas City's leaders missed numerous opportunities to dismantle inequity. According to Lucile Bluford, for example, the city's schools could have been integrated even before 1954 had the school board "made a real concerted effort."[2] Speaking of school district leaders specifically and public officials in general, Robert Farnsworth observed that they so feared controversy on racial issues that they "just buckled; [they] never faced up to the situation. And there was no guts to do it—to really make a decision." Courageous leadership in the postwar period might have eliminated some of the racial divisions that persisted long after, he believed. "It was a shame. And I think much of what we're in today is because of the lack of conviction to make a change. They were cheating in all kinds of ways within the system."[3] Black Kansas Citians had to find new ways to expose the cheats.

■ ■ The Politics of Harmony

Not surprisingly, timidity shaped the agenda of the Mayor's Commission on Human Relations in its first years of operation. Established by the city council in 1951, the commission originated in Mayor William Kemp's discovery that similar commissions in other cities had been useful in guiding public reaction to "ticklish" racial issues. The commission hired William Gremley as its first director in late 1952. The *Call* hoped that the commission would move forthrightly to combat discrimination in employment and in public accommodations, but the ordinance creating the commission indicated that it had a more conciliatory purpose. By design of the city council, the commission was created to "stimulate sympathetic understanding, harmonious relationships, a spirit of charity, and a program of practical cooperation among all groups and individuals to the end that Kansas City may grow and advance in peace and wholesome collective achievement and in the field of individual opportunity." Its official duties included investigating and conciliating complaints of discrimination, initiating projects to end undemocratic practices, and advising the city on intergroup relations.[4]

2. "Deposition of Lucile Bluford," 42, Box 102, Benson Papers.
3. Robert Farnsworth, interview with author, September 27, 1993.
4. Kemp was the candidate of the anti-Pendergast reform movement. Gremley began his career in public relations for a Catholic youth organization in Chicago. After serving

Such a roster of duties could enlist the human relations commission in making genuine social change if its members were willing to ruffle feathers. But its statutory mission statement pledged commission members to seek community concord—to alleviate only the practices and policies that "create conflicts and tensions" rather than to pursue justice for justice's sake. Beth Smith, who joined the commission in 1957, believed that the commission originated "so the administration could say it was doing something rather than making any significant changes." In fact, a public statement of its functions warned that the commission must not be a pressure group on anyone's behalf. In particular, the commission would see to it that African Americans did not create crises of conflict by challenging segregation, because "discontent about discrimination and segregation problems can lead to tension, and tension can lead to conflict."[5] Given the pacific inclinations of the city administration and its first director, the commission chose conciliation, harmony, and peace at almost any price in its first years of activity.

■ ■ Assaulting Misdirection

To halt the pious evasions that sustained segregation, black Kansas Citians launched a two-pronged assault on public and private officials' misdirection tactics. In keeping with its litigation strategy, the NAACP instituted a civil suit in 1951 to demonstrate that official anxieties over white backlash were exaggerated. Seven years later, an ad hoc group of black protesters undertook direct action to show Kansas City business owners that local blacks were fed up with misdirection and denial—enough, in fact, to make continued evasions bad for business. The NAACP suit grew out of a request in 1949 that the park board remove all remaining restrictions on the use of park facilities by black taxpayers. In typical fashion, the board replied: "Inter-racial problems, prejudices, customs and established practices are not of our making;

in the National Youth Administration and the U.S. Army, he was Director of the Department of Public Information for the Chicago Commission on Human Relations until 1952, when he came to Kansas City. "Biographical Sketch of William H. Gremley," Box 2, File 5 and Ordinance No. 15091, enacted by the Kansas City Council November 20, 1951, Box 1, File 01, KCHRC Collection-MSA; *Kansas City Call,* June 1, 1951, August 29, 1952. In 1972, the commission became the Human Relations Department, a fully funded department of city government.

5. "The Functions of a Human Relations Commission," February 12, 1952, Box 1, File 3, KCHRC Collection-MSA. Had Gremley tried to make the commission a more powerful instrument for change, he likely would have met stiff resistance. His successor, Bob Adams, "was an activist and as a result the city council cut his salary to a dollar a year," Smith noted. Beth Smith, interview with author, January 17, 1995.

they are the result of the years past."[6] Consequently, the board refused to break with tradition—ignoring the fact that the so-called customary exclusion of blacks from Swope Park dated back only twenty years and had been under almost constant legal challenge since.

With passage of the city's limited desegregation ordinance in early 1951, the Swope Park pool remained the only significant city-owned facility that officially excluded blacks. In June 1951, Esther Williams, Lena Rivers, and Joseph Moore attempted to buy tickets to enter the pool and were turned away. Two months later, the NAACP filed suit in federal court seeking an injunction to restrain the city from unlawfully barring blacks from the pool. Facing an array of legal talent that included Carl Johnson, president of the local NAACP, and Thurgood Marshall from the NAACP's national office, the city counsel's office tried to bolster the effect of its arguments by having Marshall struck from the suit on grounds that he was a member of a communist front organization. When that failed, the city admitted that the plaintiffs had been turned away because of their race but claimed that the policy was made necessary by the "natural aversion to physical intimacy inherent in the use of swimming pools by races that do not mingle socially." Decrying those who "stir up strife and racial conflict in a period of national emergency," the city's counsel explained that he had not cited case law to support his arguments because the city's case existed "in the realm of ethics," not law. Because exclusion rested on custom, not law or city ordinance, the city claimed, the Fourteenth Amendment was therefore irrelevant. Federal District Court judge Albert Ridge was not impressed with that particular smokescreen, however. Pointing out that the "custom" was operable only because the city's authority enforced it, Ridge held that segregation of Swope's pool was forbidden by the Fourteenth Amendment. Unfortunately, though he ruled in the plaintiffs' favor, Ridge equivocated in his decision. Because he ruled that the case was not a class action, the ruling admitted just the three plaintiffs to the pool and no other blacks. Encouraged by the waffling, the city promptly appealed the decision, and the park board closed the pool entirely pending a ruling on the appeal.[7]

The caution in closing the pool stemmed largely from the riot that followed desegregation of a public swimming pool in St. Louis in 1949. Shortly after the St. Louis director of public welfare ordered the city's public pools

6. Memorandum quoted in *Kansas City Call*, May 27, 1949.
7. *City of Kansas City v. Esther Williams*, 4; *Kansas City Times*, June 8, 1951, August 10, 1951; *Kansas City Star*, April 9, 1952; *Kansas City Call*, September 7, 1951, November 9, 1951, April 18, 1952, June 6, 1952.

opened to blacks, a gang of young white males had assaulted black swimmers at Fairgrounds Park, resulting in injuries to eleven persons and attracting a crowd estimated at some two thousand white hecklers. According to the *Call,* however, the city council in Kansas City drew the wrong lesson from the so-called riot in St. Louis, for an investigation by the director of Detroit's Interracial Committee blamed the incident on failure by St. Louis public officials and civic leaders to prepare citizens for the desegregation order. Had the city educated the public about the coming change and solicited its cooperation, the study concluded that desegregation of the pool could have occurred without major incident. Most important, the investigation found, St. Louis leaders must make clear their intention "to adhere to the law, and, by their example to encourage citizen respect for the law." Instead, city government in St. Louis "has no clear-cut statement of policy on the use of facilities" and "seemingly has sought to meet the problem of racial relations by sidestepping, expediency and balancing of pressures."[8] In C. A. Franklin's view, the St. Louis report indicated that Kansas City could safely desegregate its own public pools if responsible leaders educated the police and the public to accept integration. After all, he editorialized, advertising had made the patent medicine Hadacol a well-known and accepted product, and advertising could sell integration just as effectively. "The folks back of [H]adacol have the right idea. You've got to make it the popular thing to do."[9] Despite a quantity of testimony in the original suit confirming that pools had been desegregated in other cities without bloodshed, the Kansas City Council chose to spend two more years in litigation to contest the federal district court's decision.

In June 1953, the United States Court of Appeals for the Eighth Circuit denied the city's appeal. Still battling, the city took its appeal to the United States Supreme Court, which allowed the lower court's decision to stand. During that two years, the gates to Swope Park pool were kept firmly closed to white and black swimmers alike. The city's appeal failed. Yet, the *Call* reported, a city spokesman informed the *New York Times* that the city council would wait for a Supreme Court decision on five pending school desegregation cases before it opened the pool. With rumors afloat that the park board was considering building a half-million-dollar pool for blacks in order to evade the court decision, Carl Johnson announced that the NAACP

8. Letter of Mayor William E. Kemp to Dowdal Davis, May 5, 1952, Box 8, File 1, KCHRC Collection; Jack G. Nixon and Lee M. Fowler, "Kansas City's Swimming Pool Issue," May 1953, Box 8, File 1, KCHRC Collection-MSA. See also, *Kansas City Call,* August 12, 1949.
9. *Kansas City Call,* September 21, 1951.

would lodge further suits to contest a Jim Crow pool and to force compliance with the high court's decision. Since Swope Park pool was not a school, the court's stance on segregated schools was irrelevant, and the city was grasping at straws, Johnson pointed out. Kansas City had received three firm judicial answers regarding the pool, and the time had come to accept them.[10]

Finally, in the summer of 1954, Swope Park pool reopened. In the intervening months, a public education program acquainted Kansas Citians with the reasons for pool desegregation and the importance of meeting the change cooperatively. Meanwhile, the Human Relations Commission held training sessions for police and park personnel to help them accept the order and to equip them to handle possible conflicts. Gremley found the police a bit skeptical of the elaborate preparations. They readily agreed to deploy "E-Men," or squads of men trained in riot control, but police discounted the need for other measures, such as stationing black and white guards at the parking lots, bus stops, and trolley routes where blacks were vulnerable to attack. Police commanders did have an idea of their own, however. They recommended that the pools be segregated by sex, with men and women swimming on alternate days. True to black activists' predictions, the new policy sparked neither violence nor other public protest. "Kansas City can be justifiably proud of the fact that this major change has been accomplished without incident," said the *Star.* "Here a difficult problem has been handled well." Having refused mob action, however, white Kansas Citians registered their displeasure nonetheless. Attendance at the pool fell to one-third its usual level in 1954 and increased only slightly the following summer. While they might join a mixed-race audience at a prize fight or object to categorical exclusions of blacks from public facilities, most whites in Kansas City were not prepared to tolerate racial mixing in so intimate a matter as bathing.[11]

A *Call* editorial had suggested at the beginning of pool litigation that "when all of the public facilities are operated on a non-biased basis, then attention can be turned to privately-owned places of public accommodation."[12] But pressure on business owners was a long time in building. By the end of 1955, downtown hotels and theaters had largely abandoned segregation, but a report by the Human Relations Commission (HRC) found that segregation of eating establishments remained a persistent problem.

10. *Ibid.,* October 16, 1953, October 23, 1953.

11. Memo from William H. Gremley to the Kansas City Commission on Human Relations, June 22, 1953, Box 8, file 1, KCHRC Collection-MSA; Dorothy Davis Johnson, interview with author, October 7, 1991; *Kansas City Star,* August 5, 1955.

12. *Kansas City Call,* August 17, 1951.

In keeping with its philosophy of race relations, HRC censured segregated restaurants for disrupting "peace and harmony between the groups of our community." Moreover, such practices were inconvenient and unethical, an HRC resolution continued, and invited criticism of Kansas City by foreign dignitaries and conventioneers. Some large organizations refused even to bring their conventions to the city because of its segregated eateries. When the local branch of the NAACP proposed a public accommodations ordinance in August 1956, even some restaurant owners were in favor of the measure because it would allow them to open their doors to blacks without running the risks of taking steps on their own. But the city council failed to pass such a measure, despite public hearings in which a preponderance of testimony from civic organizations supported an end to segregated eateries. Instead, the Greater Kansas City Restaurant Association established a subcommittee to work with HRC's public accommodations committee, and by 1958, several downtown restaurants had begun quietly serving black patrons. However, dining facilities in downtown department stores continued to refuse service to African Americans. William Gremley, director of HRC, and Dowdal Davis of the *Call* requested a meeting with William G. Austin, manager of the Merchants' Association, to discuss the problem in March 1957. Austin stalled, however, and Davis's death enabled him to avoid a meeting altogether. In the absence of any real pressure to change their policies, the department stores continued to deny food service to their black customers.[13]

Galled by the inaction, Gladys Twine attended a regular meeting of the Twin Citians, a social club composed largely of black women professionals and business proprietors, in late 1957. At the meeting, she asked fellow members if they were as fed up as she with spending hundreds of dollars a year in stores that forbid her to sit down with a cup of coffee or a sandwich on their premises. Twine suggested that the Twin Citians make it a club project to do something about store policy, but, despite a chorus of angry agreement with her complaints, members rejected the project as too ambitious. Twine continued to talk about the problem, however, and in September 1958, new president Ruth Kerford appointed Twine to head a committee

13. Resolution of HRC, May 1958, reproduced in Dorothy Hodge Davis, "Changing Discriminatory Practices in Department Store Eating Facilities in Kansas City, Missouri: A Study of a Project in Community Organization as Illustrated by the Community Committee for Social Action of Greater Kansas City," 52; "Transcript of Public Hearing on Restaurant Discrimination," March 2, 1957, Box 13, File 3, and "Resolution to Kansas City Council," May 1, 1958, Box 13, File 1, KCHRC Collection-MSA.

to determine what action might be feasible for the club to undertake. Following recommendations of Lucile Bluford of the *Call*, the club agreed in October to take on some kind of joint project with other black organizations. Meeting with Kerford in October, William Gremley advised the women to approach the stores individually, rather than in a group, and to allow him to act as "interpreter" for each side. Kerford did speak to Macy's manager, who told her that his store would adhere to Merchants' Association policy unless other stores agreed to serve blacks. Her experience confirmed what attorney Harold Holliday had discovered in fruitless conferences with the Merchants' Association. Speaking to a meeting of club representatives, most of them women, Holliday recommended taking independent action because negotiations had achieved nothing. Accordingly, an ad hoc group of club members and black citizens who met in November 1958 targeted five department stores for a pressure campaign and organized the Community Committee for Social Action (CCSA) to carry it out.[14]

As its first step, CCSA collected letters from black store customers protesting restaurant policy at Macy's, Jones Store, Kline's, Peck's and Emery, Bird, Thayer (EBT) department stores and issued stickers for black charge account holders to affix to their bill payments protesting discrimination in the recipients' restaurants. When no store's manager would agree to take the first step, HRC's Gremley pleaded for more time for negotiations. Instead, CCSA added a parallel men's unit and began planning for direct action—a boycott accompanied by picketing of the targeted stores—and launched an all-out advertising campaign and door-to-door canvas to secure wide black support. "This could be a serious community situation," William Gremley warned the meeting. He discouraged picketing and a boycott in favor of more negotiation, to which Rev. Arthur Marshall replied, "This group has attempted to negotiate in a fair way, and it is now necessary to take overt action. If they walked in Montgomery, surely we can stop buying in Kansas City." Amid further warnings of community upheaval, the group launched its boycott but agreed to withhold picketing until Mayor H. Roe Bartle had an opportunity to intercede with store managers. In a classic example of buck-passing, the managers informed the mayor that they would leave it

14. Davis, "Changing Discriminatory Practices," 13–20, 50–52. When CCSA first appeared, Dorothy Davis (later Dorothy Davis Johnson), a former public relations director for the Urban League and HRC member, was a graduate student in social work at the University of Kansas. She elected not to join CCSA, instead winning permission to observe and document CCSA's activities for her master's thesis. The result was a thoughtful firsthand account of the group's operation.

to the Merchants' Association to decide. Meanwhile, William Austin of the Merchants' Association claimed to have no authority to decide the matter but could do only what the store managers directed.[15]

Two days later, on December 19, CCSA's pickets appeared in front of the five department stores. In spite of frigid temperatures, the pickets chose the right time to walk the cold pavements, for retailers were in the midst of the Christmas shopping season. At first, store supervisors discounted CCSA's capacity to affect sales. Fletcher Daniels recalled an indignant store president telling him, "It's typical of your people to raise sand for awhile and then it will die out and so we won't be bothered by the noise you're making." When sales did drop, managers began coming out to tell the picketers that they would prefer to open their restaurants but that the Merchants' Association "had them in a bind." The pickets were not placated, and business continued to drop. "You could hardly hear a pin fall downtown during the whole Christmas shopping time," Daniels claimed. While Daniels' recollection is somewhat exaggerated, few African Americans risked the picketers' hostility by entering the stores, and a significant number of whites stayed away either out of fear or because they honored picket lines as a matter of principle. Some took the trouble to tell picketers, "We're for you," or, "Good luck in your efforts." A number of white pastors preached in support of the boycott, and the predominantly white United Church Women registered their support by letters to the department stores. More important, however, the demonstration reached beyond its middle-class origins to attract participation from blue- and white-collar African Americans. Although Davis heard some grumbling from working-class participants that the demonstration ought to seek jobs in the stores instead of cafe seating, she and Margaret Holliday recalled that all ranks were represented on the picket lines.[16]

When this level of participation cut into post-Christmas sales as well, William Gremley tried to restart negotiations. On February 9, 1959, CCSA suspended picketing as a condition for resuming talks with store managers but began planning for a mass march on the downtown if talks failed. Then, in the midst of what CCSA described as "honest and good faith" discussions, Chamber of Commerce president Carl Rechner weighed in with an offer to negotiate a settlement if CCSA would postpone its march for sixty days. In his letter to CCSA making his mediation offer, Rechner made clear where

15. Fletcher Daniels, interview by Ella Pruitt, May 5, 1976, Black Archives of Mid-America; Davis, "Changing Discriminatory Practices," 21–32; Margaret Holliday, interview with author, January 31, 1992.

16. Interview with Fletcher Daniels; Davis, "Changing Discriminatory Practices," 36, 56, 70.

his concern lay. "We have urged your organization not to stage a parade that would cast an unfavorable reaction or publicity on our entire metropolitan community," he wrote. Having seen "excellent progress" made in local race relations, "we want to cement that progress and to prevent any deterioration, incident, violence, separation or hatred." So long as store owners negotiated under threat, however, Rechner thought that a solution was impossible—an opinion he thought he shared with "your more mature and well-known leaders." Infuriated that Rechner released his letter to the press several hours before it reached him, CCSA board chairman Rev. L. Sylvester Odom re-iterated CCSA's efforts to bring about a solution within an atmosphere of calm deliberation, and he pointed out to Rechner that the "mature and well-known" members of CCSA's board had voted to go ahead with the march if no concessions were forthcoming from the target stores.[17]

One day after this exchange, William Austin and the store managers requested a meeting with CCSA, and on February 27, a mass rally of CCSA members heard the settlement reached by the combatants. Macy's and Peck's agreed to open their dining facilities immediately. Given store managers' fears that their stores would be "overrun by Negroes" and their white business eroded, Macy's, Peck's, and Kline's further agreed to open all dining facilities after an "education and orientation program." The women of CCSA promptly organized the required tutorials for black customers in the proper dress, deportment, and table manners expected of a department store diner. The women also established a scheduling system to guarantee that a sufficient number of black diners were present every day to test the new policy without seeming to "overrun" the eateries. Apparently satisfied with the results, the Jones Store and EBT opened their dining facilities two months later.[18]

■ ■ Geography of Avoidance and Denial

The gradual erosion of segregation in downtown accommodations caused little apparent protest from white patrons. Rather than insist on continuing legal or customary rules to separate the races, whites simply practiced avoidance tactics once those strictures were removed. White swimmers abandoned a desegregated Swope Park pool, and shoppers began deserting downtown

17. Letter of Carl B. Rechner to Rev. L. Sylvester Odom, February 25, 1959, and Letter of Rev. L. Sylvester Odom to Carl Rechner, February 25, 1959, in Davis, "Changing Discriminatory Practices," 104–8.
18. Letter of Mrs. Kenneth Kerford and Mrs. George E. Walters, Jr., to Members, CCSA, March 4, 1959, in Davis, "Changing Discriminatory Practices," Appendix.

retailers for new retail centers in all-white suburbs. In 1959, Ward Parkway Center opened its first stores to customers at Eighty-Fifth and Ward Parkway, and the Landing shopping center opened at Sixty-Third and Troost in 1961. Thus began the slow but steady departure of white trade to the suburban mall. Willing to abandon patently undemocratic discriminatory practices, many whites still depended on physical separation to maintain racial boundaries. Consequently, segregated housing proved far more durable than segregated lunch counters, and blacks' deepening housing crisis made housing the sharpest issue of contention between the races during and after the Second World War.

The war years brought unprecedented employment opportunities to the black community in Kansas City, and, along with prosperity, a shortage of housing. By the end of the war, 12,701 black men and women were employed in war plants in the Greater Kansas City area—more than 10,000 of them in the four largest defense contractors. Fittingly, North American Aviation employed the greatest number, with more than 5,300 African Americans on its payroll. All together, blacks made up 6.5 percent of all war workers in Greater Kansas City in 1943, and a healthy portion of those who found war-related jobs were migrants to Kansas City. Between 1940 and mid-1943, the Federal Security Agency estimated that black population in Kansas City, Missouri, rose by 10,000 persons, an increase of 25 percent compared to a 13 percent increase for the city's population as a whole. Finding a place to live—difficult for any Kansas City resident during the war—was nearly impossible for black newcomers.[19]

The influx of war manpower produced inexorable pressures on the boundaries of the Vine Street corridor in particular. As blacks moved into white neighborhoods along the corridor's eastern and southern fringes, whites responded by breaking out windows in their homes or stoning them as they stepped off buses in white neighborhoods. In 1941, blacks received telephone calls and letters threatening infestations of termites if they did not leave their newly occupied homes, and employers reported being pressured to fire blacks who lived in white areas. Better-organized, the Linwood Improvement Association created a conflict in 1943 volatile enough to bring in the new Inter-racial Committee to try to settle the dispute. This time, LIA attempted to prosecute whites who violated their restrictive covenants. Because most covenants in the LIA area had been written so as to lapse after

19. Thomas Webster, "Community Planning to Improve the Housing Conditions of the Negro Population of Kansas City, Missouri, 1940–1947," 9–23, 117; *Kansas City Call*, August 17, 1945.

fifteen years, many property owners preferred to sell their homes to blacks for top dollar rather than renew their covenant restrictions. The LIA hoped to stem the flight.

Housing tensions also erupted in the North End during the war. Sensitive to the fact that disputes over housing had sparked the Detroit riot in 1943, the *Call* investigated the problem in the North End in 1945. According to its report, blacks and Italians had been able to "get along famously" in the North End for decades, sharing its decrepit housing stock. With expanding job opportunities during the war, however, many Italians found better paying and more secure employment. To signal newfound prosperity, Italian businessmen and community leaders joined forces to provide more housing in the North End for Italian families. The projects included buying properties the city had seized for unpaid taxes, many of those properties having black occupants. Another plan would replace Garrison Center with a housing facility for Italian newlyweds. The *Call* concluded that the North End's remaining black residents were right in thinking that the Italian community was trying to drive them out of the North End.[20] The dearth of housing meant that they had nowhere else to go.

Such crowding had its inevitable consequences. By 1940, blacks occupied 56 percent of the city's substandard housing, and the city engineer calculated that 85 percent of the areas where blacks resided was in need of rehabilitation. Seemingly, the New Deal had provided some avenues of relief for blacks' housing shortage. The Federal Housing Authority, for example, guaranteed low-interest loans by private lenders to permit families to buy new homes or rehabilitate their existing residences. But FHA's Underwriting Manual instructed its agents to honor restrictive covenants. Real estate agents in Kansas City reported that FHA would not insure loans to blacks for purchase of housing in white areas. Moreover, lenders charged higher than normal interest rates to African Americans who wished to purchase homes in black neighborhoods. Because black purchasers also were forced to pay higher than market value for substandard housing in those neighborhoods, out of lower annual incomes, lenders generally regarded black home-buyers as poor risks for FHA loans no matter where they proposed to buy.[21]

Nor was public housing a help to black families. With passage of the

20. Webster, "Housing Conditions," 101–2, 114–17; *Kansas City Call*, April 11, 1941, June 27, 1941, November 19, 1943, July 14, 1943, July 21, 1944, June 22, 1945. Thomas Webster essentially confirmed the *Call*'s suspicions about the Don Bosco project in his housing study.

21. Missouri Relief and Reconstruction Commission, "Report of the Housing Survey, Kansas City, Missouri," 11–17, 70; James L. Hecht, *Because It Is Right: Integration in*

U.S. Housing Act of 1937, cities elsewhere had begun easing their housing problems with slum clearance projects. But the Pendergast administration refused to admit that the city was scarred by blight by authorizing public housing. With the strong support of local black leaders, the city's reform administration secured the necessary authority in 1941 only to have its first housing projects (including 340 housing units for black families) put on hold due to wartime shortages in building materials. As the housing crisis worsened throughout the city, however, various federal agencies began approving projects that benefited some black residents, including T. B. Watkins Housing, completed in 1953. But there were some long-range disadvantages, for black leaders fought to reserve as many units as possible for black tenants, and the city's planning commission refused to place public housing for blacks in white neighborhoods. Practices begun in the war years became policy thereafter.[22]

Following the war, black Kansas Citians waged what the *Call* termed "an all-out fight against restrictive covenants," seemingly with the aid of the U.S. Supreme Court. The court held in *Shelley v. Kraemer* in 1948 that, because the courts were an arm of government, the use of court injunctions to enforce restrictive covenants was an exercise of the coercive powers of government and therefore an abridgment of the Fourteenth Amendment.[23] The following year, the Missouri Supreme Court ruled that the *Shelley* decision permitted civil suits for breach of contract in such cases. Fourteen property owners in Kansas City promptly brought suit asking civil damages from a couple who sold a home in the Santa Fe district. Four other such cases followed. All were dismissed for lack of proof that damages had occurred, but the possibility of civil damages breathed life into restrictive covenants in Missouri until the U.S. Supreme Court struck down a similar practice in California in 1953. Dynamiters enjoyed a reprise as well. For the first time since the 1920s a rash of bombings of black-occupied homes occurred in a lower-middle-class neighborhood near Twenty-Seventh and the Paseo in 1952.[24]

Housing, 53; Jeanne R. Lowe, "Who Lives Where? Urban Housing and Discrimination," 466.

22. Webster, "Housing Conditions," 29–64, 84–94.

23. *Kansas City Call,* December 14, 1945. See also, *Kansas City Call,* October 18, 1946, September 19, 1947, March 26, 1948. The *Shelley* case originated in St. Louis, Missouri, when J. D. and Ethel Shelley appealed a Missouri Supreme Court ruling that they should be evicted from their home in a covenanted neighborhood. Lorenzo J. Greene, Gary R. Kremer, and Antonio F. Holland, *Missouri's Black Heritage,* 163–64.

24. Thomas Gillette, "Santa Fe: A Study of the Effects of Negro Invasion on Property Values," 3, 83–84; *Kansas City Call,* December 23, 1949. The Santa Fe district extended

Most white Kansas Citians preferred flight to court fights or arson, however. The metropolitan area's postwar building boom provided their escape route as highway improvements and construction of new trafficways made it possible to work in the city and live in farther-flung suburbs that newly ringed the older core. Federal mortgage guarantees enabled white households to purchase a three-bedroom ranch in Raytown, Missouri, or an ersatz cottage among J. C. Nichols's developments in Johnson County, Kansas. One result was a wild and woolly real estate market along the city's old southeastern corridor. Fred Curls took up the real estate business in 1952, just as that market came to life. Since restrictive covenants had outrun their usefulness, whites in the southeastern corridor were anxious to sell and move to newer suburbs, removed from the line of black advance. But the availability of FHA and VA loans and the abundance of new housing stock meant that few other whites were willing to purchase homes in the old southeastern district when the suburbs beckoned. Consequently, white home-owners in the old southeast were ready and willing to sell to black families. Curls admitted that he engaged in some block-busting. In a typical ploy, he knocked on doors, telling residents that he, a black man, had had the pleasure of serving the buyer of a neighboring house and inviting the home owner to let him know if he could be of service. "And it wouldn't be long and they would let me know." Usually, whites in the area needed less prodding. Once a block was busted, "they would break all barriers." A report done for the Kansas City Human Relations Committee found other block-busting practices rampant in the Central Linwood district. Both black and white real estate agents canvassed neighborhoods by telephone, stampeding property owners with remarks like, "I'm glad you want to stay in the neighborhood; so few white people do."[25]

White realtors were still forbidden by the real estate board's code of ethics to sell a home to a black buyer on a given block unless two blacks were already living there. Eager to sell new houses to such families, and pocket their commissions, the white realtors simply telephoned black realtors like Curls to tell him a house was available. Curls, in turn, called the next name on his list of black families who were patiently waiting for a newer house in a better neighborhood. He arranged the sale. Next, he called his "investors," those

---

from Twenty-Seventh to Thirtieth Streets, from Prospect to Indiana. It lay just east of the Linwood Improvement Association area and developed similar improvement associations to resist black residence.

25. Fred Curls, Sr., interview by Ella Pruit, March 11, 1976, Black Archives of Mid-America; Beverly Breuer, "A Study of Real Estate Practices as They Relate to Population Movements in the Central-Linwood District," Box 5, File 2, KCHRC Collection-MSA.

anonymous whites who provided mortgage money for blacks at a return of
25 percent. Because private lenders were reluctant to make mortgage loans
to black families, black home-buyers readily accepted the steep terms and
paid faithfully. Curls knew nothing about the real estate business when he
entered it, but the nature of his market was such that it did not matter. "Really, it didn't take much talent real estate–wise; you just had to be a good
order-taker."[26]

■ ■ Policing and the Ironies of Reform

Just as tensions over housing resumed in the war years, relations between
the black community and the law enforcement system also deteriorated after
Pendergast's fall, for the institution of reform in Kansas City brought a re-
institution of police terror in the African American community. In 1939, on
the heels of Tom Pendergast's conviction for insurance fraud, the state legislature pushed through a bill ending home rule of Kansas City's police force.
Governor Lloyd Stark appointed a new Board of Police Commissioners, who
hired Lear B. Reed, a fourteen-year veteran of the Federal Bureau of Investigation, as chief of police. A swashbuckling devotee of J. Edgar Hoover, Reed
"combined in his person the more formidable characteristics of Fearless Fos-
dick and Paul Revere, and he was equally energetic in efforts to save Kansas
City from criminals and the nation from Reds, whom he regarded as much
more of a threat to America than the British Redcoats ever were," or so an
observer remembered. Reed launched a major cleanup of both the police
department and the city's streets. In the process, he managed to reduce the
hold of organized crime on Kansas City. Among his less successful exploits,
Reed attempted the wholesale fingerprinting of Kansas Citians, labor leaders
in particular, and proposed a paramilitary organization of civilians to work
alongside the police.[27]

But it was in the black ghetto where Reed's methods were most felt by
ordinary citizens. His purge of police ranks removed more than twenty black
officers; only three of their replacements were black. Reports of police brutality began surfacing soon after Reed's appointment. Trust in the police
department so deteriorated in the black community that, in early 1941, officers felt compelled to call in the riot squad during an arrest on a ghetto
street for fear that a crowd of onlookers would try to take their prisoner away

26. Fred Curls, interview.
27. William M. Reddig, *Tom's Town: Kansas City and the Pendergast Legend*, 365–67.

from them. Initially, C. A. Franklin was inclined to give Reed the benefit of the doubt, but the shooting of Harrison Ware in August 1941 infuriated Franklin and a sizable segment of his readers. Ware was present at the Autumn Leaf Club when the vice squad raided it. According to eyewitnesses, Officers Charles LeBaugh and Dewey Ellis, both white, began beating the unarmed Ware for no apparent reason. When Ware struck one of the officers with a cue ball, LeBaugh and Ellis shot him three times in the back, then kicked the dying man.[28]

Following a funeral march by more than a thousand protesters, the police commissioners suspended LeBaugh. Nonetheless, a delegation of black Kansas Citians prepared to meet with Governor Forrest C. Donnell to urge him to improve relations between the police and the black citizenry. Among the abuses the delegation cited were incidents of police brutality; the persistent harassment by the police of the young black men who congregated on street corners near the dance halls that white women frequented; and the resumption of arrests and insults to light-skinned women whom the police spotted in company with dark-skinned men. Donnell responded by demanding an accounting from the police commission. Amid rumors that commissioners were growing resentful of Reed's autocratic rule of both the department and the commission itself, commissioners called Reed before an executive session. Declaring to the commissioners that, "if I can not enforce the law in the colored belt, then I won't be chief of police," Reed resigned.[29] Few Kansas Citians regretted his departure, including many of the good-government reformers whose viewpoint Reed supposedly represented. As an observer and historian of the Pendergast era remarked, "Besides suppressing criminals and scattering Reds, [Reed] antagonized workingmen and union officials, Negroes, liberals and a wide variety of ordinary individuals who began to wonder if democracy could stand the strain of absolute rectitude."[30]

According to the *Call,* black residents had high hopes for Harold Anderson, Reed's replacement, and for the new relationship with police Reed's departure seemed to auger. Anderson had begun his career as a patrol officer in Kansas City in 1929, and his father was widely respected in the black community from his tenure as captain of the Flora Avenue police station. Anderson

28. Letter of Lucile Bluford to Walter White, August 23, 1941, Group II:B116, NAACP Papers, LOC; *Kansas City Call,* January 24, 1941, August 1, 1941.
29. Report prepared by Lucile Bluford for the NAACP, September 12, 1941, Group II:B116, NAACP Papers, LOC. See also, *Kansas City Call,* August 8, 1941, August 15, 1941, August 22, 1941, August 29, 1941, September 5, 1941.
30. Reddig, *Tom's Town,* 365.

promised to add black officers to the force, including black detectives.[31] Unfortunately, the board of reformist police commissioners proved as insensitive to blacks' concerns as the reforming commissioners of the 1920s had been. In response to the governor's inquiry, the board detailed nineteen allegations of police abuse of African Americans and dismissed each as exaggerations by the local black community. Officers had been justified in their actions in every case, the board reported, even in their harassment of light-skinned African American women attending a national Greek letter convention with their dark-skinned husbands. The local NAACP promptly demanded that Governor Donnell replace the entire board. Donnell did reorganize the board with a new president to replace the president who had hired Reed, and, after a grand jury failed to indict Officers LeBaugh and Ellis, a second grand jury brought an indictment. Despite what the *Call* described as an impressive body of medical evidence and eyewitness testimony, however, a jury acquitted both officers in the Ware shooting, and both were restored to active duty.[32]

Very few allegations of police use of excessive force appeared thereafter in the *Call*, whose editor commented in 1947 and again in 1954 that police brutality had declined significantly since Reed's departure. Still, there were continuing demonstrations that police officers felt responsible for upholding gender codes. In one of the most controversial cases, the police began stopping whites who tried to enter the Hot Club, a weekly jam session by black and white musicians at the Chez Paree nightclub. According to Chief Anderson, the action was merely an example of crime prevention, since violations of the law were certain to occur wherever liquor, hot jazz, and interracial dancing were found. If the club was a breeding ground of lawlessness, countered the Urban League's Dorothy Davis in a meeting of the Board of Police Commissioners, then police ought to bar blacks from attending as well. In fact, the police did just that in bars that whites patronized. Shortly before the Hot Club incident, patrolman William Todd clubbed Cab Calloway over the head with the butt of his revolver when the bandleader tried to enter the Pla-

31. In respect to staffing, the Kansas City Police Department also made separation of the races a firm policy. True to his promise, Chief Anderson appointed Leon Jordan and Clifford Warren detectives in 1942. Frustrated by the slow pace of promotion, Jordan was eventually named the city's first black police lieutenant, but he resigned rather than command a Jim Crow unit. Jordan served for a time as head of the Liberian Constabulary. He later founded Freedom Inc. in the early 1960s, the first independent black political organization in Kansas City. *Kansas City Call*, July 24, 1942, June 13, 1947, October 31, 1952, November 21, 1952, November 28, 1952.

32. *Kansas City Call*, September 12, 1941, October 3, 1941, October 10, 1941, November 14, 1941, February 13, 1942.

Mor Ballroom to hear Lionel Hampton perform. Charges of resisting arrest against Calloway were dropped, and Todd resigned, but the bandleader still sued the Pla-Mor. Arguing that Calloway had tried to inject the "New York angle" into the "Kansas City way of life," defendant's attorneys convinced an all-white jury to find in favor of the Pla-Mor.[33]

The Hot Club case raised considerable alarm among black leaders because it appeared to jeopardize interracial cooperation. If the police were free to break up social gatherings in nightclubs or on city streets simply because they included law-abiding men and women of both races, they were likewise free to arrest members of the Urban League, the NAACP, CO-POD, or Fellowship House merely for attending meetings that brought white women and black men into close contact. Moreover, the assumption by police that interracial mixing led inevitably to lawbreaking or riot lent credence to city officials' claims that desegregating public accommodations would create mayhem.[34]

It was a ticklish issue, however. As Roy Wilkins noted soon after he became assistant secretary of the national NAACP, mounting a challenge could be "interpreted as a fight to associate with white people on the most intimate social terms" that would alienate respectable blacks and whites. Several black clergy insisted that dives like the Hot Club should be shut down altogether. In the end, NAACP president Carl Johnson demanded that police commissioners issue a clear policy prohibiting the police from interfering with the actions of citizens when there was no violation of the law. Instead, the board upheld Chief Anderson's judgment that the Hot Club ban was a legitimate act of crime prevention. Board members admitted only that police were not entitled to interfere with whites and blacks who visited each others' homes and churches. Accordingly, Chief Anderson apologized after a Kansas City patrolman stopped orchestra leader Duke Ellington for questioning in 1947 when he was spotted in a cab with three light-skinned women. Little had changed three years later, however. Confirming earlier fears, a young white woman described as being "in the vanguard of the fight for civil rights and racial equality in the Kansas City area" reported being stopped by white police officers in the vicinity of Eighteenth and Vine. During questioning, one of the officers told her, "It's for your own protection. One of these n-----s might jump out of a doorway and hit you over the head." After releasing her, the officers cautioned her to stay out of black neighborhoods. "Lady,

33. *Ibid.,* September 19, 1947, January 1, 1954, December 28, 1941, February 1, 1946, January 4, 1946, May 16, 1947, May 23, 1947.
34. *Ibid.,* April 5, 1946, January 18, 1946.

you don't know these n-----s like we do," they warned. The woman reported the incident because she was frightened of the policemen and of the potential for police harassment of civil rights workers.[35]

Letters of complaint to the Human Relations Commission showed that the harassment did not abate. One letter writer, a young jazz musician and waitress, was picked up by police for sitting in her own car chatting with a young black man, also a musician. The only reason officers gave her for her arrest was that she was a white girl in a black neighborhood. She was searched at the station house and questioned by the Vice Unit for hours before being released with a warning that she would be picked up again if officers spotted her in the black district. The writer lamented that, when she moved to Kansas City from New York, "I was unprepared for the treatment I have received by the Kansas City police force due to my association with jazz musicians of the Negro race." Claiming to have been arrested three times for "riding in a car in mixed company," she was anxious "to avoid more confrontations with the ugly, prejudiced attitudes of the Kansas City Police." A second woman complained that she, too, had been arrested three times for socializing in a "colored tavern" along with other young white women. Because she and the others were very happy with the friends they had made there and wanted to continue their evenings at the tavern, the writer wanted to know if what a police officer had told her was true. Could he "as he states pick me up on investigation each and everytime he sees me their [*sic*]?!?" She hoped for an answer soon, because "I like it their and I like the people and I only hope to hear from you that we may continue to go their." Apparently she was not a singular case, for an officer told her that white girls were a constant trouble to him on his beat. Nor were the city streets the only "beat" these officers patrolled, as a white woman discovered when she was arrested in her home along with her guests, namely six of her fellow social workers whom she had invited in for coffee. Four of those guests were black—two of them black men.[36]

Sadly, another law enforcement problem returned to plague the African American community as well. During the Pendergast years, the number of black-on-black homicides declined, the result, according to the *Call*, of vig-

35. Letter of Roy Wilkins to L. Amassa Knox, April 11, 1933, Group G, Box 108, NAACP Papers, LOC; *Kansas City Call*, November 22, 1946, February 17, 1950. The woman in question asked the *Call* to withhold her name.
36. Unsigned typed copy of letter of complaint to the Kansas City Human Relations Commission, December 6, 1953, Box 14, File 6, and Letter of Shirley Morley to the Kansas City Human Relations Commission (no date), Box 14, File 6, KCHRC Collection-MSA; *Kansas City Call*, August 21, 1953.

orous prosecution of the slayers of black people. The murder rate remained low during the war, but, in 1946, the killings resumed at the rate of nearly one a week. The pace barely slackened in 1947 and 1948, when blacks committed 59 of the city's 101 homicides, taking a black life in nearly every case. An Urban League study of crime figures for 1949 showed that blacks accounted for 60 percent of arrests for murder and 54 percent of arrests for aggravated assault. The report blamed the high crime rate on the unwholesome environment of substandard housing, disorganized community life, and the lack of wholesome amusements in the black community.[37]

C. A. Franklin took a tougher stance. Noting that the great majority of black-on-black homicides followed arguments at taverns or drinking parties, he recommended that police should crack down on the carrying of concealed weapons by blacks and that watch commanders should assign station officers to patrol the taverns in the African American community to search men entering the liquor joints. So many black men carried weapons with impunity, he observed, that going armed had become a symbol of boastful manhood. "Time and again, the streets are the scenes of many night fights," he lamented, with "grinning, yelping, armed persons capering about each other, knife in hand, crying, 'I gotcha, I gotcha,' or in a blustering, bullying tone they announce to whoever will listen, 'I got the difference.'" A poll of *Call* readers showed that a majority of respondents agreed with Franklin's diagnosis and with the draconian measures he proposed to curb weapons carrying.[38]

In cases where blacks were arrested for killing or assaulting a black person, prosecutors were inclined to release them for lack of witnesses rather than pursue evidence for a conviction. Should such a case go to trial, juries often acquitted or judges levied light sentences. "So successful have killers been that it is a common boast among those so minded that they 'can do all the time standing up' that the court inflicts as a penalty for murder," Franklin observed. Until African American men and women learned to respect each other's lives, Franklin hoped that the judicial system would lock them up and throw away the key. Judicious but more frequent use of the gas chamber appealed to him as well. NAACP president Carl Johnson concurred. In 1949, Johnson wrote to County Prosecutor Henry Fox demanding that more blacks be impaneled on juries and that a black attorney be added to the

37. *Kansas City Call,* March 8, 1946; Urban League of Kansas City, "Report to the Citizens' Committee on Crime and Law Enforcement among Negroes," 1, 5.
38. *Kansas City Call,* February 14, 1947, February 11, 1948. See also, *ibid.,* August 6, 1948, January 7, 1949.

prosecutor's trial staff. A black prosecutor would be more dogged in seeking convictions in the murder and assault of black victims, Johnson argued,
and less patient with the magistrates courts, where magistrates repeatedly
dismissed black defendants during preliminary hearings, despite evidence of
probable cause. "The life of a Negro should be viewed with the same community value as any other life," Johnson asserted. For its part, the Urban
League urged the police commission to hire more black officers, who would
be less heavy-handed in treating witnesses at the scene. More black crime
witnesses would come forward to testify, the league reasoned, if the police
commanded greater respect and confidence from the black community.[39]

Responding to the demands, Fox appointed Lewis Clymer the county's
first African American assistant prosecutor in early 1949. Soon after, Fox
answered a chorus of complaints about legal laxity from readers of the *Call*
with an open letter to the paper. The prosecutor agreed with readers that
carrying of concealed weapons by blacks accounted for much of the problem. He pledged his office to relentless prosecution of crimes involving black
victims, but he claimed that he was helpless to correct some of the sources of
judicial leniency. A sufficient number of African Americans were included in
jury pools, he argued, but defense attorneys—particularly white attorneys—
regularly struck African Americans from juries in cases against black defendants. They did so on the theory that black jurors were more likely than
whites to hold the defendant to account for taking an African American life.
The same attorneys, Fox observed, "usually argue to the jury that there is a
different code of conduct for the Negro race and that they should accordingly be punished at a different standard or level than white persons charged
with similar crimes." Unfortunately, the ploy worked. The wave of black-on-
black murders continued, resuming the rate of one killing per week in the
first months of 1950.[40]

■ ■ Conclusion: Counting Costs

Patterns developed over the first half of the twentieth century persisted into
the second half. Spatial separation by residence remained an important feature of racial protocols. Removing the legal and customary segregation of
public places simply made it easier for whites to claim that theirs was not a

39. *Ibid.*, February 14, 1947, January 28, 1949; Urban League, "Report on Crime,"
5–6.
40. *Kansas City Call*, March 17, 1950, March 25, 1949.

racist social structure, while inequitable enforcement of the law legitimized separation with a myth that seemed not to spring from race prejudice or bigotry. By criminalizing certain kinds of interracial contact and by creating conditions that encouraged personal and family disorder within the black community, the magisterial system enabled whites to claim self-protection as their motive for separation. In fact, there was a good bit of truth in the claim, for the impulse to establish physical distance had originated—not in color-phobia—but in middle-class whites' yearning for a status identity and some social perks to go with it. By defining African Americans as the apotheosis of dirt, disorder, and vice, then by holding blacks at arm's length, they defined themselves as a status group. Ultimately, they defined whiteness, but their racialism was no less pernicious for being a by-product of other impulses.

Their public leaders abetted them in constructing a denial system. In the 1940s, as in the 1920s, efforts by municipal government reformers to clean up vice, crime, and police corruption created an escalation of police brutal-ity against blacks, quarantined vice to the African American community, and tightened the boundaries of racial exclusion from public places. Disclaiming either racial motives or ultimate responsibility for their acts, white leaders of every stripe deprived African Americans of clear targets for protest while helping to camouflage the racialist character of their city's social and politi-cal fabric.

Above all, white leaders acted out of expediency and fear. In their formu-lations, relations between the races served a purpose variously defined but consistently calculated in terms of what best suited the interests of whites. Just as Pendergast corrected only such abuses as would attract black votes without alienating his white constituency, race liberals of the 1920s addressed those racial disabilities that jeopardized the health and security of the white population. Civic reformers targeted blacks for rough justice and closeted vice in the African American community in order to reassure whites that their own streets were safer. Ultimately, their dread of racial violence guided public leaders both before and after the Second World War, inducing them to ame-liorate conditions for black Kansas Citians only when doing so promised to reduce the potential for interracial conflict. More often, they resisted change out of a conviction that change invited retaliation and riot by whites. Their fears were largely of their own making, but nonetheless powerful in narrow-ing the range of possibilities for public policy.

Although white integrationists of the postwar period added a new con-cept of race to the construct of racial perceptions among whites, their social ethic also reflected a degree of self-interest. They condemned racial inequal-ity because it degraded the character of whites who imposed it—inducing ignorance, intolerance, and cruelty. They did not care to live among such people. Likewise, their integration ethos harnessed race relations to the service of whites' needs by attributing to integration a therapeutic, transforming power to create the ideal white citizen. The peaceable kingdom they sought defined the community in which they wished to live—an orderly, harmonious, and secure place where the dignity of personhood enjoyed respect. The glimpses of the kingdom they experienced within their interracial subcommunities gave them pleasure and a sense of empowerment.

Although integrationists managed to delegitimize many public expressions of racism and tear away some of the masks of misdirection, still they failed to bring in the kingdom. Subtler forms of racism, and their legitimizing myths, withstood their powers to educate. They aimed at the easy targets Jim Crow offered but postponed challenges to the structural inequalities inherent in the legal and economic system and in residential segregation. Moreover, from the vantage point of three decades that were marred by riots, assassinations, and the alienation of black youth, their ethos and political culture came to appear foolishly romantic. "In retrospect I seem awfully naive," Robert Farnsworth confessed. "I don't believe at the time I was involved with a civil rights organization I had any adequate understanding of the depths of feeling in the black community about race and about how much stronger this is really seared into their consciousness."[41]

But Kansas City, Kansas–born black novelist and philosopher Julius Lester warns us that, if we dismiss integrationists, black or white, as quixotic visionaries, we commit the historian's fallacy. We assume that what happened was inevitable—that the course of events proves that some human endeavors were impossible from the start or were somehow intrinsically flawed because they did not accord with the direction that events ultimately took us. Those endeavors may nonetheless have been valid and their goals attainable. "Until the four children were murdered in the bombing of the church in Birmingham in 1963," says one of Lester's characters, "nobody told me I couldn't know what it was like to be black. . . . No one thought there was anything to gain by putting a NO TRESPASSING sign on his race."

Instead, the generation who participated in the early civil rights movement grew up believing that the values of the playground described an authentic reality—that it was good to share, that fair play mattered, that cooperation was possible. History did not prove the impossibility of achieving those ideals, Lester reminds us. Experience infected the way in which we view them. For the generation born to a knowledge of Auschwitz and Hiroshima, of

41. Robert Farnsworth, interview.

Birmingham and Memphis, the human capacity for evil looms larger and the possibilities for human nobility contract to a fatuous hope. "Without innocence, experience makes us cynics."[42]

In Kansas City, black and white integrationists practiced innocence. They believed that "truth is fatal"—that face-to-face intimacy transfigures, that exposure to brotherhood transforms, and that demonstrations of evil inspire the individual to transcend what is for what ought to be. They thought it was possible for whites to know what it's like to be black. If their expanded vision of what is possible to human society has not prevailed, the fault lies, perhaps, in our dislike of fatal truths when comfortable denials lie so ready at hand.

42. Lester, *And All Our Wounds Forgiven*, 24–25.

BIBLIOGRAPHY

■ ■ Archives and Manuscript Collections

Arthur Benson Papers, Western Historical Manuscripts Collection.
Black Workers in the Era of the Great Migration, 1916–1929. University Publications of America, 1985.
Branch Records of the NAACP Papers, Collections of the Manuscript Division, Library of Congress.
C. A. Franklin Collection, Black Archives of Mid-America.
Clifford Naysmith. "Population in Kansas City, Missouri," A. Theodore Brown Collection, Western Historical Manuscripts Collection.
Felix H. Payne Papers, Black Archives of Mid-America.
Fellowship House, Swarthmore Peace Collection.
Fellowship of Reconciliation Records, Swarthmore Peace Collection.
Jewish Community Relations Bureau Archives.
Kansas City Commission of Human Relations Collection, Missouri State Archives.
Lincoln Collection, Missouri Valley Room–Kansas City Public Library.
Native Sons Archives, Microfilm Collection, Missouri Valley Room–Kansas City Public Library.
Official Record of the Proceedings of the Board of Park and Boulevard Commissioners of Kansas City, Missouri, Department of Parks and Recreation, Kansas City, Missouri.
Panel of American Women Collection, Western Historical Manuscripts Collection.
Papers of the Congress of Racial Equality, Microfilming Corporation of America.
Patricia Wagner Papers, A. Theodore Brown Collection, Western Historical Manuscripts Collection.
Private papers of Betty Feazel.

Private papers of Reva Griffith.
Ramos Collection, Missouri Valley Room–Kansas City Public Library.
Urban League of Kansas City Archives.

■ ■ Interviews and Oral Histories

Brooks, Alvin. Interview by Sherry Schirmer, October 25, 1993.
Curls, Fred, Sr. Interview by Ella Pruitt. Black Archives of Mid-America.
    March 11, 1976.
Daniels, Fletcher. Interview by Ella Pruitt. Black Archives of Mid-America.
    May 5, 1976.
Farnsworth, Robert. Interview by Sherry Schirmer. September 27, 1993.
Feazel, Betty. Interview by Sherry Schirmer. September 21, 1993.
Holliday, Harold. Interview by Horace Peterson. Black Archives of Mid-
    America. September 27, 1976.
Holliday, Margaret. Interview by Sherry Schirmer. January 31, 1992.
Jacobson, Ann. Interview by Sherry Schirmer. June 30, 1999.
Johnson, Dorothy Davis. Interview by Sherry Schirmer. October 7, 1991.
Kalhorn, Rhea. Interview by Sherry Schirmer. October 12, 1993.
Lawrence, Anne. Interview by Sherry Schirmer. January 14, 1995.
Oldham, Virginia. Interview by Reva Griffith. 1978.
Sachs, Howard. Interview by Sherry Schirmer. June 9, 1999
Smith, Beth. Interview by Sherry Schirmer. January 17, 1995.
Swomley, John. Interview by Sherry Schirmer. October 29, 1993.

■ ■ Newspapers and Periodicals

Citizens' League Bulletin
The Crisis
Kansas City American
Kansas City Call
Kansas City Evening Star-Mail
Kansas City Jewish Chronicle
Kansas City Journal
Kansas City Labor Herald
Kansas City Labor News
Kansas City Post
Kansas City Star

Kansas City Sun
Kansas City Times
Kansas City World
Missouri Mule
Rising Son
Social Improvement News

■ ■ Government Documents

Annual Reports of the Board of Education of the Kansas City Public Schools.
Charter and Revised Ordinances of Kansas City, Missouri.
Manuscript Schedules of the Census of the United States.
1909 Missouri Laws.
1969 Missouri Laws.
Reports of the Superintendent of Schools, Kansas City, Missouri.
Revised Statutes of Missouri.
Senate Journal of the Twenty-Fourth General Assembly. January 2, 1867.
U.S. Department of Commerce. Bureau of the Census. *Census of the United States.*

■ ■ Books and Articles

Adler, Frank J. *Roots in a Moving Stream: The Centennial History of Congregation B'nai Jehudah of Kansas City, 1870–1970.* Kansas City: The Temple Congregation B'nai Jehudah, 1972.

Anderson, Alan B., and George W. Pickering. *Confronting the Color Line: The Broken Promise of the Civil Rights Movement in Chicago.* Athens: University of Georgia Press, 1986.

Anderson, Jervis. *A. Philip Randolph: A Biographical Portrait.* New York: Harcourt Brace Jovanovich, Inc., 1972.

Baker, Paula. "The Domestication of Politics: Women and American Political Society, 1780–1920." *American Historical Review* 89 (June 1984): 620–47.

Baron, Harold M. "Racism Transformed: The Implications of the 1960s." *Review of Radical Political Economics* 17 (1985): 10–33.

Baylor, Ronald H. *Race and the Shaping of Twentieth-Century Atlanta.* Chapel Hill: University of North Carolina Press, 1996.

Beasley, Maurine. "The Muckrakers and Lynching: A Case Study in Racism." *Journalism History* 9 (autumn–winter 1982): 86–91.

Bettelheim, Bruno, and Morris Janowitz. *Dynamics of Prejudice: A Psychological and Sociological Study of Veterans.* New York: Harper and Bros., 1950.

Binder, A., and P. Scharf. "The Violent Police-Citizen Encounter." *The Annals of the American Academy* 452 (November 1980): 111–21.

Bledstein, Burton J. *The Culture of Professionalism: The Middle Class and the Development of Higher Education in America.* New York: W. W. Norton and Co., 1976.

Bluford, Lucile. "The Lloyd Gaines Story." *Journal of Educational Sociology* 32 (February 1959): 242–46.

Blumer, Herbert. "Race Prejudice as a Sense of Group Position." *The Pacific Sociological Review* 1 (spring 1958): 3–7.

Board of Public Welfare, Bureau of Labor Statistics. *Report on the Wage-Earning Women of Kansas City.* Annual Report of the Factory Inspection Department, April 15, 1912, to April 21, 1913.

Board of Public Welfare. *Social Prospectus of Greater Kansas City.* Kansas City Board of Public Welfare, 1913.

Bodnar, John, Michael Weber, and Roger Simon. "Migration, Kinship, and Urban Adjustment: Blacks and Poles in Pittsburgh, 1900–1930." *Journal of American History* 66 (December 1979): 548–65.

Bodnar, John, Roger Simon, and Michael P. Weber. *Lives of Their Own: Blacks, Italians, and Poles in Pittsburgh, 1900–1960.* Urbana: University of Illinois Press, 1982.

Borchert, James. *Alley Life in Washington: Family, Community, Religion, and Folklife in the City, 1850–1970.* Urbana: University of Illinois Press, 1980.

Boyer, Paul. *Urban Masses and Moral Order in America, 1820–1920.* Cambridge: Harvard University Press, 1978.

Branch, Taylor. *Parting the Waters: America in the King Years, 1954–1963.* New York: Simon and Schuster, 1988.

Briggs, John W. *An Italian Passage: Immigrants to Three Cities, 1890–1930.* New Haven: Yale University Press, 1978.

Brody, David. *The Butcher Workmen: A Study of Unionization.* Cambridge: Harvard University Press, 1964.

Brown, A. Theodore, and Lyle W. Dorsett. *K.C.: A History of Kansas City, Missouri.* Boulder, Colo.: Pruett Publishing Company, 1978.

Bullard, Robert D. *Dumping in Dixie: Race, Class, and Environment.* Boulder, Colo.: Westview Press, 1990.

Burton, Clarence A. *Autobiography of Clarence A. Burton: A Story of His Life and Experiences.* Bound manuscript, 1927. Missouri Valley Room–Kansas City Public Library.

Case, Theodore S. "Kansas City before and during the War." *Annual Report of the Board of Education of the Kansas City Public Schools, 1898–99.*

Cecil-Fronsman, Bill. *Common Whites: Class and Culture in Ante-bellum North Carolina.* Lexington: The University Press of Kentucky, 1992.

Cell, John W. *The Highest Stage of White Supremacy: The Origins of Segregation in South Africa and the American South.* Cambridge: Cambridge University Press, 1982.

Chalmers, David. *Hooded Americanism: The History of the Ku Klux Klan.* Chicago: Doubleday, 1965; Quadrangle Paperbacks, 1968.

Chevigny, Paul. *Police Power: Police Abuses in New York City.* New York: Pantheon Books, 1969.

Clinton, Catherine. "Caught in the Web of the Big House." In *The Web of Southern Social Relations: Women, Family, and Education,* edited by Walter J. Fraser, R. Frank Saunders, Jr., and Jon Wakelyn. Athens: University of Georgia Press, 1982.

———. *The Plantation Mistress: Women's World in the Old South.* New York: Pantheon Books, 1982.

Cowherd, Fletcher. "Experiences and Observations of a Long-Time Kansas City Realtor." Address to the Real Estate Board of Kansas City, Missouri, April 28, 1939, Vertical File, Missouri Valley Room–Kansas City Public Library.

Davis, Angela Y. "Reflections on the Black Woman's Role in the Community of Slaves." *The Black Scholar* (December 1971): 2–15.

———. *Women, Culture, and Politics.* New York: Random House, 1984.

Davis, Dorothy Hodge. "Changing Discriminatory Practices in Department Store Eating Facilities in Kansas City, Missouri: A Study of a Project in Community Organization as Illustrated by the Community Committee for Social Action of Greater Kansas City." M.A. thesis, University of Kansas, 1960.

DeBenedetti, Charles. *The Peace Reform in American History.* Bloomington: Indiana University Press, 1980.

Department of Superintendence. *Kansas City and Its Schools.* National Education Association, 1917.

Dickerson, Dennis. *Out of the Crucible: Black Steelworkers in Western Pennsylvania, 1875–1980.* Albany: State University of New York Press, 1986.

Dollard, John. *Caste and Class in a Southern Town.* New York: Harper and Bros., 1937. Reprint, 1949.

Dorsett, Lyle W. *The Pendergast Machine*. New York: Oxford University Press, 1968.

Duis, Perry. *The Saloon: Public Drinking in Chicago and Boston, 1880–1920*. Urbana: University of Illinois Press, 1983.

Ehrlich, George. *Kansas City, Missouri: An Architectural History*. Kansas City: Historic Kansas City Foundation, 1979.

The Federation of Colored Charities. 1914.

Feldstein, Ruth. *Motherhood in Black and White: Race and Sex in American Liberalism, 1930–1965*. Ithaca: Cornell University Press, 2000.

Fields, Barbara J. "Ideology and Race in American History." In *Region, Race, and Reconstruction*, edited by J. Morgan Kousser and James M. McPherson. New York: Oxford University Press, 1982.

Findlay, James F., Jr. *Church People in the Struggle: The National Council of Churches and the Black Freedom Movement, 1950–1970*. New York: Oxford University Press, 1993.

Finkle, Lee. *Forum for Protest: The Black Press during World War II*. Rutherford, N.J.: Farleigh Dickinson University Press, 1975.

The First 100 Years: A Man, a Newspaper and a City. Kansas City: The Kansas City Star Co., 1980.

Flynn, Charles L., Jr. *White Land, Black Labor: Caste and Class in Late Nineteenth-Century Georgia*. Baton Rouge: Louisiana State University Press, 1983.

Fogelson, Robert M. *Big-City Police*. Cambridge: Harvard University Press, 1977.

Formisano, Ronald P. *Boston against Busing: Race, Class, and Ethnicity in the 1960s and 1970s*. Chapel Hill: University of North Carolina Press, 1991.

Foster, Matthew A. "Effective Police Protection for Residential Sections." *American City* 25 (July 1921): 31–32.

Fox, Greer Litton. "'Nice Girl': Social Control of Women through a Value Construct." *Journal of Women in Culture and Society* (1977): 805–17.

Frazier, E. Franklin. *Black Bourgeoisie*. Glencoe, Ill.: The Free Press, 1957.

Fredrickson, George M. *The Arrogance of Race: Historical Perspectives on Slavery, Racism, and Social Inequality*. Middletown, Conn.: Wesleyan University Press, 1988.

———. *White Supremacy: A Comparative Study in American and South African History*. Oxford: Oxford University Press, 1981.

Garfinkel, Herbert. *When Negroes March: The March on Washington Move-*

ment in the Organizational Politics for FEPC. Glencoe, Ill.: The Free Press, 1959.

Gates, Henry Louis, Jr. "Introduction: Writing 'Race' and the Difference It Makes." In *"Race," Writing, and Difference,* edited by Henry Louis Gates, Jr. Chicago: University of Chicago Press, 1986.

Geller, William A. "Police and Deadly Force: A Look at the Empirical Literature." In *Moral Issues in Police Work,* edited by Frederick A. Elliston and Michael Feldberg. Totowa, N.J.: Allanheld Publishers, 1985.

Giddings, Paula. *When and Where I Enter: The Impact of Black Women on Race and Sex in America.* New York: William Morrow and Company, Inc., 1984.

Gillette, Thomas. "Santa Fe: A Study of the Effects of Negro Invasion on Property Values." M.A. thesis, University of Kansas City, 1954.

Gilmore, Glenda Elizabeth. *Gender and Jim Crow: Women and the Politics of White Supremacy in North Carlina, 1896–1920.* Chapel Hill: University of North Carolina Press, 1996.

Glover, Virginia Louise. "Negro Education in Missouri, 1865–1900." M.A. thesis, University of Illinois, 1951.

Gossett, Thomas F. *Race: The History of an Idea in America.* New York: Schocken Books, 1963. Reprint, 1965.

Gottlieb, Peter. *Making Their Own Way: Southern Blacks' Migration to Pittsburgh, 1916–30.* Urbana: University of Illinois Press, 1987.

Grantham, Dewey W. *Southern Progressivism: The Reconciliation of Progress and Tradition.* Knoxville: University of Tennessee Press, 1983.

Greenbaum, Susan D. *The Afro-American Community in Kansas City, Kansas: A History.* Kansas City, Kans.: City of Kansas City, Kansas, 1982.

Greene, Lorenzo J., Gary R. Kremer, and Antonio F. Holland. *Missouri's Black Heritage.* Rev. ed. Columbia: University of Missouri Press, 1993.

Grenz, Suzanna M. "The Exodusters of 1879: St. Louis and Kansas City Response." *Missouri Historical Review* 73 (October 1978): 54–70.

Griffith, Reva. "Going Forth: Quaker Women and Resistance." *Friendly Woman* 9 (autumn 1990): 17–19.

Grossman, James R. *Land of Hope: Chicago, Black Southerners, and the Great Migration.* Chicago: The University of Chicago Press, 1989.

Grothaus, Larry. "Kansas City Blacks, Harry Truman and the Pendergast Machine." *Missouri Historical Review* 69 (January 1975): 65–82.

———. "The Negro in Missouri Politics, 1890–1941." Ph.D. diss., University of Missouri, 1970.

Guy-Sheftall, Beverly. *Daughters of Sorrow: Attitudes toward Black Women, 1880–1920.* Black Women in United States History Series. Brooklyn: Carlson Publishing, Inc., 1990.

Hall, Jacqueline Dowd. "'The Mind That Burns in Each Body': Women, Rape, and Racial Violence." In *Powers of Desire: The Politics of Sexuality,* edited by Ann Snitow, Christine Stansell, and Sharon Thompson. New York: Monthly Review Press, 1983.

————. *Revolt against Chivalry: Jesse Daniel Ames and the Women's Campaign against Lynching.* New York: Columbia University Press, 1979.

Halpern, Rick. "Race, Ethnicity, and Union in the Chicago Stockyards, 1917–1922." *International Review of Social History* 37 (1992): 25–58.

Haskell, Henry C., Jr., and Richard B. Fowler. *City of the Future: The Story of Kansas City, 1850–1950.* Kansas City: Frank Glenn Publishing Co., 1950.

Hecht, James L. *Because It Is Right: Integration in Housing.* Boston: Little, Brown and Company, 1970.

Herberg, Will. "America's Civil Religion: What It Is and Whence It Comes." In *American Civilization,* edited by Russell E. Richey and Donald G. Jones. New York: Harper and Row, 1974.

Higginbotham, Evelyn Brooks. "African-American Women's History and the Metalanguage of Race." *Signs* 17 (winter 1992): 251–74.

————. *Righteous Discontent: The Women's Movement in the Black Baptist Church, 1880–1920.* Cambridge: Harvard University Press, 1993.

Hine, Darlene Clark. "Rape and the Inner Lives of Black Women in the Middle West." *Signs* 14 (1989): 912–20.

Hoggins, Olive L. "A History of Kansas City Churches." Missouri Valley Room–Kansas City Public Library

Horowitz, Roger. "The Path not Taken: A Social History of Industrial Unionism in Meatpacking, 1930–1960." Ph.D. diss., University of Wisconsin–Madison, 1990.

Huber, Joan, and William H. Form. *Income and Ideology: An Analysis of the American Political Formula.* New York: The Free Press, 1973.

Independent Commission on the Los Angeles Police. *Report of the Independent Commission on the Los Angeles Police Department,* July 9, 1991.

Jackman, Mary R., and Michael J. Muha. "Education and Intergroup Attitudes: Moral Enlightenment, Superficial Democratic Commitment, or Ideological Refinement?" *American Sociological Review* 49 (December 1984): 751–69.

Jackson, Kenneth T. *The Ku Klux Klan in the City, 1915–1930.* New York: Oxford University Press, 1967.

Jones, Lila Lee. "The Ku Klux Klan in Eastern Kansas during the 1920s." *The Emporia State Research Studies* 23 (winter 1975): 10–40.

Jordan, Winthrop. *The White Man's Burden: Historical Origins of Racism in the United States.* Oxford: Oxford University Press, 1974.

Kelleher, Daniel T. "The Case of Lloyd Lionel Gaines: The Demise of the Separate but Equal Doctrine." *Journal of Negro History* 56 (August 1971): 262–71.

Kennedy, Lyle. "The First Flight to the Suburbs." *Westport Magazine* (July 1980): 6–7.

Kousser, J. Morgan. *The Shaping of Southern Politics: Suffrage Restriction and the Establishment of the One-Party South, 1880–1910.* New Haven: Yale University Press, 1974.

Kovel, Joel. *White Racism: A Psychohistory.* New York: Random House, 1970. Reprint, Vintage Books, 1971.

Kusmer, Kenneth L. *A Ghetto Takes Shape: Black Cleveland, 1870–1930.* Urbana: University of Illinois Press, 1978.

———. "Urban Black History at the Crossroads." *Journal of Urban History* 13 (August 1987): 460–70.

Landmarks Commission of Kansas City. "Hyde Park Historic District." National Register of Historic Places Inventory—Nomination Form.

———. *Kansas City: A Place in Time.* Kansas City: Landmarks Commission of Kansas City, Missouri, 1977.

Lane, Roger. *Roots of Violence in Black Philadelphia, 1860–1900.* Cambridge: Harvard University Press, 1986.

Larsen, Lawrence H., and Nancy J. Hulston. *Pendergast!* Columbia: University of Missouri Press, 1997.

Law Enforcement Association of Kansas City, Missouri. *Crime Survey and Comment,* 1929.

Law Enforcement Association. *Report to Members,* 1925.

Lawrence, Sidney. "United We Stand." *Kansas City Jewish Chronicle* (December 13, 1948).

Lester, Julius. *And All Our Wounds Forgiven.* New York: Arcade Publishing, 1994.

Levine, David Allan. *Internal Combustion: The Races in Detroit, 1915–1926.* Westport, Conn.: Greenwood Press, 1976.

Lewis, Earl. *In Their Own Interests: Race, Class, and Power in Twentieth-Century Norfolk, Virginia.* Berkeley: University of California Press, 1991.

Lipset, Seymour Martin. *Political Man: The Social Bases of Politics.* New York: Doubleday and Company, Inc., 1960.

Litwack, Howard, and Nathan Pearson, eds. "Goin' to Kansas City." Catalogue for the *Goin' to Kansas City* Exhibit, Kansas City Museum, 1980.

Loewenberg, Peter. "The Psychology of Racism." In *The Great Fear: Race in the Mind of America,* edited by Gary B. Nash and Richard Weiss. New York: Holt, Rinehart and Winston, Inc., 1970.

Long, Herman H., and Charles S. Johnson. *People vs. Property: Race Restrictive Covenants in Housing.* Nashville: Fisk University Press, 1947.

Lowe, Jeanne R. "Who Lives Where? Urban Housing and Discrimination." In *Cities in American History,* edited by Kenneth T. Jackson and Stanley K. Schultz. New York: Alfred A. Knopf, 1972.

McKay, Nellie Y. "Alice Walker's 'Advancing Luna—and Ida B. Wells': A Struggle toward Sisterhood." In *Rape and Representation,* edited by Lynn A. Huggins and Brenda R. Silver. New York: Columbia University Press, 1991.

Martin, Asa. *Our Negro Population: A Sociological Study of the Negroes of Kansas City, Missouri.* Kansas City: Franklin Hudson Publishing Company, 1913.

Martin, Dwayne. "The Hidden Community: The Black Community of Kansas City, Missouri, during the 1870s and 1880s." M.A. thesis, University of Missouri–Kansas City, 1982.

Matscheck, Walter. "Kansas City Studies Its Police Department." *National Municipal Review* 18 (July 1929): 453–57.

———. "Kansas City Wins Police Home Rule." *National Municipal Review* 21 (August 1932): 342–43.

May, Elaine Tyler. *Great Expectations: Marriage and Divorce in Post-Victorian America.* Chicago: The University of Chicago Press, 1980.

Meier, August, and Elliott Rudwick. *CORE: A Study in the Civil Rights Movement, 1942–1968.* New York: Oxford University Press, 1973.

Metcalf, George R. *From Little Rock to Boston: The History of School Desegregation.* Westport, Conn.: Greenwood Press, 1983.

Miller, S. M., ed. *Max Weber.* New York: Thomas Y. Crowell, 1963.

Mintz, Steven. *A Prison of Expectations: The Family in Victorian Culture.* New York: New York University Press, 1983.

Missouri Relief and Reconstruction Commission. "Report of the Housing Survey, Kansas City, Missouri." 1934–1935.

Monchow, Helen. *The Use of Deed Restrictions in Subdivision Development.*

Chicago: The Institute for Research in Land Economics and Public Utilities, 1928.

Morton, Patricia. *Disfigured Images: The Historical Assault on Afro-American Women*. New York: Praeger, 1991.

Naysmith, Clifford. "Quality Hill: The History of a Neighborhood." Missouri Valley Series, no. 1 (1962).

Noel, Thomas J. *The City and the Saloon: Denver, 1858–1916*. Lincoln: University of Nebraska Press, 1982.

O'Sheel, Shaemus. "Kansas City, the Crossroads of the Continent." *The New Republic* (May 16, 1928): 375–78.

Osofsky, Gilbert. *Harlem: The Making of a Ghetto, Negro New York, 1890–1930*. New York: Harper & Row, 1963; Harper Torchbooks, 1966.

Painter, Nell Irvin. *Exodusters: Black Migration to Kansas after Reconstruction*. New York: Alfred A. Knopf, 1977.

———. "'Social Equality,' Miscegenation, Labor, and Power." In *The Evolution of Southern Culture,* edited by Numan V. Bartley. Athens: University of Georgia Press, 1988.

Parrish, William E. *A History of Missouri, 1860–1875*. Vol. 3 of *A History of Missouri*. Columbia: University of Missouri Press, 1973.

Pearson, Nathan W., Jr. *Goin' to Kansas City*. Urbana: University of Illinois Press, 1987.

Peretti, Burton W. *The Creation of Jazz: Music, Race, and Culture in Urban America*. Urbana: University of Illinois Press, 1992.

Pfeffer, Paula F. *A. Philip Randolph, Pioneer of the Civil Rights Movement*. Baton Rouge: Louisiana State University Press, 1990.

Phillips, C. A. "A Century of Education in Missouri." *Missouri Historical Review* 15 (January 1921): 298–314.

Philpott, Thomas. *The Slum and the Ghetto: Neighborhood Deterioration and Middle-Class Reform, Chicago, 1880–1930*. New York: Oxford University Press, 1978.

Polenberg, Richard. *War and Society: The United States, 1941–1945*. Philadelphia: J. B. Lippincott Company, 1972.

Powdermaker, Hortense. *After Freedom: A Cultural Study in the Deep South*. New York: Viking Press, 1939.

Rabinowitz, Howard N. *Race Relations in the Urban South, 1864–1890*. New York: Oxford University Press, 1978.

Reams, Bernard D., Jr., and Paul E. Wilson. *Segregation and the Fourteenth Amendment in the States: A Survey of State Segregation Laws, 1865–1953*. William S. Hein and Co., 1975.

Reddig, William M. *Tom's Town: Kansas City and the Pendergast Legend.* Columbia: University of Missouri Press, 1947. Reprint, 1986.

Reed, Laura Coates, ed. *In Memoriam: Sarah Walter Chandler Coates.* Kansas City: Hudson-Kimberly Publishing Company, n.d.

Reese, William J. *Power and Promise of School Reform: Grassroots Movements during the Progressive Era.* Boston: Routledge and Kegan Paul, 1986.

Report of the Board of Park and Boulevard Commissioners of Kansas City, Missouri. Kansas City: Hudson-Kimberly Publishing Co., 1893.

Research Department. *Economic Growth in Kansas City.* Kansas City: Federal Reserve Bank, 1953.

Rice, Roger L. "Residential Segregation by Law, 1910–1917." *Journal of Southern History* 34 (May 1968): 179–99.

Robinson, Joann Ooiman. *Abraham Went Out: A Biography of A. J. Muste.* Philadelphia: Temple University Press, 1981.

Roediger, David R. *The Wages of Whiteness: Race and the Making of the American Working Class.* London and New York: Verso, 1991.

Rosenzweig, Roy. *Eight Hours for What We Will: Workers and Leisure in an Industrial City, 1870–1920.* Cambridge: Cambridge University Press, 1983.

Rotundo, E. Anthony. *American Manhood: Transformations in Masculinity from the Revolution to the Modern Era.* New York: Basic Books, 1993.

Rudwick, Elliot M. *Race Riot at East St. Louis, July 2, 1917.* Carbondale: Southern Illinois University Press, 1964.

Rush, Barbara J. "The Ku Klux Klan in Kansas City during the Twenties." M.A. thesis, Marquette University, 1970.

Russell, Ross. *Jazz Style in Kansas City and the Southwest.* Berkeley: University of California Press, 1971.

Sachs, Howard F. "Seeking the Welfare of the City: A Survey of Public Relations, Economics, and Social and Civic Activity." In *Mid-America's Promise: A Profile of Kansas City Jewry,* edited by Joseph P. Schultz. Kansas City: The Jewish Community Foundation of Greater Kansas City and the American Jewish Historical Society, 1982.

Savage, W. Sherman. "The Legal Provisions for Negro Schools in Missouri from 1865–1890." *Journal of Negro History* 16 (July 1931): 309–21.

Schlafly, James J. "A History of the Catholic Church in the Diocese of Kansas City." Jubilee Edition. *The Register* (October 28, 1955).

Schruben, Francis W. *Kansas in Turmoil, 1930–1936.* Columbia: University of Missouri Press, 1969.

Schultz, Joseph P. "The Consensus of 'Civil Judaism': The Religious Life of Kansas City Jewry." In *Mid-America's Promise: A Profile of Kansas*

City Jewry, edited by Joseph P. Schultz. Kansas City: The Jewish Community Foundation of Greater Kansas City and the American Jewish Historical Society, 1982.

Scott, Anne Firor. "Most Invisible of All: Black Women's Voluntary Associations." *Journal of Southern History* 56 (February 1990): 2–22.

———. *The Southern Lady: From Pedestal to Politics, 1830–1930.* Chicago: The University of Chicago Press, 1970.

Senechal, Roberta. *The Sociogenesis of a Race Riot: Springfield, Illinois, in 1908.* Urbana: University of Illinois Press, 1990.

Sennett, Richard. *The Uses of Disorder: Personal Identity and City Life.* New York: Alfred A. Knopf, Inc., 1970.

Skolnick, Jerome H., and James J. Frye. *Above the Law: Police and the Excessive Use of Force.* New York: The Free Press, 1993.

Slavins George Everett. "A History of the Missouri Negro Press." Ph.D. diss., University of Missouri–Columbia, 1969.

Sosna, Morton. *In Search of the Silent South: Southern Liberals and the Race Issue.* New York: Columbia University Press, 1977.

Spear, Allan H. *Black Chicago: The Making of a Negro Ghetto, 1890–1920.* Chicago: The University of Chicago Press, 1967.

Swofford, Ralph P. *Important Facts about Kansas City.* Kansas City Real Estate Board, May 1923.

Swomley, John. "Christian Dynamic for Social Change." In *War, Peace and Justice: The Prophetic Record.* Kansas City: Smith Grieves Co., 1985.

Takaki, Ronald. "The Black Child-Savage in Ante-bellum America." In *The Great Fear: Race in the Mind of America,* edited by Gary B. Nash and Richard Weiss. New York: Holt, Rinehart and Winston, Inc., 1970.

Thernstrom, Stephan. *The Other Bostonians: Poverty and Progress in the American Metropolis, 1880–1970.* Cambridge: Harvard University Press, 1973.

Trotter, Joe William. *Black Milwaukee: The Making of an Industrial Proletariat, 1915–45.* Urbana: University of Illinois Press, 1985.

———. *Coal, Class, and Color: Blacks in Southern West Virginia, 1915–32.* Urbana: University of Illinois Press, 1990.

Tuttle, William M., Jr. "Contested Neighborhoods and Racial Violence: Chicago in 1919, A Case Study." In *Cities in American History,* edited by Kenneth T. Jackson and Stanley K. Schultz. New York: Alfred A. Knopf, 1972.

———. *Race Riot: Chicago in the Red Summer of 1919.* New York: Athenaeum, 1985.

Urban League of Kansas City. "The Negro Worker of Kansas City." July 1940.

———. "Report to the Citizens' Committee on Crime and Law Enforcement Among Negroes." June 1950.

Vollmer, August. "Survey of the Metropolitan Police Department of Kansas City, Missouri." Report to the Kansas City Public Service Institute, March 1929.

Ward, David. "The Emergence of Central Immigrant Ghettos in American Cities, 1840–1920." In *Cities in American History,* edited by Kenneth T. Jackson and Stanley K. Schultz. New York: Alfred A. Knopf, 1972.

Webster, Thomas. "Community Planning to Improve the Housing Conditions of the Negro Population of Kansas City, Missouri, 1940–1947." M.S.W. thesis, University of Kansas, 1949.

White, Walter. *Rope and Faggot: A Biography of Judge Lynch.* New York: Alfred A Knopf, 1929.

Whitney, Carrie Westlake. *Kansas City, Missouri: Its History and Its People, 1808–1908.* Chicago: The S. J. Clarke Publishing Co., 1908.

Wilder, Craig Steven. *A Covenant with Color: Race and Social Power in Brooklyn.* New York: Columbia University Press, 2000.

Wilkins, Roy, with Tom Matthews. *Standing Fast: The Autobiography of Roy Wilkins.* New York: Viking Press, 1982.

Williamson, Joel. *The Crucible of Race: Black-White Relations in the American South since Emancipation.* New York: Oxford University Press, 1984.

Wilson, William H. "Beginning of the Park and Boulevard Movement in Frontier Kansas City, 1872–1882." *Missouri Historical Review* 56 (April 1962): 255–73.

———. *The City Beautiful Movement in Kansas City.* Columbia: University of Missouri Press, 1964.

Woodward, C. Vann. *The Strange Career of Jim Crow.* Oxford: Oxford University Press, 1955.

Worley, William S. *J. C. Nichols and the Shaping of Kansas City: Innovation in Planned Residential Communities.* Columbia: University of Missouri Press, 1990.

Wright, George C. *Life behind a Veil: Blacks in Louisville, Kentucky, 1865–1930.* Baton Rouge: Louisiana State University Press, 1985.

Wyatt-Brown, Bertram. *Southern Honor: Ethics and Behavior in the Old South.* New York: Oxford University Press, 1982.

Wynn, Neil A. *The Afro-American and the Second World War.* London: Paul Elek, 1976.

Young, William H., and Nathan B. Young, Jr. *Your Kansas City and Mine.* Kansas City, 1950.

INDEX